Memoirs Of A Black Englishman

By Dr Paul Stephenson OBE
and Lilleith Morrison

◬ Tangent Books

First published 2011 by Tangent Books (978-1-906447-39-4).
This edition published 2021 by Tangent Books.

Tangent Books
Unit 5.16 Paintworks, Bristol BS4 3EH
0117 972 0645
www.tangentbooks.co.uk
richard@tangentbooks.co.uk

ISBN 978-1-910089-97-2

Authors: Dr Paul Stephenson OBE and Lilleith Morrison

Design: Joe Burt, Wild Spark Design

Front cover image: Adam Gasson

Production: Shirley Brown, Richard Jones

Assistant publisher: Sol Wilkinson

A CIP record of this book is available at the British Library.

Printed on paper from a sustainable source.

For my late wife Joyce who was a support and strength to me and to my wonderful children Paul Junior and Funmilayo.

Acknowledgements

Thank you to all the people who supported this venture with encouragement, information, photos and advice and with special appreciation to the following:

Edna Allen

Paul Barnett

Owen Batchelor

BBC Archives

Tony Benn

Bristol Black Archive Partnership (BBAP)

Bristol Museums, Galleries & Archives

Shirley Brown

Tony and Lalel Bullimore

Sonia and Vincent Burgess

Richard Burley

Sir John Dankworth

Barbara Dettering

Madge Dresser

Sherrie Eugene

Karen Garvey

Roy Hackett

Heritage Lottery Fund (HLF)

Rupert Hopkins

Eric Jay

Brian Julian

Nicholas A. Juravich (Christ Church, Oxford)

Asif Khan

Neil Kinlock

Dame Cleo Laine

Ros Martin

Reverend Wayne Massey (Christ Church, Clifton)

Rob Mitchell

Prof. Chris Mullard CBE

Trevor Phillips OBE

Guy Reid Bailey

Karl Ritchie

Tennis Russell

Sam Ramsamy

Gavton Shepherd

Sir Jay Tidmarsh

John Williams

About the book

The concept of this book was to put Paul Stephenson's life into a political perspective and was a collaborative work. Lilleith Morrison did the background research and the first few sessions began with Lilleith taking notes while Paul recalled events in his early childhood. At this point Paul suggested using a recorder and most of the other sessions that followed were recorded. During the process of the book the sessions became ones where Paul would either talk about a period in his life with the occasional question from Lilleith or answer questions Lilleith had already prepared as a prompt.

The recordings of Paul's spoken words were at first typed up verbatim and then edited into a written form and restructured where appropriate but the recordings had the effect of making Paul's voice and turn of phrase a strong and clear element of the book, with Lilleith dovetailing the background research into his personal memoirs. This was to enable the reader to see the inter-relationship between the personal and political in Paul's life.

Rob Mitchell read through an early draft and made some useful comments before the book was completed and the final version submitted to the publisher. In this book the term Black is capitalised where it refers to a race i.e. people of African descent including the African diaspora. The term BAME is also used to refer to people of Asian, African, and minority ethnic groups.

Lilleith Morrison MSc

Lilleith Morrison came to England from Jamaica as a child in 1955 and achieved a BEd at Cambridge University in 1971. She arrived in Bristol in 1981 and in 1983 she pioneered the teaching of Black History in Further Education and voluntary projects and wrote the Open College Network's module on Black History.

In 1992 she produced a video, *Black n' Write* on Black writers from Bristol and Manchester and a radio feature, *Positive Images of Black Men,* for a Media course at the University of the West of England. In the 1990s she also worked with parents and their children in a school setting to produce stories they wrote together and from 1991 to 2000 and was project co-ordinator for the Books for Babies Project in Bristol. She was Access Course Team Leader and member of Diversity and Equality Steering Group at Filton College until 2006 and has a Social Science MSc in Media, Culture and Conflict.

In 2007 she served as Project Officer for Bristol Black Archives Partnership where she worked with many of Bristol's Black achievers. In 2008 she completed a diploma at Bristol University in Creative Writing for Performance and has had one of her short plays performed on a building site. She has completed a year-long project with PATH (Positive Action Training Hub) into Teaching with local universities to recruit more Black students into teaching. She strongly believes in an inclusive society where everyone has the opportunity to fulfil their potential.

Foreword

By Tony Benn

In 2008 Paul Stephenson was given the Freedom of the City of Bristol in recognition of the work he has done there to bring the black and white communities together.

It was an honour that he richly deserved because his campaign for a boycott of the buses in Bristol in 1963 against racial discrimination opened up the question of Bristol's role in the slave trade which the city had never really been ready to accept.

The refusal of the Bristol Bus Company to employ black drivers was an issue that had been ignored and it was Paul who brought it into the public domain by discovering there was a vacancy for a bus driver and putting in the name of a black man, who was then told there was no vacancy. Instead of accepting it, Paul decided to make an issue of the matter and he organised a boycott of Bristol buses based on his knowledge of similar boycotts that had occurred in the United States as an early example of their campaign for racial equality.

As one of the MPs of the city at that time I was approached by Paul for my support which I willingly gave and it was a very interesting experience.

The trade union involved at the time was my own union, the Transport and General Workers' Union, and we made little progress with them until the campaign became public. I approached the Bishop of Bristol who told me Paul was a trouble maker, and I was delighted when Harold Wilson, the leader of the opposition in parliament, gave his support and the boycott was successful with a black driver appointed.

Paul himself was responsible for making this campaign succeed and his memoirs give some background to his life and work. Born in 1937 Paul was English and black, joined the RAF and when he was demobilized, his first job was as a youth worker in Bristol which led him into his campaign against discrimination on the buses. Later he went to America and on to Jamaica and when he returned to Britain he married Joyce who was a Jamaican living in Bristol. Later he was appointed as a community relations officer and served in that capacity in Coventry and from there to become a national youth officer for the National Community Relations Council in London where he won the support of Muhammad Ali for his plan to promote sports development among the ethnic minority.

But it was, later, in Bristol that he campaigned to build the Bristol Black Archives Partnership and he worked with the Empire and Commonwealth Museum in Bristol to commemorate the abolition of Slavery winning financial support to make it possible.

By this time Paul had moved from being a trouble maker to something of a local treasure, widely respected and admired and it was singularly appropriate that two centuries after Wilberforce's campaign against the slave trade, Paul should be rewarded by receiving the Freedom of the city.

His life, as readers of this book will see, offers living proof that history is made by the people who make the effort. It also shows that the initial hostility that they provoke is replaced by respect and goodwill if the effort continues for long enough.

Paul Stephenson's life confirms that expectation and I strongly recommend his book.

Years Of Childhood Joy

1937-1947

I exploded into the world of Rochford Essex on 6th May 1937, the same day that the Hindenburg air ship blew up over New Jersey, USA. That catastrophic accident brought an end to that kind of transport for the general public but there were other significant changes taking place at that time too. This was a period in which Black people were becoming prominent as international figures on the world stage, even though Nazi ideology was growing in Europe. The year before I was born, Jesse Owens, a Black American track athlete and grandson of a slave, had won four gold medals at the Berlin Olympics, much to the dismay of Hitler who witnessed this event.

In 1937 Joe Louis, the Black American boxer, had been defeated by a German boxer called Schmeling. The Nazis had claimed this as evidence of Aryan superiority. In the return match in 1938 however, Joe Louis knocked out Schmeling in the first round and his victory was seen as a major repudiation of Nazi Germany's claim to white superiority. These events were a prologue to the unfolding drama that was to take place in the post-war years after the Nazis were defeated.

The race card was on the political table in a new and dynamic way and my life was to become intricately intertwined and interwoven with this issue. During the era of my birth, it was not only in the field of sports that Black people were becoming distinguished. Paul Robeson, the son of an escaped slave, was a multilingual actor, singing star and civil rights activist, who was at that time living in England and making films here. He was to be an important role model for me in my teenage years.[1]

As a child I was innocently unaware of the role race and equality issues were to play in my life. As a black-skinned person but culturally an English one, my life and identity were to be influenced and intricately involved with the British government's redefinition of its concept of what it was to be British and how this related to race. In fact, over the coming years this was to become a continuous process of acknowledgement and rejection. It was to have an impact on my life, as I was to also help shape those definitions and re-definitions. But this story started long before I was born.

Its source is in Africa but for my part we will take up the story here in England. I will begin with the British Empire that ruled the waves and the Britons who 'never, never, never will be slaves', yet here lies a contradiction. Colonial subjects were theoretically equal to whites but in practice they were segregated and treated as inferior. In fact, some colonial subjects were descendants of those previously enslaved by the Britons of the mother country.

This ambiguous relationship is illustrated when in 1914 and 1939 the British Government accepted into the Royal Navy its colonial subjects as equal to whites. The 1914 British Nationality and Status of Aliens Act declared "any person born within His Majesty's dominion and allegiance "is a natural-born British subject.

In practice however, this was not the case because BAME colonials were segregated during the war and when it ended, unlike their white counterparts, were expected to return to their

---

1   Paul Robeson was the epitome of the 20th-century Renaissance man. He was an exceptional athlete, actor, singer, cultural scholar, author, and political activist. His talents made him a revered man of his time, yet his radical political beliefs all but erased him from popular history. http://www.pbs.org/wnet/americanmasters/episodes/paul-robeson/about-the-actor/66/ Retrieved 27/10/2020

own country. Not all BAME Britons chose to follow the Colonial Office directives though and during the inter-war years several BAME communities developed in port cities such as Liverpool and Cardiff. Like me, during my early years, BAME Britons, in those times, were still a rarity.

In 1925 the British Government enacted the 'Coloured Alien Seamen Order' (CASO) which was theoretically to stop alien seamen falsely claiming British nationality but what it really did was to effectively make BAME seamen from the colonies lose their privileges of citizenship. It was the first instance of the state sanctioning racial subordination inside Britain, not just in its colonies[2].

I was of course oblivious to this as a child, but over the next two and a half decades, my experiences and particular circumstances would be preparing me to play my part, with others, in the changes that would come about in Britain's race relations. The civil rights of BAME Britons would develop as I too developed my own identity and found my place in the country of my birth; a country where being English and Black were then viewed as mutually exclusive.

I feel my unique childhood helped prepare me for the role I was to play in future years. After the age of two years I had no contact with my West African father, Joseph Stephenson, who had been a medical student studying here. That is why I was brought up as a Black English boy but without links to a Black family. My mother, Olive, who like me had an African father, also like me had little to do with her male parent.

As my mother was in the Women's Royal Army Corps I only saw her from time to time when she was on leave, so she wasn't a strong influence in my early years. My other significant relative

2   Kathleen Paul, Whitewashing Britain, 1997

was my grandmother who was dual heritage but looked white, so I had a very English childhood with no references to my African heritage. I also had no contact with other Black children. In retrospect, I see I was a Black English boy of a very rare kind. People around at the time tended to regard me as a cuddly curiosity. It was only in later years that I would find people's perception of me change and instead I would to some people, be considered a racial threat, trouble maker or political activist.

The Second World War started when I was two years of age. After the attack on Pearl Harbour the American forces joined the war and stationed troops here in England. They insisted that their units serving here were segregated until 1944. The American military leaders insisted on segregation of facilities and particularly pubs and dance halls that their servicemen frequented despite the fact those Black soldiers took the same risks as white ones.

During the war years BAME GI soldiers in Bristol were billeted in Old Market, Ashley Down, Great George Street, Brockley, Nailsea and Failand. They were subject to segregation and were not allowed in the same pubs and clubs as white American soldiers. In July 1944 a group of Black soldiers were involved in a fight with white soldiers. There were four hundred soldiers fighting when a hundred and twenty military intervened. The tragic result of this altercation was the death of a Black soldier who was shot dead in Baldwin Street.[3]

Later in life I was to play a part in changing the kind of injustice that led to Black people being turned away from pubs, clubs and hotels purely on the basis of their race.

It is understood that Churchill complied with Roosevelt's request that there should be segregation of Black GIs who were

3 Evening Post 4/3/05)

keen to fight against Hitler on British soil. The British colonial forces, though not subjected to official segregation, were subjected to racial discrimination as I discovered from Dr Arthur Wint, a Jamaican, who served in the RAF from 1941 to 1945 as a pilot. He was a world record setting, 400 metre runner and gold Olympic medallist known as the Gentle Giant [4]. I was to establish a relationship with him when he was Jamaican High Commissioner in the 1970s and heard about his wartime experiences then.

My own life took on a dramatic, if more personally auspicious, turn of events because of the war. I became an evacuee in 1940 and this experience was to have a far-reaching influence on me. It was to shape and form me into the person I was to become as well as opening up new horizons for me. I was sent to Dunmow, a rural market town in Essex, and there I was the only Black child out of the eight East End children. As an evacuee I was in the care of Essex County Council. It wasn't possible to find homes for all the children, especially Black children, so I went into a care home. When my mother visited me there, people would say 'That must be Paul's mum'. It was obvious because of her colour she stood out as my mother, so from a very early age I also stood out as easily identifiable. She later told me that she felt quite angry when the local people there had mistaken her for a man because she was in British army uniform. They hadn't seen a Black woman in an army uniform before.

One of my earliest memories was in the coal cellar of the Dunmow children's home. The first thing I can really say I remember is a wartime recollection of being deep in this shelter

---

4   There were 400 Caribbean aircrew in the RAF during the Second World War. 103 were given distinguished service medals. There seems to be no official record of the contribution of volunteers from the Caribbean at the Ministry of Defence, the Air Ministry or the National Archives so the following site makes an attempt to redress this oversight: www.caribbeanaircrew-ww2.com Retrieved 27/10/2020

and wearing a gas mask. At three I wasn't aware of the danger as we children were having fun trying on each other's masks, while all the time oblivious of any possible gas attack or the fact that Chamberlain and Hitler were weighing up the possibility of using chemicals and gas as weapons. Obviously, the surrounding adult's excitement and tension had imprinted this otherwise meaningless event on my young mind. In retrospect I now see that I had started life in a fragile world torn by war and in the middle of a struggle for a free world that would have dire consequences if lost.

It was also a world that would change dramatically after the war and the boundaries of freedom and equality would be pushed even further in the post-war period. Former colonies around the world were to emerge from the war demanding their freedom. Local Black-led equality activities were linked to national movements which were in turn connected through people and the media to international movements. These connections strongly influenced the nature of this movement, the kind of strategies, choice of tactics and targets as well as the outcome and effect it would have on British society and legislation. As a small child in that shelter, however I had no idea that I would be part of that new struggle in future years.

Dunmow was to become very special to me, the place I would return to time and time again when I was living in post-war London. It was a rural, middle-class farming community where I attended a Church of England school. On my way home from school I used to watch the cattle auctions. The deep lowing noise of the cattle, the smell of them, the rumble of human conversations and the switching of cow's tails as they flicked flies away, all formed part of my earliest memories.

At my infant school in Dunmow the teachers were very

affectionate, but treated me differently. One teacher found me a source of curiosity, which led her to cut locks off my hair as a good luck charm. The village children unaccustomed to anyone of my colour asked me whether I was black all over. On one particular occasion at school there was a girl who asked me that question but directed it to a particular part of my anatomy, requesting a view of it in return for a similar favour.

In another particularly unsettling experience I was standing in a butcher's shop during rationing. I must have been about four or five years old at that time when a large white woman kept staring at me. She then turned to the butcher who was holding an enormous knife and said, 'I could eat him'. It went through my mind that the reason there weren't any Black children like me around was because they had all been eaten up. Fear, curiosity and self-consciousness played on my mind in the infant years of my life.

I was nevertheless treated kindly there and have very fond and affectionate memories of the place. Those were happy days. It was this mixture of being different but lovingly treated that was to have a profound effect on my development. Like most children I accepted the world as it was. I was new and the world was new to me.

The people responsible for my care treated me with kindness and for this I am very grateful. Even officials who did not attend to me daily still had time to make me feel special. The Senior Child Welfare Worker, Miss Snowden, was very influential and always asked about me every time she visited. Miss Wansborough-Jones, the Essex children's officer who visited various children's homes, would also seek me out to see how well I was doing and appeared to give me her particularly caring attention. It was she who ensured that I returned to London after the war with the hope that I would renew the bonds I had with my mother. Even though I looked different and was sometimes treated differently I felt wrapped in a blanket of caring affection.

As children we attended a Congregational Church of our own accord and unchaperoned as it was opposite the care home, we evacuees lived in. Our teachers would also take us to the Anglican church a mile away because it was the same denomination as our school. It was at the latter that I remember being fascinated, as only a five-year-old can be, by the golden eagle statue inside the church. We all appreciate magnificence and beauty in objects of art, and this is the first time I can remember experiencing that feeling of joy and wonder a remarkable piece of art can engender in someone open to using their imagination. For me this eagle symbolised the power and authority of God. When I returned to Dunmow in later years, I went straight to the church to look at the eagle as it captured a moment of my past for me and struck a thunderous chord deep inside me.

This was a time of childhood discovery and the world lay around me yet to be explored. When Rev. John P. Carol arrived as a new minister, we were all very respectful of this newcomer. One Sunday he said 'People believe life is not worth living.' I remember thinking to myself in my youthful innocence. 'How can anyone believe that? I'm having a great time.' This memory illustrates how happy and secure those days were for me.

Rev. Carol lived in the Manse across the road from our home and showed an interest in us evacuee children and would visit us from time to time to look after our well-being. He was a caring person and we had a deep regard for him. He was very concerned about the outcome of the war, it seemed to me, more so than other adults around.

The first Church of England vicar who was to have a

memorable influence on my attitude to religion and Christianity was the Rev. Mellish. He was an interesting person. He was the vicar of Dunmow and he had won the Victoria Cross (V.C.) during the First World War. For an Anglican vicar to have a V.C. was something I didn't understand at the time because I thought a vicar would be a man of peace, not someone who could also be a war hero. He left a strong impression on me because many people told me he was a hero. I had a feeling that he was someone who was spiritually important though I wasn't aware of the social and influential importance of his V.C. He was a man of some authority with an austere personality and must have been a very well-known vicar in the Anglican Communion. I now wonder how this affected his relationship with the Bishop of Chelmsford, his superior, who perhaps looked up to him. I was becoming aware of people's relationships with each other and the inherent contradictions these relationships sometimes held and developing a grasp of these protocols.

As I attended a Church of England school there was a link between Rev. Mellish and the teachers, Mr and Mrs Banks, whom I remember vividly. Mr Banks, who we children called 'Trotter', because of the way he walked, was captain of the Home Guard. It was his wife who would read stories from the Old Testament to us children. As an adult I was to tell Mrs Banks how important those stories were to me and that I would never forget them. Mr Banks was both Headmaster and Captain of the Home Guard and could be seen marching through the town. He had all the farm workers and others marching through Dunmow creating an atmosphere that was later to be captured in the television series *Dad's Army*.

I was aware of a connection between Mr Banks and Colonel Gibbons who owned a brewery so near the school you could smell the hops from the playground. Colonel Gibbons was chair of the governors at my school and I felt the Colonel seemed to have some influence over Mr Banks. I then realised why, the Colonel was a captain in the First World War and Mr Banks was a captain in the Home Guard during the Second World War. As a young boy I was becoming aware of these power relationships between adults.

Mr Banks was from the North of England with a northern accent and had been a Church of England missionary in Canada. He was responsible both to Colonel Gibbons and Rev. Mellish. My young mind was observing and taking in relationships between people and getting to understand how people commanded influence over others and especially how people could have power in different ways.

At school I led a gang as we called ourselves (though we were all very well behaved) made up of Primrose and Mavis Peacock, Freddy James and Peter and June Markwell. We would enjoy the usual activities that children did in those days. We would go down by the stream and play fives with clay squares, seeing how many we could get on the back of our hand. We would go rabbiting in the cornfields, hitting rabbits on the head with sticks. I even got a few. In those war-torn days rabbits were considered pests rather than pets so our attitude to them was different than today.

Mrs Hails, my actual teacher, was young and attractive. She showed a personal interest in my educational development and encouraged me a great deal and helped my self-confidence to grow by treating me with warm affection. Miss Cross was also another teacher who was important to me in showing a deep interest in my progress. Like all children our creative endeavours were sometimes directed at our teachers and this is a poem we made up about them.

'Mr. Banks sat on the bank and it began to hail. Mrs Cross got very cross and that's the end of my tale.'

One story Mrs Banks would read to us struck a chord with me, the story of David and Goliath, a popular theme in many epics. It was a symbolism that was not lost on me in my struggles in later years. I was deeply enthralled by David's relationship with King Saul's son Jonathan. Indeed, King Saul was, at the time, a bogeyman for me who struck dread in my heart and I feared him immensely, if ever I was alone. My housemates who were aware of my fear of King Saul, would laughingly joke, 'Don't go in there, you might find King Saul'. The story of King Saul reaching for a javelin and throwing it at David struck me with foreboding. *'And Saul sought to smite David even to the wall with the javelin.'* This image of Saul attempting to murder David in a jealous rage even though he had saved his kingdom left me cold with terror.

For me it was the greatest story to unfold in the Old Testament, since it dwells on all the themes humanity wrestles with – relationships, jealousy, love, betrayal and bravery – which teaches you the nature of God. Like most children I learnt about these great themes from stories, and this particular one I found compelling, as it had a powerful effect on me though I was not aware of it at the time.

As young children we also joked about other stories in the Old Testament such as Aaron and Moses about whom we had a rude and irreverent poem.

Moses and Aaron went down a dark hole.
Moses set fire to Aaron's arsehole.
Moses came up with a terrible fright.
Aaron came up with his arsehole alight.

There were a few poems going around and one was dedicated to me. Primrose who was ten at the time and her sister Mavis who was my age gave it to me. This made me feel singular but cherished.

I had a babe as black as ink
He is an African I think
His hair is black
His teeth are white
This song I sing to you tonight
Sleep my little darling boy
Thou art mother's dearest joy
Moon shall shine and stars will keep
Watch over darling darkie's sleep

My presence in Dunmow drew a lot of interest and another example of being singled out as different was when during the war there was a ringworm and head lice epidemic. We were transported to Braintree isolation hospital where the matron Miss Tordoff singled me out from the rest of the children.

Miss Tordoff was a short woman with a middle parting in her hair and an authoritative manner, which made even the nurses terrified of her. She questioned why I was thought to have caught ringworm given the tight knots in my hair. She nevertheless said I may as well be kept under observation. This incident illustrates the misconceptions about Black people that abounded at the time and how very little some white people knew about Black people. My fellow housemates and myself stayed at the hospital for two weeks before returning to Dunmow.

It was also at this stage in my life that I was to meet two women, who had a strong influence on me and on my growing perception of the world. As a young evacuee I was to become aware of the English class system and it is Joan Piggott and Kathleen Stubbs I must thank for this particular part of my education. They were acting foster carers in Dunmow, responsible for our day-to-day care. This was where my understanding of the English class system began to take form.

Joan, who was strict and not as warm to us London East Enders as Kathleen, would take us to her home, a manor house in Abbess Roding, Essex. In contrast Kathleen, a tall woman older than Joan but very gifted in the way she understood young children, would take us to her working-class terraced cottage in the village of Manuden, Essex. I could see that although these two women got on well together, Joan's way of life contrasted radically with Kathleen's ordinary working-class background.

With Joan we children would play in the grounds of her parents' Manor House and were allowed to pick plums and pears from the orchard. She introduced us to English traditions such as May Day and dancing round the Maypole as well as the habit of Sunday walks. At this time, I took my first steps towards understanding the English middle class. At the same time the other children around me were mainly from the working-class background of the London East End. As I was exposed to both these contrasting experiences, I was able to gain confidence in relating to and in understanding the perspective of both these classes from an early age.

Mrs Christine Custerson, who was chair in the late 1940s of the Children's Committee of Essex County Council, was another person who took an interest in me. She attended the Congregational Church in Saffron Walden and we established a long-standing and unique connection, so much so that she attended my wedding in Bristol when she was in her eighties. When she came, she stayed with the then Bishop of Bristol, Oliver Tomkins. My wife and I also spent some of our honeymoon as her guest.

She was the president of the Saffron Walden Liberal Party and in the 1960s I used to stay with her at 'Farmadene', her house in Saffron Walden. It was she who influenced my political views later in the Sixties by showing me that she was trying to understand the position of young Black people in Britain like myself. Later she was to introduce me to her Liberal friends and would have liked me to join the Liberal party but they weren't radical enough for me.

Dunmow was peopled with some interesting characters and Mr Culpin was one such. He and his wife together with Mr Lawrence were the local Sunday school superintendents at the Congregational church. Mr Culpin was also the manager of Dunmow's pig factory. The factory would help organise the famous Dunmow Flitch Trial. This competition entailed choosing every leap year the happiest couple in the town. If they could prove to a judge and jury that they had lived harmoniously for a year and a day, without quarrelling, they would win a flitch of bacon (half a pig). It was also at Sunday school in Dunmow that I met David Fisk who was to become a good friend of mine and whose family was to virtually adopt me.

I remember my first ever drive in a car was with the Sunday school superintendent, Mr Lawrence. I was five or six at the time and Mr Lawrence used to take us evacuee children out as a treat. He would thrill us by taking us out in his Ford Popular after Sunday school around the small villages of Essex. He was the manager of a gas company and was very good to us. A devout Christian, he was also a man with a great sense of humour who was easy to communicate with. My impression of him was that he was a very able person. I first met him when I was five years old but he was to become crucial in my life in later years when I left the RAF to start a civilian career in 1960.

Looking back, life in Dunmow seemed like a series of treats. The Crittall family, the metal windows manufacturers, arranged another treat. They had a vast estate and a large house in Great Easton two or three miles from Dunmow. It was in these grounds that I saw my first Punch and Judy show. They had several cars in their house and as a young child I was impressed when they would announce the times the various cars were coming to pick us children up and take us back to the village. Val Crittall was particularly interested in where I was coming from and always inviting me to come and see her as I got older and was a young teenager.

My stay in Dunmow, although somewhat strange because of my unique status, was nevertheless a very happy and formative period in my life, in which I was lucky enough to meet interesting people who gave me the attention every young child needs. My experience of the diversity of English life as seen through its class system was to stand me in good stead in later years because I felt able to relate with confidence to the rich and powerful, an opportunity I might not have had if my circumstances had been different. In retrospect, I feel uniquely placed to develop certain character traits and connections with people there which would serve me well throughout my life.

When it was time to leave Dunmow it was more traumatic than I first realised. I felt very alone as a young boy having to leave a place in which I had so many positive experiences. The Jesuits say, 'give me a boy for the first seven years of his life and I will give you the man', well the seven years I spent in Dunmow were my most formative years. As a young boy my childhood, despite being in a care home, was a very rural middle class one.

I used to weep secretly at the thought of leaving the place I had grown to love. It was a very lonely experience and yet I held on to God. It was spirituality that helped me through as a seven-year-old. Dunmow was a place I valued and cherished and I would keep the links with people I had met there over the coming years. I now realise this was my first home. I was not just leaving a place but people who I had bonded with and who I cared about and who cared about me, so that leaving home came for me at a much younger age than for most young people.

The next period in my life was to prove a very important wake up call. We children were taken to London in an old Ford Poplar car by an Essex Social worker called Mr. Boreman. There I was to experience overt racism of a kind I had not encountered before. Again I was the only Black boy in my school but in London I was not an interesting curiosity – quite the contrary!

Every free time I had I'd leave Forest Gate, London and catch a bus and go up to Dunmow and when I got there, I'd get a bike and cycle to Great Bardfield where I had my first holidays. I loved these regular visits to the countryside and the people who had shown me the affection and that warmth sustained me during the troubled times in London. Those excursions brought back a lot of good memories and were a wonderful relief from the hostility to my colour I found on the Romford Road in London.

A Wake Up Call:
The Post-War Years
1947-1953

1947 heralded significant changes in my life when I returned to London to live in Forest Gate. At that time I was still under the care of Essex County Council and lived in a cottage home for boys and again I was the only young Black person around. There were six boys living there and two became my close friends, Tony Mills and Kenneth Cornell. Although I didn't live with my mother, who was looking for a flat for us, I saw a lot of her. She explained that she had joined the war effort to assist in Hitler's defeat because she knew that a victory for Hitler would have dire consequences for Black people living in Europe and that included us.

It was during this, another very formative period in my childhood, that I first became aware of the negative and personally painful aspects of race. I started to experience on a regular basis being called such names as 'blackie', 'monkey' and 'nigger' on my walk to school in the neighbourhood streets. There were certain roads such as the Romford Road I couldn't walk down because I would be pelted with bricks and bottles, luckily most of them missed. These were the children destined to be the future 'Teddy Boys' who would lock horns with the newly arrived immigrants from the Caribbean. These clashes during the 1950s would lead to the riots at Notting Hill. The attacks on me in 1947 and the following years were to be my wake-up call of what being Black and living in London meant at the time. In 1948, a year after I returned to London, the Windrush landed on the 21st June with 492 Jamaicans on board. Although I wasn't from the Caribbean, in later years I would find my fate and the fate of the newcomers bound together by civil rights issues.

In the years 1947-1962 the causes of migration from the Caribbean were the growing population, unemployment, and the fact that the United States had restricted migration from the Caribbean with their 1952 McCarran-Walter Act. On arrival in England the migrants faced two crucial and related problems, those of employment and housing. Later the education of their children was also to become an issue.

The first Caribbean settlers in Bristol were ex-servicemen who either stayed or returned after a temporary stay in their birth countries. Avonmouth was a known destination for Caribbean produce, which at the time was primarily bananas. One hundred and fifty nine stowaways were arrested there between 1955 and 1959 on boats from Port Antonio and other Caribbean ports.[5] But many more came to Britain because they were invited by the British Government who saw them as a source of cheap labour to solve their post-war lack of manpower.

When Churchill was Prime Minister, he warned that if Britain's future as a nation were to be the centre of a great empire then it would depend upon an improvement in the birth rate. In the post-war years workers were a scarcity, so this led the Government to recruit labour from the Commonwealth countries. Caribbean workers were being recruited by the British Transport Commission, London Transport Executive and British Hotels and Restaurants Association and the Regional Hospital Boards.

But here again there was an ambiguity in the indigenous population's attitude to Black migrants. When in 1955 a shortage of labour in transport and catering had been identified, the British Transport Commission suggested recruiting Italians to

5   Dresser and Fleming 2000

avoid the race 'problem'. The National Union of Railwaymen was opposed to this, so the Transport executive subsequently focused on Ireland and the Caribbean.

The opportunities offered to Caribbean migrants often under rated their talents. In 1953 the Government set up a working party on the Employment of Coloured People in the UK. A survey undertaken gave questionnaires to area officers whose opinions often reflected gross stereotyping and this became the basis on which BAME people were placed in jobs. A recruiting team was sent to Barbados in 1956 but most migrants were downgraded in jobs they were offered as newcomers, even though the trade unions were officially opposed to discrimination. Between 1950-1955 there were 36,000 BAME immigrants compared to 250,000 from Southern Ireland and thousands of Italians and other European workers, yet the focus of alarm was on BAME immigration [6].

On the one hand the British Government was feeling twitchy about having too many BAME migrant workers arriving at *"This throne of kings, This sceptred isle, This Earth of majesty,"* but they also wanted to maintain their international influence while balancing several different, competing communities of Britishness within the Empire. Therefore in the same pivotal year, 1948, the year of the Windrush's arrival, and the year of the United Nation's declaration of Universal Human Rights [7], the British also passed the 1948 Nationality Act. This Act conferred on colonial subjects the right to enter Britain and stay for the rest of their lives.

The 1948 Nationality Act bolstered Britain's international stature without imposing too much strain on either the goodwill

---

6   Carter et al. 2000

7   On December 10, 1948 the General Assembly of the United Nations adopted and proclaimed the Universal Declaration of Human Rights

of the United States towards the Empire or Britain's own limited financial resources. It created a new entity, the United Kingdom and Colonies, whose residents shared a common citizenship and ostensibly conferred equality of status to subjects in its colonies with its subjects in the mother country. The Conservatives criticised the bill for undermining Britain's imperial nationality by ending the period when birth within the king's dominion and allegiance, i.e. the UK automatically conferred the proud status of a British citizen.

By its terms alien women marrying British men no longer automatically became British. The bill also changed the manner of acquiring British citizenship and devised a scheme to permit Irish aliens to benefit from British nationality. It extended the rights of women, regarding nationality, if they married foreigners and created a mechanism for strengthening the Empire and Commonwealth.

In 1949 the Attlee Government discussed how to prevent unwanted colonial migration without endangering the strength and unity of the Commonwealth. There was a conflict between Britain's formal nationality policy, which gave the right to all its members to enter Britain, and its informal national identity that reserved this right only for people who they believed really belonged, the white British.[8]

The rights of Commonwealth citizens were not always what they appeared. In West Africa for instance, the British Travel certificate which confirmed the holder as a British subject was issued, but by the latter half of 1951 arrangements were made to omit references to British subject status so the holder could be sent back as an alien.

Other parts of the Commonwealth also had problems with

8   Kathleen Paul, 1997

their right of entry. In the West Indies they delayed the issue of passports to migrants and in India and Pakistan the government refused passports to those without jobs or homes to come to, effectively differentiating between them and the indigenous British. Shipping companies were also instructed by the Ministry of Transport to terminate seamen's contracts at their homeport.[9]

It seems to me that there was a formal definition of being British as stated in the 1948 Nationality Act which embraced BAME subjects abroad but there was also a racial notion of belonging constructed when Britain had conquered other races and this was based on race and colour. This had not yet changed. It was shown in the attitude of the Government, employers and unions towards the incoming Caribbeans. Some elements felt that if Black people were unemployed it was not because of discrimination but because they were irresponsible, quarrelsome and lacked discipline. They lived in slums not because of discrimination and the unwillingness of the government and local authorities to tackle the housing shortage but because they knew no better.

This attitude was evident from the opposition to Fenner Brockway's[10] bill seeking to outlaw discrimination. Had the British Government been sincere about the terms of the 1948 Nationality Act conferring citizenship on their BAME colonial subjects they had plenty of opportunity to ensure that these newcomers were protected by the law. The constant defeat of Fenner Brockway's bills tells us differently. In those days being BAME was to be perceived as a foreigner, hence my treatment on

---

9   Carter et al 2000
10   Fenner Brockway won the Eton & Slough seat in the 1950 General Election. In the House of Commons Brockway was a member of the left-wing group Tribune Group led by Aneurin Bevan. Brockway disagreed with Bevan on the issue of nuclear weapons and in 1958 joined with Bertrand Russell, Victor Gollancz, J. B. Priestley, Canon John Collins and Michael Foot to form the Campaign for Nuclear Disarmament (CND).

the Romford Road.

It was also in 1948 that a white crowd of two to three hundred people attacked Caribbean people outside an Indian restaurant. The next day a crowd of two thousand attacked a BAME seamen's hostel, which led to the BAME community barricading themselves in a club, called Wilkies, on the third day. A white crowd gathered outside, and the police forced their way in to arrest the BAME defenders and beat them up. Independent witnesses were charged with an offence when they came forward to testify in support of the BAME seamen.[11]

This incident illustrates how the authorities' reaction to any confrontation between races was a tendency to come down heavily on the side of the indigenous people irrespective of the rights and wrongs of the individual case. Two days after the arrival of the Windrush, eleven Labour MPs wrote to Clement Attlee urging immigration control. Furthermore in 1950 the Labour Cabinet Committee was set up to review immigration checks[12] and though these were later shelved, it illustrates how despite wanting BAME labour, the government did not seem to want the BAME labourers themselves.

Intentionally or not the British Government had constructed a framework to view BAME people as threatening and alien. In fact, both political parties did this by not investing sufficiently in the infrastructure to prevent a strain on resources, and to make matters worse social services were sometimes cut to resource other policy areas. In addition to this, government spokespeople referred to colonial immigration in terms suggestive of disapproval or alarmist.

It is bitterly ironic that MacMillan, who as housing minister

11   Fryer 1984
12   Carter et al, 2000

in 1951 achieved a target of building 300,000 houses a year, was to reverse this policy in 1954 when his cabinet discussed the social and economic problems caused by immigration. They also cut between twenty-five to thirty million pounds in the budget for social investment which affected housing, education and hospitals.[13] These were all areas where the BAME newcomers were perceived as being in competition with the indigenous white working class. The Government caused the very problem that was blamed on BAME presence.

Although the British government's policies aggravated the racist reaction that met the newcomers the Government only stepped in when under pressure by other forces to try and address a problem they themselves had helped to construct. In 1954 the Government appointed five internal investigation studies into Commonwealth migration but none into Irish or Italian immigration and neither Labour nor Conservative Governments took any measures to facilitate the settling in of the newcomers.[14] There were also several officials and politicians willing to convince the public of the benefits of legislative control of immigration and this often took a racist form playing on people's fears.

The only constraint the Government had on their policies towards the BAME newcomers was their desire to preserve the Commonwealth and this was to be useful to my campaign for civil rights in later years. At that time the creation of the Commonwealth was a precursor to the struggle for national independence in the British colonies. The impact of the 1948 Nationality Act and the new arrivals from the Commonwealth was to herald a change in attitude that was to affect me as a child in London.

13   Kathleen Paul, 1997
14   Kathleen Paul, 1997

Unaware of the forthcoming struggle between Britain and her colonies I had my own childhood battles. During this time I attended Odessa Primary School just off the Romford Road. There I got into a playground fight over a Jewish boy called Martin Englemann – though I didn't know it at the time this, was my first political fight.

Although I was not subjected to name calling and racist treatment in school itself, when I saw Martin Englemann being subjected to the treatment I was receiving on the streets of London, because he was Jewish, I stood up for him in that playground fight. After that action, no one wanted to provoke me into fighting. In retrospect this was my first awareness of racism towards another race. I instinctively knew from my own experience that this was an injustice even before I had developed a political philosophy.

'Whenever you hear anyone abuse the Jews, pay attention, because he is talking about you.'[15]

I might not have articulated this perception in the same way but I must have felt this same sentiment at the time when I stood up for Martin Engelmann.

There were some positive influences during my childhood days in London, and Major Stanley McNelly was one of them. He was an insurance loss adjuster and I believe an assistant recorder at Chelmsford, Essex County Court and someone who shaped my early life. His mother lived in the East End and was a great fan of the popular singer and entertainer Donald Peers whose famous record at the time was 'In A Shady Nook By A Babbling Brook'. Major McNelly devised summer holidays for the East End children to go on during those post-war years. Later in my life I was to organise just such events for inner city children in Bristol, Coventry and Brixton. It was this kind of wholesome opportunity

15   Fanon,1986 p.60

that engendered self-sufficiency and confidence that I wanted to give the children of immigrant families when I became a youth worker.

In those post-war days I visited and stayed with middle-class families, for instance the Douglas-Smiths at their large detached country home The White House in the village of Great Bardfield, Essex. Mr Douglas-Smith was I believe a Cambridge don who invited me back each summer between 1946 and 1948. The family I understood was approached with the possibility of fostering me but while I was happy there, they felt I might have become too isolated so did not foster me.

When visiting the Douglas-Smiths I would pop across the road from The White House to an old thatched cottage where a frail and slightly hunchbacked old lady called Nellie Bright lived in what I can only describe as a hovel. When I look back on it the Douglas-Smiths must have been very liberal to allow me to go to this woman's house where she would give me tea. In her home there was no electricity or sanitation; her only light came from candles. I felt sorry for her and would sit talking to her. I got to know her, and she would tell me about her times.

That was quite an experience for a young boy. She had an amazing personality and was well known all over the village. Everyone there knew Nellie Bright. She was a popular person who would greet everyone with her characteristic and cheerful "Hello Dearie". Looking back, I find it amazing that Britain claimed to have brought all these improvements and innovations to the colonies and yet had on their own doorstep senior citizens living in very poor conditions. I think this was my first experience of having a human concern for disadvantaged people

The Douglas-Smiths were surprised that I was in dialogue with this well-known village woman and that I would spend summer nights talking to her. Her poverty and how she dealt with it fascinated me. I felt sorry about the poor condition she lived in and I asked myself did she really need to live like that? When I revisited the village later in the 1960s, I took my wife, Joyce, to meet her. When she died, I think the local council converted her cottage into a village museum.

My activities during this period included camping in The Rodings and in Epping Forest, and like many young people I was also interested in films and music. I used to go to the Odeon's Saturday matinee shows and watch cowboy films which featured Hop Along Cassidy and Roy Rogers. It was also at the Odeon that I saw 'My Brother Jonathan' and 'Scot of the Antarctic'. It was a happy feature of the week meeting up with other children and singing songs.

I remember going into a popular record shop in Woodgrange Road in Forest Gate to buy my first record, an Al Jolson one. In fact, I was featured in the Stratford Express because I won a competition for miming to an Al Jolson song. At that time no one felt uncomfortable about seeing white people black up, at least I was unaware of any issues about it then. The irony of being a Black person imitating a white person who was imitating a Black person I felt was amusing. This was the first time I saw my picture in the paper. I would put black make up on and use toothpaste to whiten my lips, which amused the other contestants. Looking back it must have been a great laugh as it was long before Lenny Henry's debut in the Black and White Minstrel show. I was a fan of Jolson and was very taken by his fortitude as played by Larry Parks in the film *The Jolson Story*.

Like most boys at the time my imagination was also caught by the swashbuckling Errol Flynn who I wrote to and he answered by sending me a picture of himself which featured him sword fighting. I particularly liked Flynn in the film *The Three Musketeers*. It was years later that I found out the author of the book *The Three Musketeers*, Alexander Dumas, was a Black French writer.[16] I was also very much a fan of Paul Robeson and admired Frankie Laine and Doris Day. We used to watch black and white television and I was also mesmerised by Mario Lanza when he appeared in films on television.

In July 1948 Britain was going through radical political changes during the post-war period and Aneurin Bevan had got the National Health Service Act through Parliament. The Act had enabled my mother to secure work in the newly established NHS. It was during this period that she introduced me to early migrants from the West Indies. I was not used to seeing Black people and my mother's associates at first intimidated me because of my late introduction to people who were visibly like me. This was an important step in my awareness of race and understanding how white people might perceive me. Their manner and appearance felt different to the adults I was used to but gradually as we met Black families with children I was to develop an appreciation and a great affection for Caribbean people and culture. It also gave me great confidence because these Black youngsters mostly living in Notting Hill were new arrivals from the Caribbean and I was able to show them the ropes. I not only felt I could identify with them but also had some standing among them as my peers.

We weren't a close-knit family – the war had shattered that. Back in London I was told I had a baby sister, Josie, who was privately fostered by a friend of my mother's. My mother at the time was struggling to re-enter civilian life after being demobbed.

---

16 Alexandre Dumas's grandfather married a slave he fell in love with in San Domingo (now Haiti), named Marie Louise Cesette Dumas, her son Thomas took her name and enlisted with the French army. His son Alexander became the famous French author of the three Musketeers and other well-known popular novels.

From time to time I saw Josie during those childhood days, but it was later as young adults that we saw more of each other and began to relate as siblings.

In the post-war years my mother would also take me to visit my grandmother Edie Johnson, an actress in the West End. Edie took to me personally even though she had issues about race. She was dual heritage herself but could pass as white and there was a tension between her and my mother who clearly looked Black. Edie was uncomfortable with being Black and that was passed on to her daughter, my mother. Nevertheless Edie and I got on like a house on fire. She lived in the Kings Road in Chelsea and accepted me totally, probably because I was an articulate, confident young boy and of course her grandson. She was English, her daughter and grandson were English, and she made it clear she was against the immigration of Black people from the Caribbean.

At the time I was puzzled by the fact that she was attached to me but not welcoming to Black immigrants. I believe that was due to her insecurity. The race issue in our family was emotional as well as genetic. Despite this I was very impressed that she was on the stage, though I never saw her perform. She had shared the stage with Sir George Arliss, the Shakespearean actor who was the first British actor to win an academy award. Sadly I was in Germany doing my National Service when she died.

When I was old enough I attended Whitehall Secondary School where again I was the only Black person. I was put in the lowest class 1D, perhaps because of racist stereotyping, but I eventually worked my way up to 4A. At Whitehall School some teachers did express racism towards me and on one occasion when I was being caned across both hands for talking in class I was also asked by a certain teacher, who took relish in making a racist pun, 'What are you looking so black about Stephenson?'

This was also the teacher who wrote on my last school report that I was 'a disturbing influence'. The change from being perceived as a cuddly curiosity to a racial threat had begun.

These experiences taught me that colour mattered and that it was wrong for people to judge you on that alone without finding out about your personality or what you were really like. I also knew that racial discrimination was harmful, unjust and should be confronted. My school experiences were not purely negative however as I did make friends with several white school chums and stayed at their homes with their families from time to time. I was also popular with the girls; some of them would wave and scream as I went past their classrooms.

In my early teens I adopted Black role models, men I could look up to and admire such as the cricketer Sir Learie Constantine who was later to become a personal friend. Other role models were Paul Robeson, the singer and Sugar Ray Robinson, the boxer. They were people in entertainment and sport, the two fields that Black people were allowed to excel in at the time.

Alfred Garrett was the foster father at my Forest Gate foster home and he encouraged me to take up a career in the Royal Air Force. His wife was very positive towards me. She took me under her wing and gave me a lot of support, as did he, but their son, who had been physically affected by polio, had a negative attitude towards me. While his parents did not show any racist attitude, his envy towards me manifested itself in a racist way. Once, seeing me in sunglasses and observing the impact it had he said, 'What's a nigger wearing glasses for? You're just a nigger.' I was shocked by his remark.

On another occasion we were all on holiday on the Essex coast in Clacton and the Garrett's daughter Madeline, who was an attractive girl of about nine years old, was with us. While we were at an open-air show, we were asked to say who we thought was the most attractive person, so I took Madeline on the stage. There were immediately murmurs of 'What is that little Black boy doing up on the stage with that little white girl?' People don't realise you are picking up these negative reactions to your colour as a child, but you are, they affect you and you remember them.

Alfred Garrett had been a physical training instructor in the RAF, and his experience there had inspired him to advise me to join the Air Force. He had been influenced by the fact that many Caribbean people had joined the RAF after the battle of Britain in 1940. Here we have a picture of a white man influenced by Caribbeans joining the Air Force who in turn influenced me to take up a career in the RAF. He was a strict disciplinarian, NCO and amateur boxer representing the RAF and he was keen that I followed in his footsteps. He also felt I would be severely disadvantaged as a Black person in the labour market and wanted me to have the opportunity of a good career. His experience of seeing Caribbeans in the RAF during the war made him feel it would be a suitable path for me. I owe the next stage of my unfolding life story to his advice.

There was another person who also influenced my decision to join the Air Force cadets. Tony Mills, a great friend of mine living at the children's home in Forest Gate, had a father who was a young sergeant in the RAF and his father would take us both out together on trips. On one occasion he took us to meet Air Commodore Frank Whittle, the inventor of jet propulsion who was renowned in Bristol. He had already been knighted at the time. I was about eleven and aware that I was meeting someone very important, but I didn't know quite how important. This in my young mind gave the RAF a sheen of glamour.

I went to night school to prepare myself for the exams to get into the cadet apprentice scheme in the RAF. Tony Mills, who I thought had a better chance because his father was already in the RAF, also took the exam. But when we went up for our three-day examination and physical and psychological tests I got through and Tony didn't. However, his father prevailed on the Force till he got in.

I stayed from 1953 to 1955 when I did my cadet training, which included rifles. It was the same course any cadet would do whether from a local school or Eton. We had the same military training course in the use of firearms as officers or those doing National Service. The officer's course however would contain more theory on military tactics. Though we both went into the cadets together I didn't see much of Tony Mills and we eventually lost contact with each other after being posted to different places.

My time in the RAF was a pivotal period in my life and one which would have a far-reaching effect on my future, but for quite the opposite reasons I anticipated at the time.

Finding A Path:
The Formative Years
1953-1962

The seven years in the Royal Air Force (RAF) from 1953 until 1960 were to change my life. I saw another world travelling around Europe and large sections of England I never knew existed. Of course, I also had to face racism, but I also experienced extraordinary things in the Air Force and my experience there led to me identifying my real path in life.

I went into the Royal Air Force, a fifteen-and-a-half-year-old boy cadet. I was stationed in RAF Cosford Staffordshire near Wolverhampton, which is well known for its indoors athletic championships. I spent eighteen months there as the only Black cadet in my flight. I was aware of the insecurity of the other white members of the flight who seemed to miss their homes in various ways. They expressed this by crying at night or wanting to leave the Force. In contrast, for me it felt more like going up to a boarding school given my background in post-war London. When I first left Dunmow, Essex I used to cry a lot because I missed all my friends and the supportive relationships I had around me at the time, but I had come through that phase. I could now adjust to my new environment, but many of these other lads were experiencing leaving home for the first time. I didn't feel the same; I had already left the place I thought of as my home.

I made several friends, but I did find it embarrassing when my flight sergeant would call out at assembly time to ask me how I was getting on but referred to me as Sambo. I was embarrassed as much by his concern for me, as the only Black cadet, as his derogatory use of language. It was understood, given the culture of our belonging together as a flight, that his use of the term Sambo was a warning to parade training corporals and many of the other cadets in my peer group that I was not to be victimised or abused. It was implicitly known that if I were, they would answer to him. It was a perverse form of deterring bullying or racial abuse by using the racist term Sambo in this way, but I came through the eighteen months there without too much abuse from my fellow cadets.

On 2nd June 1953 as cadets we had the day off to watch the Coronation. It was a wet day and like thousands of people in Britain, we saw it on television. They mentioned during the programme that Colonel John Hunt was the leader of the Everest expedition that sent Edmund Hillary and Tenzing Norgay to the summit for the first time. I was impressed but did not know then that John was to become the Director of the Duke of Edinburgh Award and that this same John Hunt and I were to become very close friends and guests in each other's homes. When I first heard of him, we were worlds apart but only ten years later, we were on the Youth Service Development Council chaired by Countess Albemarle.

I found while a young cadet that I became interested in religion and the Church of England chaplain took a keen interest in my attitude to it and so I eventually became a candidate for confirmation. It was the Bishop of Lichfield, the Right Reverend Dr A.S. Reeve who confirmed me into the Church of England as a Christian. He took the salute after the confirmation prayers with our Commanding Officer who was an Air Commodore and who we regarded as a tin god.

I was surprised that the Bishop and the Air Commodore were on the parade dais together as we marched past after the confirmation service. Not for the first time it struck me as ironic that the church and the Air Force went hand in hand, as did the concept of a 'just war'. I felt my spiritual life was different to my military one. I thought that the Bishop and the Air Commodore were fundamentally separate, because Christians were given the commandment 'Thou shalt not kill'. In my view the Air Commodore was signalling the opposite. In those days of course Sunday parades were compulsory and even if you were an unbeliever you were perceived as Church of England. Many people have contradictory beliefs when you examine them carefully. That was one of those moments in time when that particular irony was brought home to me.

I must say that the Church of England had a profound impact on my thinking about religion and humanity. I was pleased that I had become a member of the Church since it gave me a sense of confidence and a form of understanding of what humanity was about. It was also great fun as we went on retreats, visited theological colleges and I could get out of some of the parades.

I also felt that not being racially abused and being accepted by my Flight was very helpful and I made very close friends with cadets from Scotland and Wales. For the first time I had come into touch with young boy cadets who weren't English but defined themselves as Scottish and Welsh.

I passed out in 1954 and Princess Marina, the Duchess of Kent, was the guest of honour at the passing out parade. It was understood that as I was the only Black cadet in the Flight, Princess Marina may well speak to me, and she did. I was surprised to find, as this was the first time I had spoken to a member of the royal family, that she had a heavy foreign accent, which was miles apart from the British upper class accent I'd been used to hearing.

My first posting was to Royal Airforce Waterbeach just outside Cambridge; here I developed a strong affectionate relationship with an officer's daughter. We saw each other during Church of England RAF station parades. I knew I was taking a risk with my affection for an officer's daughter, particularly being a Black airman, but we somehow managed to keep it quiet. Waterbeach was interesting because of its close proximity to Cambridge University. I was completely fascinated by the young students all riding on bicycles around the city.

When in Cambridge I saw a great deal of the Fisk family who I first met in Dunmow, Essex. They lived then in Great Easton, Essex. Mrs Fisk, I knew as Ma Fisk. She had three sons, David, Peter and Jim and a daughter who died of polio. David was closest to me as we had met in Sunday School in Dunmow and kept our link over the years. I spent much of my leave with them and they would take me out on trips in their Ford Popular.

My next posting was to Manston, Kent, which I really enjoyed, as it was an American Air Force base. I was to come into contact with many Black American GIs at the base who would entertain me with their music, and I felt very much at home there.

I was part of a small contingent at the base looking after RAF interests and re-fuelling aircraft that were going on to Germany or to various parts of Europe. I well remember one occasion when the Queen Mother flew in, in an emergency. She was to take the parade in Deal at a training camp for the Royal Marines, but the weather was bad. As a consequence of this, they had arranged to send a car up to Manston to drive the Queen Mother down to Deal. I was on duty as a young NCO to ensure things ran smoothly.

It was understood that the Queen Mother wouldn't leave the aircraft until the car came up to collect her. However, I saw her looking at me from the window of the aircraft and she gave a sort of wave. Later she came out of the aircraft and came up to me and asked where in America I was from. I was bit stunned as I was in RAF uniform and had saluted her very stiffly in a mark of respect and yet she thought I was an American GI. In those days of course nationality was associated with skin colour so I stood out as an anomaly, but it is interesting how people's preconceptions can sometimes outweigh reality and the evidence of their own eyes.

I also encountered the Bolshoi Ballet when they had to divert to Manston to get to London. I was on duty and responsible for their transfer from the aircraft on to the coaches to take them to London. At the time I was unaware of the prestigious reputation of the Bolshoi Ballet. I only knew we had to look after them until the coaches arrived.

Manston was very important to me because it was here that I was to renew my links with Mr Lawrence, my Sunday School teacher at Dunmow. I remembered fondly my earlier childhood days during the war when he was manager of a gas station and of the general welcome I had in Essex. Hence this reconnection with Mr Lawrence and his wife meant a lot to me. They were wonderful; they introduced me to Margate Methodist church where they were active members. I made several friends in the church there and was warmly received into it. During my leave when I had time off from working at Manston, I would stay overnight with the Lawrences who gave me a second home, and this was really important to me. Manston was a great posting as I enjoyed every moment of it, going into the sea on summer days and working with youngsters from the Methodist church.

I also made a close friend of Martin Prater, a devout Methodist who was very active in the church, while I was stationed at Manston. His father was a churchwarden and worked alongside Mr Lawrence in Margate. Martin's father was very supportive of what I was doing, and I was able to take an active part in the church. Martin and I kept our friendship going even after I had left the RAF and in later years Martin who became a chartered account worked for Notting Hill Housing Association as a finance director when I too worked in London.

My next posting was to Germany in March 1957 we journeyed there by troop ship and arrived during Lent. There was a feeling that we shouldn't fraternise with the *'Deutsches'* and so we couldn't go out. It was felt that as the Germans were celebrating Lent, if we fraternised with them it could lead to frustrations and perhaps violence. I stayed in a transit camp for a couple of days and after that I was told that I would be posted to Oldenburg in North Germany.

I was fascinated by the Germans; I liked them funnily enough. I took to them and for them I was a curiosity piece in the same way that I was in my early years of the war to the English. Many of them had never seen Black people and particularly because I was now a junior NCO, this spiced their interest. The children, in particular, would point to me and say, "Look Mum there is a schwarz man" – a Black man, "a neggar", a Negro. This had echoes of when I was a six or seven-year-old when people in England would say "Look Mum there is a Black boy." Once again, I felt I was being perceived as someone different.

My colleagues in the RAF were those doing National Service and others who were regulars pursuing a career in the RAF. Although I was being trained as an electrical technician on aircraft, I wasn't really interested in this. I wanted to get out and do things without all the military restrictions, so I decided to learn the German language.

Some National Service airmen persuaded me that I could join the Rover Scouts. They were working with children of regular airmen who were having their children educated in military schools and so I eventually joined up with the Scouts. This experience was to be very influential and had a major impact and influence on my future career.

Rudyard Kipling's, 'The Jungle Book' was used as a motivational book for the Cub Scouts and the adult leaders of the Cub Scouts were named after the main characters in this novel. I was known as Baloo and had an enormous impact on the youngsters and so Baloo came to mean more to those young Cub Scouts than Akela their leader.

The youngsters would listen to what I had to say as Baloo. My commandant, Group Captain Julian Cribb, the station Commander, had a son also called Julian who was about eight. The younger Julian was fascinated when I told the Cubs they had to go on camps and do various things like make their own beds, clean their shoes and if they did it correctly would get badges for all this.

I did not realise how inspired young Julian was by my description of Cub life until subsequently I had a message from the commanding officer that they were having difficulties with their son. Julian the younger had insisted on making his bed and doing his shoes when, in reality, a commander had a batman to do all that. This was creating havoc in the commander's household and while we were on parade the Group Captain stopped and asked if I would like to go over to his home and talk to his wife about his son Julian. The problem was that his son wanted to do all the domestic work and it was upsetting the servants. I agreed to go and talk to him but was very amused by this incident.

I used to take the RAF children to youth hostels. They loved coming away on scouting expeditions I organised for them, where they would have the opportunity to take tests and get their badges. They would also have fun camping in the many woods, which abound in Germany. I got to know their leaders well and would sometimes be invited to stay with them.

I knew I wanted to leave the RAF but knew I also needed an education, so I decided to take some GCEs. I spoke to my education officer and he could do the core subjects with me but not the Constitutional History and other subjects, so I had to do many of the subjects myself. I studied what was available in the library but with Constitutional History all I had to go on was the white papers of Britain dismantling its Empire. I was particularly interested in this subject, as this was a time when Britain was changing her relationship with her former colonies and African countries were becoming independent. I wanted to know why it was all happening.

I studied in the evenings on my own listening to Shirley Bassey singing songs on the radio such as 'I Will Love You'. I got through my 'O' level exams whilst in Germany. I also did my exams in London including an 'A' level Constitutional Law while I was in the RAF and got through.

I was also linking up with the German scout groups and youth groups and being entertained all over the place as well as going to Mittenwald with my scout friends. When we went skiing, I had a terrible accident and they had to stop the ski lift, take me down, get me to hospital and bind up my leg. This was the time of Manchester United's Munich air disaster. That was in January 1958. I was in plaster for two months. There was a lot of dismay at the time when they saw the lift stop and they were putting me on a stretcher on the lift. When I was being carried down some people said in German 'Broken your foot?'

The German family I was staying with in Mittenwald came to see me in hospital and asked me what I wanted, rather cheekily I told them wine. They duly obliged and got me a bottle but unfortunately, I drank too much of it and the nuns got really annoyed and had me discharged, so I returned to the German family. I mixed really closely with the Germans and loved every moment. They were always so delighted to see me and related to me in a warm and sympathetic manner. I was learning German, and this surprised many Germans because I didn't have too heavy an accent.

One fascinating person I became acquainted with was Fritz Wolff. I met him when I was hitch-hiking from Heidelberg, and he stopped to pick me up and took me to his home in Osnabruck. He was very warm, very helpful and informative. He loved a good debate and I met him at a time when I was just putting on my political colours. I shall always remember that very important meeting for me as a young Black NCO making a connection with a very influential German citizen.

Fritz Wolff turned out to be a political cartoonist who worked for the prestigious newspaper Die Welt. This national paper had been founded in Hamburg by the occupying British forces and was modelled on *The Times*. Fritz Wolff, who also worked in Osnabruck, invited me to stay with him at his lovely home where he told me a lot about the work he did as a political cartoonist. This was at the time of Harold Macmillan who was the British Prime Minister from 1957 to 1963 and Dwight Eisenhower who was the American President from 1953 to 1961. For me this was a unique and treasured contact with someone who was so distinguished.

I bought a car when I was in Germany, a Mercedes diesel, so I was able to drive around and do what I wanted to do. I stopped to visit the German families I knew, to catch up on their news and enjoy their company.

I was still in Germany when the Notting Hill riots of 1958 occurred. It featured strongly in the German press but didn't surprise me because I had seen it coming. The reaction I had engendered during the early years of the war had alerted me to the danger Black people were in from some elements of white society. The reaction to me as a young Black boy wasn't as strong because I was not in a position to be considered a threat. As a boy I was just a cuddly curiosity who was seen wandering around for miles and miles in the Essex countryside. The Notting Hill riots were much more dramatic, as were the Nottingham riots[17] where a similar incident occurred.

I felt that some of the children who had been attacking me on the Romford Road were the same element that was now creating trouble in Notting Hill. It was an attempt by some Teddy Boys at the time, coming from the white working class, to humiliate and subjugate the Black immigrants from the Caribbean who were now living in their midst with their own culture, Blue Beat music, and different ways of walking and talking.

Some elements of the white working class found this intimidating and wanted to terrorise Black people. This happens in situations where people are in competition for scarce resources such as jobs and housing. But the migrants fought back, particularly the Jamaicans, and they had to work out a way where the Black migrant workers were given a sense of protection. That is where my campaign was to come in because I was to campaign on the same level as the Americans. We needed civil rights protection under the law against discrimination. Before that it was how we keep the white working-class content and not threatened. There is no doubt that the Nottingham and Notting Hill riots left the English working class with the feeling that the immigrants, especially the Jamaicans, were not going to put up

---

17   Disturbances sparked off in the St Ann's area of Nottingham led to violent clashes between Black and white people.

with discrimination easily.

The Jamaican population made up a large per cent of the immigrant population. There were small groups from Barbados and Antigua, but they didn't come in large numbers like the Jamaicans. The latter came in greater numbers to the inner cities and were able to imprint their culture there. Much to the annoyance of the police and local politicians, they were going to fight for their rights. Later in the 1960s the non-violent Bristol Bus Boycott campaign gave them a breathing space and the Government an opportunity to look particularly progressive, by bringing about the first Race Relations Act to protect Black people from the more openly racist attitudes of some elements of the white population.

The Notting Hill Carnival had started in 1954 and was at first an indoor affair that became an outdoor carnival. By the summer of 1958, however, there were frequent clashes between Blacks and whites, which culminated in a white gang's attack on an interracial couple. Local whites were spurred on by local fascists and there was a riot for two days, with windows smashed, houses burnt and Black men and women assaulted while police and white crowds looked on.

On the second night Black residents struck back. At the Calypso Club Michael de Freitas (Michael Abdul Malik or Michael X)[18] suggested self-defence, and support came from other Black neighbourhoods. They fought a pitched battle with Molotov cocktails, bottles, bricks and metal that drove the white rioters back to their neighbourhood. The police then intervened, and the riots subsided.

This stripped some Caribbeans of their image of being British

18   Michael X was a Trinidadian and a spokesman for Black militancy. He was implicated in two murders and hung in Trinidad in 1975.

citizens. They were taught the lesson that they were Black first and British last. This had a galvanising effect on Black leadership as the riots brought people together socially and politically. After the riots new organisations for Black equality grew, a small group of intellectuals and well-connected activists formed the West Indian Standing Council (WISC). It was conceived as a channel of communication between existing Caribbean organisations in London and the Caribbean High Commissions to develop leadership in the Caribbean community and foster integration and improve relations between the races. WISC was a precursor in fact to organisations like the Community Relations Commission (CRC) and Commission for Racial Equality (CRE); organisations that would later be intertwined with my own life.

As Britain was disassembling her Empire, she was trying to stay a world power, so had formed the Commonwealth in order to keep her influence. Ironically this connection with her old colonies meant Britain cared about her image with the Commonwealth leaders and so Caribbean leaders could bring some influence to bear on the British government.

Caribbean leaders flew to London to show solidarity with the Black community and met with the Home Secretary R.H. Butler[19] and the Prime Minister Harold MacMillan. In one rather telling incident policemen moved in on the Jamaican Prime Minister, Norman Manley, when he was talking to someone in the street. He was naturally outraged. Manley described racism as a world phenomenon. American civil rights leaders also gave support and showed solidarity with the Caribbeans in Notting Hill. Later this support of new nations for their migrant communities was to be

---

19   Richard Austen Butler known as RAB because of his initials, was a Conservative MP who served as Chancellor of the Exchequer in 1951-55, Home Secretary 1957-62, Deputy Prime Minister 1962-63 and Foreign Secretary 1963-64.

very helpful in my own struggles for Black equality in Britain.

The British Government's response to both the Notting Hill and Nottingham riots was not at all supportive to the immigrant population. Neither working parties nor cabinet reports suggested that educational measures to familiarise the public with the new migrants were necessary. Remember they had been invited to England because their labour was needed. After the Nottingham and Notting Hill attacks on Black people the government saw migrants as the 'problem', not the racism which caused the attacks, and instead of tackling racism they started fashioning an Immigration Act which eventually became the 1962 Commonwealth Immigration Act.

The Act set up a voucher system allowing only those who had a job to come to England. Some of its sections carried deportation penalties for migrants from the West Indies, Asia and Africa. It removed non-commonwealth Irish immigrants from provisions of the Act – effectively making it a 'colour bar'.[20]

This was a knee jerk reaction to the Nottingham and Notting Hill riots where white people attacked Black people but the Government's response was to start undoing what its Nationality Act of 1948 had ostensibly created – British citizenship for all members of the Commonwealth. In addition, Conservatives blocked a total of nine times Fenner Brockway's bill to outlaw racial discrimination in public places, lodgings, dance halls, and to set up of penalties for incitement to racism. It was the beginning of an on-going process that was to introduce a caste system in British nationality that was to ensure that some British subjects were more British than others.

Meanwhile in Germany, I left Oldenburg for another part of that country, Gutersloh RAF base, where I continued to maintain

20   Jones 2000

the good relations with the German Scout movement and their leaders that had come to mean so much to me. I was increasingly invited to their homes whereas my other RAF colleagues would just go to the local NAFFI and stay in their billets. My last link with the scout movement in Germany was with English Scouts from Norwich who had an exchange partnership with the German Scouts. That partnership was very powerful as it helped the English Scouts to get a better understanding of Germany because there was still a lot of animosity by English service men towards the Germans because of the war. I was much struck and duly impressed by the way the Norwich Scouts contingent was pursuing a very positive partnership.

It was in Gutersloh where I first met Arthur English, who was then a well-known British post-war comedian from the music hall tradition and who specialised in playing spivs. He was later to play Mr. Harman the maintenance man in 'Are You Being Served'. It was here that I did an Al Jolson act before an RAF Christmas audience in 1958. Arthur was very supportive and keen for me to do the Al Jolson act. I was proud to be on the same show as him and he was keen to have me on. In a way, looking back on it, that Al Jolson act was to give me self-confidence with which to relate to crowds and an audience in a way which affected them.

I remember one particularly amusing occasion when I was doing a show a lady said to me, "I have no racial prejudice. I watch the Black and White Minstrel Show as much as I can." Despite that particular woman's ignorance of Al Jolson's race I believe in his twenties he was one of the greatest living showmen. This was in spite of the fact that, Black actors were often refused parts while their fellow white actors blacked up to depict Black people in a stereotypical way; this was an insult to Black aspiration. The social revolution caused by the Civil Rights Acts rightly put an end to the practice.

I left Germany in October 1959 to take up a posting in RAF Finningley in Yorkshire. When there I contacted the Methodist church in Doncaster where they had a very charismatic young preacher, Len Barnett, for whom I developed a great respect. It was through him that I was influenced to go on a retreat at Christmas in 1959, which was to change the direction of my life.

It was also in Finningley that I met up with Al Saxon who was an old friend from Forest Gate. After I left Dunmow I had worked for his parents in a grocery and florist shop near my school. I got along well with both him and his brother Tony Fowler. The Fowlers were Jewish, and they were very interested in where I was going and what I was doing, and they kept in touch with me after I left school. Now Al had become Al Saxon, a well-known rock singer, and had a hit with 'She's Only Sixteen'. He knew I was in the RAF and knew I was going up to Doncaster, so we arranged to meet up. During that period in Finningley because of him I also met Cliff Richard, who was appearing at the Doncaster Odeon.

Al, who had just got a hit record, took me backstage. Cliff Richard, who had been in a state of sheer nerves having to go on stage with girls screaming like mad, was very easy to talk to, and afterwards I asked him how he could go on the stage literally shaking. He said, 'Oh don't worry when I get on stage after I split my trousers it all changes and I get my nerve back.' Of course this is before Billy Graham influenced him.

At Christmas 1959 I went on a retreat with the Methodists in North Yorkshire and had an exquisitely enjoyable Christmas. While there I met people who were keen to assist me in getting out of the RAF and going to college. It was a life changing moment for me when one of them said that I might be able to get a place at Westhill College in Birmingham, which specialised in the training of youth leaders. After Christmas I lost no time applying for a place there in the following September.

When the Principal wrote to say I had been accepted at West Hill College the RAF were reluctant to let me go but eventually they relented partly due to the influence of Mrs Custerson who wrote to them. She had some influence because of her friendship with Rab Butler. I had to pay £250 to the RAF because they had trained me. I was given an outstanding reference by my commanding officer and I left the RAF in early March 1960. I had been told what to do all my life, first in the care of the County Council and then in the Royal Air Force. Now I was free to live my life as I wanted to. I was a free man alone and a civilian. It felt joyous! I could make decisions for myself and accept the consequences.

I had experienced some racism in the RAF such as name-calling, but I didn't let it impinge on my lifestyle or my ambitions. The best period of my time there was in Germany. It opened my mind to what people could do to each other. I was aware of the atrocities of the Nazis, but I couldn't quite match up the contradiction of the German's affection for me with the cruelty they allowed to happen in Europe.

I remember reading a book called 'The Scourge of the Swastika'. It had been written by Lord Russell of Liverpool, a barrister who headed the British legal team at the war crime trials at Nuremberg. This book revealed the cruel inhumanity of some German people towards the Jews and yet somehow, I was able to feel they were redeemable as not all of them were involved in this terrible genocide. It nevertheless left a terrible impression on me, what humans were capable of doing to other human beings. Even though I was treated well by most people in the RAF I'd suffered psychologically from having my colour always pointed out. I was therefore able to empathise with the Jews.

The Nazi ideology promoted by Hitler could never have been so terrible had it not been for the fact that the ordinary German people remained silent. It is this silence towards terror that allows the evil of 'Lebensraum'.[21]

As a civilian I was homeless, determined and independent. The Lawrences who were very good to me lived in Cliftonville, which was considered a good part of Margate. I stayed with them during my first weeks out of the RAF. In preparation for my two years Youth Work course at Westhill College in Birmingham, I spent a few weeks consolidating my experience of working with young people.

During that life changing Christmas in 1959 when I found out about the professional training I could get as a Youth Worker. I was also told about a Methodist holiday camp in Norfolk. I had links with Norfolk during the post-war years because I used to camp there during the summer when I was still being looked after by Essex County Council in a boys' foster care home. Hence, when I was told that at the Methodist camp in Mundesley-on-Sea I could work my ticket as a student there, that is exactly what I did in Easter 1960. I drove up there and loved it. In later years I was to return to it with my wife and children for summer breaks.

I became the entertainment officer at Mundesley Holiday Youth Camp and enjoyed organising bonfires on the beach, going to Great Yarmouth and sailing on the Norfolk Broads where the young people would enjoy jumping into the water. There were two old houses there converted into lodgings, so later as a young student at Selly Oak I never had to worry about having a place to stay because I could just drive off to Mundesley as there was

---

21 'Lebensraum' was an ideological principle of Nazism, used to justify German territorial expansion into Central and Eastern Europe to support Germany's 'natural development'.

always a place there for me to sleep.

In preparation for college I started supply teaching. The first school I taught in was the Charles Dickens School in Broadstairs, Kent followed by schools in Margate. While I was teaching in Margate Junior School the Head was surprised that I was signing on the dole and said that this was outrageous, and that the education committee should be paying me. I was the only Black teacher in the school and was very popular with the children. He insisted that I was paid by the education committee and made this happen. I didn't mind who paid me because I loved teaching in schools.

I got on well with the children in Kent and Margate schools but was not always as popular in the staff room as in the classroom. I was liberal and tended to clash with the authoritarian trend of some teachers who considered me out of phase with their viewpoint. As a young temporary teacher I don't suppose I had much effect on their entrenched views.

I then moved to Essex and was given accommodation by Christine Custerson at her large manor house 'Famadene'. It was there that I met Rab Butler and his wife Mrs Courtald. Butler had been the victim of polio and consequently had to use his left hand to shake hands rather than his right. Rab Butler had just lost his Tory leadership challenge and his wife was visibly shaken by this.

During the summer term, wanting my own digs, I looked round for accommodation in Thaxted but the local pub there refused me, because I was Black. Since the pub was opposite the vicarage, I asked the vicar if I could rent a room there. He was known as the red priest because he had communist views, so he said, 'Yes.' I was rather pleased, as to stay in the vicarage at Thaxted was rather something! I lived there from Easter to the summer. I did supply teaching at Saffron Walden High School and started an after-school club there. I also took the children swimming to a private swimming pool in Little Bardfield.

I then got a job as a supply teacher at Saffron Walden Technical College. I was living in the same village as students who attended the college so I would give them lifts in my car when I saw them waiting at the bus stop. There were occasions when they were late for their bus and missed it so I would give them a lift, but teased them by saying to them sternly, 'Right you're late for college". This was all done in fun as I got on very well with those young people and set up a Youth Club in the Mill in Thaxted and they would come camping and on cycling expeditions at the weekends. They took to me and I took to them.

In September 1960 we had groups of young Austrians and Germans from Europe coming over to Mundesley and a group from Austria invited me to stay in their home just outside Vienna. Subsequently, before starting at Westhill, I hitch-hiked from Mundesley to Vienna and back. On the way I visited friends I had known in Germany when I was in the RAF. I didn't have trouble hitch-hiking as cars would stop, even though they were not used to picking up Black hitchhikers, and I got a lift across to Vienna Forest where I camped with the students who I had met in Mundesley, Norfolk.

When I returned to England, I began to prepare myself for student life and my two-year course at Westhill, Birmingham. For the first time I felt the excitement of real independence and that I was at last treading a path of my own making. Shouldering the responsibility for my own future was a thrilling prospect.

At Westhill I had to share a room with a devout Methodist who told me he was making a great sacrifice sharing a room with a Black person and that I was privileged to do so because he was liberal. That was my introduction to college. I realised I had arrived in a new environment and again I was to be reminded that objectionable racism also existed here. Years later he was to apologise to me for saying that. This made me feel optimistic about the progress that had been made in how white people perceived Black people and that real equality between different races could be achieved.

It didn't come as any surprise that of our intake of students, who were mature students, I was the only Black person. By that time I had two 'A' levels and six 'O' levels. When I realised that most of the students were trainee female students from white middle-class backgrounds and they only had five 'O' levels and no 'A' levels I asked whether I could do the Teachers Training course as well as the Youth Workers course. I was refused and told I had to do the two-year Youth Workers course because it wasn't possible for me to take up the Teacher Training course even though it was a Teacher Training College.

I think this was another form of racism because I was better qualified than many of the student teachers. I felt very disappointed by this as I felt they were denying me an opportunity that I was more than qualified to undertake. It was with some satisfaction therefore that I was later to pass the course with distinction as the first Black student to do so.

Today people refer to glass ceilings in terms of the upper echelons of Industry and government but it existed then and to a large extent still exists now for young Black people as a glass door excluding them from appropriate qualifications. Let us not forget that in America in 2000 a Justice Policy study[22] was published by a Washington DC based think-tank which found that that there were more Black men in prison there than in College – 791,600

22   www.justicepolicy.org/research/2046 'Cellblocks or classrooms?: The Funding of higher Education and Corrections and its Impact on African American Men' (Retrieved 22/6/2020)

were in jail and only 603,032 in Colleges.

Westhill College's focus was mainly on primary school aged children. In my group I got on quite well with the other students and didn't meet up with much day-to-day racism. I was also able to connect with Birmingham's disadvantaged white youngsters in the city and took them out to different places to camp, where we spent weekends in various hostels.

It was a Methodist-sponsored youth course so there was a strong feeling that we had a duty to instil the youngsters with Christian ideology. I could however understand when the youth said to me at the end of the day, 'Paul I don't want to say my prayers'. When I look back on that, I really feel sorry for them. My feeling was that the College was doing it out of Christian love and charity and so the youth ought to recognise that, but I certainly saw that the youth were mainly secular and didn't really want to be railroaded into Christian ideology.

Dr Fred Milson was my tutor. He was a brilliant man and a wonderful wit who gave me a great deal of encouragement. One of the things he asked me to do was to look after children who were going to Davos Dorf in German speaking Switzerland as a holiday. I guess he chose me because I could speak some German. He asked me if I would take charge of them when they arrived in Davos Dorf.

By a strange coincidence I had been given the book 'Die Zauberberg' ('The Magic Mountain') by Thomas Mann in January 1961. This novel about ideas and lost humanism depicts the fight between liberal values and conservative values and is set in Davos. Thomas Mann describes the Magic Mountain where Germans went to be treated for TB. The book tells how the protagonist, Castorp, went from Hamburg to Lanquart on the German-Swiss railway travelling on this magical rail line with all its tunnels and snow-capped mountains.

It seemed amazing to me that here I was doing exactly the same journey from Hamburg to Lanquart where I got off and had a beer and then took the train to Davos. It was exactly how I envisaged it from the book. Thomas Mann talks about Davos Dorf where annually industrialists, bankers and politicians go to make their world-shaking decisions.

When I arrived there, just as the book describes, there was a nun as you emerge from the train and striking snow-capped mountains surround you with horse and carriages and drivers that greet you and take you where you want to go. I had just relived a very real experience from Thomas Mann's book by going through the same journey that he depicts. I spoke to one of the drivers in German and he was surprised by the fact that I could speak some German. He took my luggage and so I arrived at the children's home in preparation for the youngsters from Bedford who were going to have their holiday there.

Unfortunately, the Bedford youngsters didn't care about the breath-taking beauty of the views and the picturesque snow-capped mountains. They were totally unimpressed by the scenery from the ski lift or the mountain rides; all they wanted to know is if there were any fish and chips at the end of it. I was trying to say can't you see the beauty and splendour of your surroundings. I tried to spark them with some enthusiasm for the inspiring loveliness of the landscape around them, but they had no cultural understanding or sense of beauty about their environment.

The matron in the home they were staying was very authoritarian and that put them off completely. When they started saying 'We want to go home, we want to go back. We don't like it here.' I knew I was in the middle of a crisis. The matron didn't understand exactly what was wrong with them and she felt they were undisciplined and didn't know how to take orders. I had to liaise between the matron and the children who were writing home saying, 'Get me out of here'.

In the end I managed to calm the children and recommended that they return home. After this mini misadventure the parents invited me to meet them in Bedford and so I went there as a guest of the company. Some of the children had written to their parents saying 'Paul is great' but didn't mention that I was Black so this was a surprise to the parents when they saw me, which just shows how little skin colour matters to children.

At this time I also became alerted to the position of the African Caribbeans in Birmingham who had started to come here. The youngsters were often leaving their grandparents and joining up with their families but coming here to live in the ghastliest areas. I used to take some of these youngsters out to various places, but they didn't live in areas I thought was suitable, as they were frequently open to racial abuse. As I have mentioned before the national government had done nothing to ensure there was enough invested in the infrastructure to prevent a strain on resources. In fact, social services were sometimes cut, which meant the newcomers were perceived as competing for resources with white working-class locals and wrongly accused of being given preferential treatment when the reverse was true.

Through my Youth Work studies I was also to meet up with the late Denis Howell who was leader of Birmingham City Council at the time. He was very outgoing and friendly and took an interest in how my life was going. We kept in touch – he always had a healthy curiosity about what I was doing and so I maintained links with him. He was to become very important later in my life when he became Sports Minister and backed me in the campaigns, I was involved in such as the anti-apartheid campaign.

As students we were studying the effects of disadvantage on young people in society. I was investigating how the police dealt with the disadvantage, how seriously they took this into consideration and its relationship to the crime rate and generally what the police's attitude to these things were. I was trying to see things from the police point of view, as they were having a difficult time. My attitude was that these youngsters were being made criminals because of a system of social inequality and they were no worse than I would have been had I been brought up in that situation.

Some of the police perceived Black youths as potential criminals. The onus seemed to be on the youth to prove they weren't criminals. However, I showed such concern and enthusiasm for the subject that I was almost in trouble with police myself. Some youngsters were having problems with the police and when I supported the young Black immigrants the police felt I was being biased against them. This incident led to the police speaking to Westhill College about me. This I think without knowing it at the time, may have been my first political brush with authority.

I was one of the few students who had a car and I think I was a little envied because it was a Mercedes. It was very useful, as I was able to get around. I met up with some of the Scouts in Birmingham who were sympathetic to me recruiting more young Black people into the Scouts.

Generally I had great fun and made friends during my two years at Westhill, Birmingham. I took an apolitical attitude to what was going on in the world. I was probably right of centre at that time. In the headlines were the Cuban revolution, communism and socialism but issues of racism were only beginning to surface as a social, political and economic force in Britain. Those who were upwardly mobile saw racism as an individual problem and not a collective one. For me that was about to change.

Bristol Bus Boycott
And The Bay Horse Incident
1962-1964

I left Westhill in July 1962 having successfully passed an interview for the post of Youth and Community Development Worker in St Paul's, Bristol. This post was advertised in a Birmingham newspaper and it asked for a Youth Worker to especially address the needs of Black youth. I was not particularly interested at the time as I saw myself returning to London or staying in Birmingham and threw the newspaper in the wastepaper bin in my room.

While we were at Westhill we were very privileged students. We had our individual rooms and we had cleaners who made our beds and cleaned our rooms out. On the day I threw the paper away the cleaner was off sick. That minor incident in her life acted as a chain reaction having an impact on mine and on race relations in Bristol and then Britain itself.

One of the other students asked me if I'd seen the advertisement and said it would suit me. I replied that I didn't really know Bristol and, in any case, I'd thrown the paper out. When I got back to my room later in the evening, the cleaner hadn't been in, so the paper was still there. I took it out of the wastebasket and looked at it again. I decided I wouldn't lose anything if I went for an interview, so I decided to apply and subsequently got the job.

The Joseph Rowntree Trust funded the post for an initial three years. Anne Hewer, a magistrate, was a member of the Bristol Education Committee and on the steering group that appointed me. She was very upper class and married to Professor Hewer who was a Professor of Medicine at Bristol University.

She had a warm, endearing personality and was very supportive of what I was doing. Although she didn't like the publicity that my campaign on the bus issue would attract, nevertheless she was loyal and proved supportive in the future, which annoyed the powerful establishment of Bristol. She was a great liberal. She really didn't want me to leave when I went to take up a post in Coventry. My line manager was Edward Seath, Bristol City Council's principal Youth Service officer.

When I arrived in Bristol the Black population there was overwhelmingly Jamaican but there were people from other Caribbean islands as well. St Paul's where I was working was, and still is, the main Caribbean area, although Easton too has a large Caribbean population. Today people are more dispersed over the city but both St Paul's and Easton retain their cultural identity. In those days people would send for family and friends to join them. It was possible then to do that as the Government had only just began to put in place their immigration legislation with the 1962 Commonwealth Immigration Act, previously mentioned, which was effectively a colour bar on people coming from the colonies.

In November 1963, immigration was the subject of much debate behind the scenes at Westminster. Tony Benn states in his diary that at a meeting of the Parliamentary Labour Party Harold Wilson criticises the Conservatives' new Commonwealth Immigration Bill as racist. It discriminates between Commonwealth and European immigrants and is not based on an agreement with Commonwealth countries but unilateral in character. At the same meeting Wilson outlined his views, stating that he felt control was necessary, but that racial discrimination should be made illegal and greater help given with housing and education. He also wanted to see proper control of rents and the national Government helping local authorities, especially with establishing working parties. Wilson also thought there should be maximum facilities for Commonwealth students, including the interchange of visits, and felt controls alone would not solve the 'problem' as immigration was provoked by poverty in the Commonwealth. He felt the solution lay in an increase of aid through the Commonwealth, the United Nations and trade.[23]

This attitude was not shared by all, even the unions still urged the General Council to give special attention to the problems caused by the influx of fellow workers of other races, despite the fact that in 1955 the Trades Union Congress (TUC) condemned all manifestations of discrimination. It is clear from this that they still saw the Caribbean migrants, not the racist reaction to them, as the problem.

The Indian and Pakistani Governments co-operated with restricting immigration as they didn't want low caste Indians arriving and spoiling the reputation of the well-to-do or the students. Caribbean countries were also urged to adopt tougher tactics on migration, but Michael Manley rejected a proposal for a passport moratorium on grounds that the rationale for this was not about jobs or houses but race.[24]

My concern, at the time, was however with Black people already here. They had to be resident in the city for one year to qualify for a five-year waiting list for houses so most Caribbean migrants were forced to live in overcrowded conditions, especially when they first arrived.

It was very much a period when people were settling in, finding jobs and making their mark in a new country. Even though this was the only country I knew, I felt a great sympathy for their concerns, and I could strongly identify with the

23   Benn, 1987
24   Paul, 1997

irrational prejudices and racism they faced. Today racism can still be about colour, we unfortunately still have the fascist British National Party getting voted into the European Parliament, but racism is often more about culture now, than colour. In those days it was all about skin tone so of course I had a great rapport with these newcomers who looked more like me than my fellow-countrymen and women.

In St Paul's, Bristol a small number of white proprietors began to sell Caribbean food in and along Grosvenor Road and were later replaced by Caribbean shop owners themselves as the community grew. They had a Caribbean cricket team and Black churches had also been established. People made their own entertainment, such as blues clubs which were often run from someone's cellar as they could be turned away from the pubs and clubs outside St Paul's or risk being beaten up by Teddy Boys. This discrimination in places of public entertainment was something I would tackle head on two years after arriving in Bristol.

Owen Henry, a Jamaican was someone who started social events in a basement room in St Paul's. People would meet friends on a Saturday evening, play dominoes, chat and listen to blue beat records. Henry also had a sound system called Honeybee, which he played at basement parties. He was a popular community leader and organised trips back to Jamaica, which evolved into a travel business. He was also to play a major part in the Bristol Bus Boycott campaign.

At that time, Jamaicans here were saying, 'I'm going to make money and send it back to help the children'. They wanted to return prosperous, so they weren't prepared for a confrontation, especially as they came with a sense of belonging – after all this was their mother country. They had been taught this was the seat of civilisation. They had no idea about racism, the way it operated in England. When I later visited Jamaica to speak about racism that subject didn't have the same meaning or relevance for them. Their injustices stemmed from class, and even though skin tone may be an issue, the blanket racism they faced here was different.

There were, however, slow realisations that for most people the prosperity they had expected, which would allow them to return wealthy, wasn't happening. That is why people started bringing their children over here and so a small but growing population of Black children started arriving here. This was a very crucial step for these migrants, as this meant people became less tolerant and complacent about their conditions here and so it engendered a desire to improve life for themselves in their new home. I think this changing shift in attitude helped the Bristol Bus Boycott campaign to gather grassroots support.

I saw how the young immigrants who were growing up or who were born here were being treated. I foresaw that if we didn't intervene and recognise what was happening to them that thousands of young people would experience the racism I faced when I first got back to London just after the war. I didn't want them to grow up going through the nightmare I went through, a curiosity at first then a figure of unjust hostility. I wanted them to be treated equally and have the same rights and opportunities as white English people.

In my first job as a qualified youth worker I was based in Great George Street in the Youth Service Office. At first, I stayed at the St Agnes vicarage in Badminton Road, St Paul's and joined the church there. The Bishop of Bristol, the late Oliver Tomkins, thought the vicar, who had been a missionary in Africa, was the person to help immigrants from the Caribbean. I found this not to be the case. In fact, the vicar, in my opinion, was very right wing so I got a flat with another youth worker in Clifton.

My flatmate worked in Southmead. There were two appointments paid for through the Joseph Rowntree Trust. One was my appointment in St Paul's and the other was my flatmate's who was working with disadvantaged young white people in Southmead. We both shared an office in Great George Street. For the first year I worked among the families in St Paul's with their many issues that showed the city as being openly racist and quite proud of being so.

During this time I was also teaching as a supply teacher in Baptist Mills and running a Youth and Community Centre there while developing relations with the Asians and Caribbeans. My links with the school meant that I was able to engage the children at the Youth Club to take pride in their club and they did this by decorating it and doing it up. This was very encouraging. I had a tremendous rapport with the young school children who were not used to seeing a young Black man teaching. I still get stopped today by ex-pupils who remember me from those days.

That was a time when John F Kennedy was in the middle of the missile crisis with Cuba. I was saying to them this is a very serious time for the world and it had an enormous impact on them because when ex-pupils stop me in the street, they often mention this. I taught English, Geography and History. 'That Was The Week That Was', a satirical news programme, was on the television and I would explain to students how you could use satire effectively to make a point.

It was a very interesting time in education because there was a move towards comprehensive school and that debate was raging. People had begun to object to the segregation of children at the age of eleven who would, after being tested, be divided into those considered academic enough to go to a grammar school and those who failed, who would go to a secondary modern school. Comprehensive schools were being introduced which taught children of all abilities together and this meant that late developers did not find themselves disadvantaged.

At one time I was the only Black teacher in Bristol and I sometimes heard racist remarks in the classroom. They had no idea about the cultural background of the young Black children who would sometimes be left with grandmothers in the rural districts of Jamaica and then later come to join one or both parents, fathers or father's partners in Bristol. They didn't understand their language, music, culture or their food.

Some members of staff were very ignorant about Black culture. Teachers often didn't know where Jamaica was on the map or thought St Kitts was in Africa. I heard remarks such as 'Is Jamaica in Africa or Trinidad?' By and large most teachers were unconcerned about meeting the needs of the new migrant children they found in their care. Sonia Burgess was a student in one of my classes and was around at the time of the Bristol Bus Boycott campaign. One of Sonia's teachers said she was so bright that she wanted to keep her in the class to stimulate the rest so did not encourage her to go into a higher class but kept her there. Those kinds of things were going on all the time. Despite this Sonia eventually became a successful businesswoman.

Often their parents didn't understand that their children were in fact being robbed of an education. Some of these youngsters had to deal with hostility, abuse, strange weather, and difficulties with relationships with their families. It was a very hard time for them.

How did the education establishment react? Many of the teachers in school had no idea of the cultural background of their students. Black children were often inappropriately designated with special educational needs and placed in special schools. This assessment was based on prejudice rather than science, and we are still living with that legacy today. Even as late as 1972 Caribbean children accounted for only 11% of children in state schools but 4.95% of all children in (SEN) Special Educational Needs schools. This underachievement was the result of language, curriculum, teacher's attitudes and material disadvantage compounded by racism and its effects.[25]

There were teachers who did struggle to understand the culture of their newly arrived pupils from the Caribbean; the headmaster of Baptist Mills School was one. He was very sympathetic with what I was trying to do and was concerned regarding the Black children's educational prospects. After the Boycott campaign however his attitude to me changed.

Once I had established the youth club in Baptist Mills dozens of youngsters would come and visit the club to listen to music and to dance. It became very popular with them. I had no problems relating to the white children. They were very warm and friendly and there were no issues with race or anything with them. They saw me as one of the teachers at school running a youth club and the Black children who had recently arrived in England were happy to have somewhere they could play their music. I would take the youngsters camping into the forests and farms around Bristol. This was something the Black children could connect to as they had mostly arrived from rural areas in the Caribbean.

Remembering my early childhood in Essex. I wanted to give them the positive experiences I had as a child in the countryside, not the negative ones of the city streets after the War. I identified with nature in a very real way and especially wanted these young immigrants to have this kind of wholesome and confidence-building experience. I would sometimes take them on wild

25   Ramdin, 1987

nature study walks showing them wildflowers such as bluebells, buttercups, celandines, cowslips, primroses and such beauties of nature.

On September 27th, 1962 the Bristol Evening Post published an article about a scheme I had organised with the youth. I had arranged for a group of fifteen English, Indian and Caribbean boys from Baptist Mills Youth Club and Dockland Settlement to work at Howarth Fruit Farm in Cleeve and get paid in fruit. We stayed at Goblin Coombe, a rural hostel which was run by Bristol's Youth Service in Somerset. It was just before they went back to school and the weather was sunny and mild. They really enjoyed themselves, after picking the fruit the boys turned it into jam. They had a wonderful time making the jam and then putting it in jars. They then gave half the jam to pensioners and the other half they sold and donated the money to charity. They had a lot of fun doing that and it helped build their confidence and self-esteem.

Recently I got a taxi and the driver, a grey bearded Sikh wearing his turban, reminded me of the trip to Goblin Coombe that he went on as a young teenager, all those years ago when I was teaching at Baptist Mills.

Back in 1962 I was doing community development work as well as teaching in school and I was meeting up with people and parents who brought their children into school. I was helping with extra classes in the evenings, as there was an enormous appetite for education from Caribbeans who had come here to make the most of their opportunities. I got to know some of the community leaders, and many complained about the Bristol Bus Company. It had a ban on employing Black people even though there were people coming from London who had been recruited and trained on London buses but couldn't get a job on the Bristol buses. I found out later that Owen Henry and others had made a complaint about this but did not get anywhere.

This experience had a profound impact on me and effectively politicised me. I was really concerned about the way racism was taking hold of the city and the effect it was having on Black parents and Black children and of course my own experience of being Black. It was after seeing what was happening to Martin Luther King and his followers in Alabama who were being set upon by the police with dogs, being beaten up and worse, that I found the inspiration for the fight against racism.

In my own life experience, though I was completely English, my colour made me realise that there were no rights for Black people, no legal protection from discrimination and injustice. At that time of course Black people here were not welcomed in the Police Force or the Fire Service or in any of the main public institutions except as cleaners or such low paid work with no prospects. In addition there was no law against racial discrimination.

Rosa Parks'[26] refusal to move to the back of the bus on 1st December 1955 and her ensuing arrest had led to the formation of the Montgomery Improvement Association with Martin Luther King, as its president and head of the civil rights movement. It was this fight, the manner in which he engaged with racism and took on Washington ensuring that the American Government knew Black people were no longer willing to endure being second-class citizens, that inspired me.

Seeing what was happening in the USA I decided we should

26   Rosa Parks was a Black American from Montgomery, Alabama where Black people were only allowed to sit in a few seats on the public buses and if a white person wanted their seat, they had to give it up. On one bus journey in 1955 Parks was asked to move for a white person. She refused, the police were called, and she was arrested and convicted of breaking the bus laws. The Black people of Montgomery decided that the best way to show their anger at what had happened and how they were being treated was to organize a bus boycott.

draw more attention to what was happening here with Black people, particularly in Bristol. I then decided to take on the Bristol Bus Company because it was a symbol of all that was wrong with Bristol because it advocated and defended racism and was the most notorious racist employer in the city. I was walking on the Downs when the idea of a bus boycott in Bristol, inspired by Rosa Parks and Martin Luther King, came to me.

Everyone knew about the ban and I understand there was even an article in the Bristol Evening Post in 1961. Three residents of City Road, St Paul's namely Fianzo Clarke, Henry Patrick and Patrick Shillingford had complained about racism including the Bristol Omnibus Company's failure to employ Black people[27] but no one had tried to lift it. I knew something had to be done about the situation so in April of 1963 I decided to address the issues of racism and the civil rights of people in this country through this piece of blatant discrimination. I wanted to move the debate on from the clashes with Teddy Boys in the streets to the rights of Black people in this country.

My first step was to prove a ban existed. I was doing night classes at Baptist Mills and Guy Bailey was a student there, so I invited him to prove that the Bristol Omnibus Company was being racist. When he agreed, I rang the Bristol Omnibus Company to arrange an interview for Guy Bailey, recently arrived in Britain, who had been a boy's brigade officer in Jamaica. I knew he was suitably qualified, a very good quality candidate with an impeccable character and a member of the cricket club. I also knew there was a vacancy. I made the call because I had a very English accent and I did not tell them when I rang that Guy was Black. When Guy arrived, they refused to interview him on the grounds of his race. I then went to see Ian Patey, the

27   Samuel, 1989

Bus Company's general manager, and established that there was indeed a company policy not to employ Black people so there was a second witness to the ban.

I was aware of all the arguments he produced. This ranged from, white people won't work with Black people, white women conductresses won't work with Black drivers, they would lose customers, the unions wouldn't tolerate it, they were worried about jobs being taken away, pay would decrease, it would cause violence between passengers and crew. I responded that he was playing on people's fear.

I felt like David facing Goliath. Thank goodness for those childhood images we can draw on during difficult times. It took me back to my early childhood years and thinking about justice and injustice in the stories of David, Goliath and Saul I had heard during the war in Dunmow. At the time they were just stories, here these themes were being played out in my own life. I had no doubt, however, that we would win our campaign given the impact Martin Luther King's campaign was having on the other side of the Atlantic. He was David with only the slingshot of justice on his side, but he was toppling the giant of segregation.

In fact, time has proved Mr Patey utterly wrong as Black and white people do work together in all kinds of scenarios across Britain today. Not only was Patey hiding behind the unions, but he was also making assumptions about the nature of people, who often turn out to have more integrity and moral fibre than they are given credit for. That is not to say that fears aren't currently being whipped up against new immigrant work forces such as white Eastern European workers or that Black workers do not still struggle for opportunities to work, for higher education or against glass ceilings in the work place. Nevertheless people are often better than they think.

At that time my meeting with Ian Patey was to end with me informing him that we would be mounting a campaign against this racist ban and publicly opposing it. His reaction was to say, 'Go away with your campaign, we are not employing Black people.'

What I didn't know at the time, but which was uncovered in Madge Dresser's pamphlet on the subject[28], was that previously in February 1962 a question was raised by Councillor Langham in the Council about 'coloured labour' on buses. His question must have been referred to committee and soon after, Ian Patey was invited to attend a mid-March session of the Joint Transport Committee.

There Patey justified the ban by stating that he had 'evidence' that 'coloured' crew would downgrade the job and that white labour would go elsewhere. Mr Gailey, a Bristol Omnibus Company official, also said because of better employment opportunities in the West Indies the better type of 'coloured' labour was not available now or already employed in London. On this rather spurious evidence the Council decided not to oppose the ban. Well, Ian Patey's reactions to Guy Bailey's interview, opened Pandora's Box for the Bristol Omnibus Company and it came in the form of a political campaign.

Wally Jenkins, the leader of Bristol City Council and local councillor for St Paul's was very hostile to the campaign. In fact, he was very hostile to the kind of progress I wanted to see happen. After the success of the Bristol Bus Boycott campaign when I tried to establish a community relations committee in Bristol he was totally opposed to the idea. However, when the idea was taken up in London, he changed his mind and became chair of the one we set up here. This was, I believe, mainly to keep me out.

28   Dresser, 1986

Back in 1957 the Caribbean Association had taken over from the older Colonial Association with Bill Smith, a conservative Jamaican, as its chair. He was someone who genuinely believed that the Bristol Bus Boycott campaign undermined racial harmony in the city. To a certain extent our campaign was disruptive, but you can't have true racial harmony without racial justice, so our protest was essential as a step towards racial harmony in not just Bristol, but the nation. However, the Caribbean Association refused to endorse the campaign and because of their hostility and Wally Jenkins' attitude it was crucial to bring another voice into the arena.

I realised that getting support for the campaign would be a key factor in any success, so I set about doing just that. I knew I could count on the support of the local Caribbean community leaders such as Owen Henry, Prince Brown, Audley Evans and Roy Hackett and we had a meeting in my flat and called a Press Conference at the Triangle in Clifton.

I saw a new group was needed and decided to set up a group called the West Indian Development Council (WIDC) to manage the campaign against the Bristol Omnibus Company. Owen Henry, Roy Hackett, Prince Brown, Audley Evans and other supporters I knew, because of the work I had done in the local community, were enthusiastically on board for a campaign. That was how the WIDC was set up. We were all unaware that this would eventually lead to changes in British legislation

I also marshalled support from people such as the Bishop of Bristol, Oliver Tomkins who I knew quite well and lobbied Bristol MPs Tony Benn and Stan Awbery. Jamaica had just become independent and Trinidad had too so their High Commissioners would also become involved. Henry Hennessey was a councillor who was also very supportive about what I was doing. He spoke out against Patey and the unions and faced expulsion from the Labour party the very next day as a result. The official explanation was that he made offending remarks about housing.

Owen Henry was a strong supporter of a ban on using the buses. He had a tremendous amount of support from his fellow Jamaicans in Bristol. He would take part in marches and accompany me on speaking engagements. He made a several speeches in support of the campaign and would win over newly arrived immigrants who did not know about the issue, so he could give them a clear understanding of what was going on. Many of them had not been exposed to racism in the way that they were now being exposed to it in Bristol.

On one occasion I was speaking at an event when a group of fascists were being very hostile to us and Owen Henry made it clear he was prepared to take direct action in my defence even if it meant facing violence. He also stood by me at a time when I was receiving death threats. He strongly opposed racism and wanted his fellow Jamaicans to support the boycott. After the success of the campaign he invited me to become president of what is now known as the Caribbean Parents and Friends.

Prince Brown was also a staunch supporter of the campaign. He was no stranger to struggle as he had worked against discrimination in housing, which was quite a problem for Black people, especially youngsters who could sometimes get thrown out of home. This was usually due to a culture clash between the youngsters and their immigrant parents under the pressure of poverty. He spent a lot of time drawing attention to homelessness amongst Black youth and trying to get something done about it. He had been a policeman in Jamaica and cared deeply about unemployment and homelessness. He was genuinely concerned about these issues.

Obviously, I supported what Prince Brown was trying to do in the community. In fact, in later years when I was working for the Commission for Racial Equality (CRE) Bristol was part of my regional responsibility so I recommended that the church in Trinity Road received a grant, so it could be converted to a community centre for young people and the elderly. We had the support of the local churches with this and it is still a thriving community centre to this day.

During the Bristol Bus Boycott campaign Audley Evans also came to demonstrations and marches and attended meetings. He was an ambitious entrepreneur who wanted to advance himself but finally became disillusioned with England and migrated to Canada. Some of the most promising youngsters were moving out then.

Roy Hackett was another person concerned about racism who gave the Bristol Bus Boycott campaign a hundred per cent backing. We worked well together as he was easy going and good for a laugh and at the same time a man of complete integrity. We had first met at a social event at the Transport and General Workers' Union premises in Victoria Street. He also showed me real kindness when I returned from my trip to Jamaica and I had nowhere to stay so, he put me up.

With the West Indian Development Council (WIDC) established, the campaign began with a press conference to announce the beginning of the boycott and the formation of the WIDC. The campaign caught the imagination of the local press, then the national press and it became known as the Bristol Bus Boycott. Although the Bishop and sometimes the press were to turn against me, I had the support of Tony Benn and other influential people.

I first met Tony Benn after I wrote to him asking him to back the campaign. We then met and I gave him a whole lot of leaflets and posters. He was very keen to be involved and very obliging and gave me a tremendous amount of active support. We rapidly became close. He went around giving leaflets out to people using the buses and used his position as a popular MP to influence Bristol public opinion

In early May when the Bus Boycott hit the headlines Tony Benn spent time writing to Oliver Tomkins, Bishop of Bristol, Frank Cousins, Ernest Marples the Conservative Minister of Transport and others in Bristol about it. He also spoke with Ron Nethercott, Regional Secretary of the Transport and General Workers' Union (TGWU), who refused to speak to me about the ban. Nethercott was very angry with Tony Benn because of his support for our campaign. Benn was unequivocal in his stand against the ban and saw through the arguments that Nethercott and the Bishop of Bristol made against the boycott.

Once Tony Benn got involved the regional committee of the Transport and General Workers' Union TGWU told him I was a communist, an agitator, unrepresentative of the Caribbean community and that they had been working for years behind the scenes to have the colour bar lifted. Tony Benn's response was to get Harold Wilson, leader of the Opposition, on side. Wilson was a powerful person to have involved. With him on board, Tony Benn ensured that it was clear the campaign was not communist led. Both Harold Wilson and Tony Benn gave me a lot of moral support too.

I had written to Harold Wilson asking him to publicly deplore the racist employment policy regarding the ban of Black workers on the buses. His reply to my letter was prompt and later, at a rally in Trafalgar Square, he took the opportunity of referring to the situation in Bristol whilst deploring the selling of arms to the

South African Government. In fact, Harold Wilson telegrammed me his support with the words 'The last of the colour bar - Bristol has it.'

My first personal encounter with Harold Wilson was when I was invited to the House of Commons where I sat next to him at a dinner given for the leaders of the immigrant Caribbean community. Also present was Baroness Gaitskell, who had just returned from the House of Lords after taking her seat there for the first time. She was the widow of the former Labour leader, Hugh Gaitskell. It was Hugh Gaitskell who had led the Labour Party into deploring the Commonwealth Immigration Bill, on the grounds that it was too hastily conceived and that control on immigrants to Britain could best be exercised by negotiations with Commonwealth countries.

Other people there were Harold's wife Mary, Jocelyn Barrow, Tony Lester, Julia Gaitskill, Baroness Gaitskell's daughter and Lawrence Lindo, Jamaica's High Commissioner. It was a jovial evening and people were in good spirits. There was a friendly, informal and relaxed atmosphere there. What was unique was a British Leader of the Opposition actively supporting Black people in promoting civil rights. I thanked Harold Wilson for his support, and he promised that he would introduce laws against racial discrimination if he became Prime Minister. I knew then that the growing elements of racism in Britain were a social evil that Harold Wilson was deeply concerned and disturbed about, so I was delighted to learn that one of the first pieces of legislation in the Wilson Government would be to enact a law against racial discrimination. I felt that on this issue he could confidently count on Liberal Party support, since the Liberal leader Jo Grimond believed this piece of legislation was long overdue. This was my first inkling of how far this thing could go and I felt all the thrill of starting on an exciting new road that opened possibilities of real change.

The press had a mixed reaction to us but their discussion about the boycott in both local and national press kept our campaign in the public eye. The Evening Post ran an article headlined 'Bristol Bus Crews Back the Boss' in which it stated that the Bristol bus drivers and conductors are nearly 100 per cent behind their chief Mr Ian Patey in not wanting to work alongside 'coloured' labour.[29] On the other hand their comment on April 30th, 1963 asked, 'What are trade union leaders doing to get the race virus out of the systems of their rank and file? There is an urgent job of education here. The union has plenty to say about South Africa. They should take a look nearer home.'

During the campaign I was criticised by both Black and white people. Some Black people criticised me for making things more difficult for them as new arrivals and reminded me that this was a white man's country and as a Black man I had no say in what they wanted to do. I felt differently, this had always been my country. I felt confident that I could change things and had ideas about whom to contact. I had already established friendships with both middle class and working people and was not afraid to approach the press and MPs or network with local community leaders. And in a few years down the line the newly arrived immigrants would have children whose only country would be this England. I felt we had to make it a better place for everyone.

There was confusion among some members of the Black community, who thought I had gone too far, and I would make things difficult for them. But the majority of the local community supported us and more than one hundred staff and students from Bristol University marched with many members of the Caribbean

29   Bristol Evening post, 2/5/1063

community from the Victoria Rooms to the centre of Bristol where university lecturers and myself made speeches. In my speech I urged Bristol not to go down the same road as Alabama but to stand up to racism as Martin Luther King had done. On the march we brought the city to a standstill as we walked down Park Street – probably the first time ever the traffic had been stopped for an issue of race. Joining us on the march were women from the Caribbean community including Olive Osborne, Mrs Delores Campbell, Joyce Bernard and Joyce Morris-Wisdom who was then only a school girl. Barbara Dettering joined us on other local marches and gave us her full backing. It was a very educating and healing experience. There was also another march, which blockaded the road and the bus station in Eastville.

Paul Boateng[30], a young law student at Bristol University, also gave his support. Later he was, in his professional capacity, to help defend the eighteen youths accused of 'rioting' in Bristol in 1981. He has the distinction of being the United Kingdom's first Black Cabinet Minister and is now a personal friend.

Sir Learie Constantine's involvement was pivotal to the success of the campaign as the Bristol establishment was now coming out and had decided to attack me as being unfit to lead the campaign. Not only was his advice useful but he came at a time when I felt pretty swamped by the attacks on me in the press and from characters like the Bishop of Bristol, Nethercott and Jenkins. To have the support of one of my childhood heroes gave me a tremendous feeling that we could win. This gave me a renewed vigour for the struggle as he was a man passionate

---

30   Paul Boateng was the first Black MP along with Bernie Grant and Diane Abbott. In 1997, he made history when he was appointed Parliamentary Under Secretary of State at the Department of Health, the first Black person to hold ministerial office in the Government. In October 1998, he became the minister of State for Home Affairs. He was appointed Chief Secretary to the Treasury on 29 May 2002. After retiring from Parliament he was appointed ambassador to South Africa for four years and in 2010 became Baron Boateng.

against racism and would not compromise.

Learie Constantine was a famous Trinidadian cricketer before the Second World War who had become a BBC commentator after retiring from cricket. He was extremely well connected, so was a great asset to the campaign. At the time of the Bristol Bus Boycott he was the first High Commissioner for Trinidad, well known for his stand against racial discrimination and a popular figure. His sympathy with our campaign was understandable because he had, despite his fame and popularity, faced discrimination at close quarters.

In 1943 he had travelled to London to play cricket at Lords, having made a reservation for his family at the Imperial Hotel in Russell Square. However, white American servicemen staying there objected to the presence of his family and they were asked to leave. Learie brought a civil action against the hotel for breach of contract as at the time racial discrimination was not illegal in Britain. He was awarded costs, but the law was not changed.

I was shattered when Eric Williams' the Trinidadian Prime Minister at the time, fell out with Sir Learie, forcing him to resign. Williams felt Sir Learie should not have involved himself in a local dispute in the United Kingdom, especially as most of the people involved in the dispute were Jamaicans and not Trinidadians. Yet Duncan Sandys, who was Commonwealth Secretary for the Conservative government at the time, made it clear he had no objections to Sir Learie's involvement in the campaign. In fact, he was very surprised by the bitter irony that Eric Williams could effectively get Sir Learie, a senior diplomatic and popular figure, to resign for taking a stand against racial discrimination.

Harold Wilson was furious with the way Sir Learie was treated and subsequently made the him the first Black person to be given a life peerage and in 1967 he became Baron Constantine of Maraval in Trinidad and Tobago and Nelson and Colne in the County Palatine of Lancaster.

On one of Sir Learie's visits to Bristol I took him round Cadbury's Chocolate factory where there was a cricket match going on in the grounds. When we walked into the stadium several thousand people all stood up and applauded as we walked across the pitch to the pavilion. That was the first time I saw a Black man being admired by the English. I hadn't had that experience before.

On the race issue the Bristol Omnibus Company appeared to have an understanding with the Transport and General Workers' Union although it was not an openly acknowledged relationship. They did however seem to be singing from the same hymn sheet. Both saw the issue of having Black drivers on the buses as something white drivers were fearful of and something the management were not prepared to go along with. The Eastville bus crew threatened to walk out if Black labour was employed and to withdraw voluntary contributions to Labour Party funds because of Tony Benn and Harold Wilson's intervention.

The Union reaffirmed its national policy of opposing racial discrimination in any form and because I was the spokesperson for the WIDC, accused me of jeopardising the welfare of the city's coloured citizens. Ron Nethercott said I didn't represent the Caribbeans in the city and the WIDC was only a small pressure group, which was almost entirely disowned by the Caribbeans. They stated that they considered Bill Smith the spokesman of the Caribbean population not me.[31] More criticism of me followed the report and revealed that my employers, the Bristol Youth Committee, had carpeted me for using its offices as headquarters for the boycott campaign.

In a report in the Daily Herald on May 4th 1963, Nethercott

31   The Times, 7/5/1963

stated I had been irresponsible and dishonest. I took Learie Constantine's advice to sue him and Odhams Press for libel. I was successful and awarded compensation and costs. I received £500 and an open apology from Odhams Press and Ron Nethercott. I was the first Black person to have upheld a victory in court against a trade union over the issue of race.

The move to isolate me and the WIDC was taken not by hard-liners like Patey and the Eastville TGWU but so called liberals like Ron Nethercott and Oliver Tomkins the Bishop of Bristol. The city's Labour clique preferred Bill Smith to me but Bill Smith's own organisation, the Caribbean Association, called on Nethercott not to use Smith as a 'stooge' and considered me their spokesman.[32]

The Bishop of Bristol, Oliver Tomkins, came out in public and said I was a troublemaker. This was very disappointing for me personally, as we had been friendly previously and in fact, I had had dinner with him only the Christmas before. He knocked on my door in Frederick Place and told me he was going to come out against my campaign and me over the Bus Boycott issue. He said, 'I hope you understand sometimes it's difficult being a bishop'. He was a lovely person and I don't think he really wanted to attack me in the way he did. I think he did this on the advice of his industrial Chaplain who was a white South African. I still rate Oliver as being a warm and lovely person but ill advised.

The leaders of the Bristol Council of Christian Churches had offered to mediate and issued a statement signed by the joint presidents, the Bishop of Bristol, Dr Tomkins, the president of the Free Church Federal Council, the Rev. J. Newton Holder and the acting chairman, the Rev. Rupert Davies blaming a 'group of unrepresentative Caribbeans' for causing trouble and deploring

32 Western Daily Press 14/5/1963

the busmen's attitude and asking for a Christian approach. This stirred up Tony Benn who was vigorous in his support for the boycott. He noted that nowhere in the statement did the Bishop say the ban was wrong and should go.

The reaction to the statement was that forty-two members of the WIDC carrying banners marched from the Dockland Settlement in City Road, St Paul's to picket St Mary Redcliffe church after morning service when worshippers were leaving. While on the march I heard on the radio that only a few Caribbean protesters came out to give their support to the campaign but there were about eighty to a hundred of us. We would have been a larger group but a Black church leader who had promised his support changed his mind at the last minute.

The Bristol Council of Churches also accused us of 'engineering the row'. They saw that we had taken a strategic approach to the issue and used this against us to make it look as if we had 'engineered' the situation. This was preposterous as the issue was already there and it was immoral and unjust, we only engineered the protest against it, not the 'row' itself. After the campaign however Oliver Tomkins and I quickly became reconciled.

The attempt to isolate the WIDC and myself might have worked except for Learie's intervention. He made the connection with Bristol and slavery and met with the Lord Mayor but didn't get very far with him. He did the right thing by snubbing Patey and going straight to the Transport Holding Company in London, which had ultimate control over the Bristol Bus Company management. This alarmed Patey who contradicting himself, denied the colour bar by stating that the company employed Black cleaners and maintenance workers. Learie also put Nethercott under pressure as he involved Frank Cousins, the National Chair of the Transport and General Workers' Union. Frank Cousins made it clear that discrimination was not a union policy.

Frank Cousins was very concerned about the South West's Regional Secretary, Ron Nethercott's attitude. Nethercott seemed to believe Black workers would undercut the pay of white workers while maintaining the oxymoron that this was nothing to do with race but only about pay. At the same time Ian Patey was giving them reasons why Black people shouldn't work on the buses such as, they would drive out the white conductresses. There were also elements of the workforce themselves who were opposed to the campaign.

In the meantime I tried to get the Caribbean cricket team, who were visiting Bristol, to support us publicly but they had a strict 'Don't mix sports with politics' policy at the time. However, they were willing to be photographed with Sir Learie Constantine and myself and agreed to meet the Caribbean community.

With Sir Learie's intervention there was a murmuring from the Jamaican community that their High Commissioner should be doing something, so Laurence Lindo the Jamaican High Commissioner came to see me to find out what was happening in Bristol. He was a quietly spoken man who didn't do things from the front line like Sir Learie but preferred to work behind the scenes, and in fact this modus operandi was very effective for him as he got things done.

Jamaica had become independent in 1962 so this was probably his first major event after becoming High Commissioner in London. I got to know him well after the end of the campaign and there was a time when I felt like going over to Jamaica and doing some youth work there but he told me it was needed here more than Jamaica and persuaded me to stay here. He was devoted to Jamaica and its people and became the oldest and longest serving

Commonwealth ambassador.

I felt there was some tension between the High Commissioner of Jamaica, Laurence Lindo and Sir Learie. Lindo felt the issue was a matter for Jamaican nationals and concerned them, not Trinidadians. Sir Learie on the other hand saw the issue as a racial one across the board regardless of nationality.

Once he was involved, Laurence Lindo set about holding discussions with Sir Philip Warter, the chair of the Transport Holding Company, and Sir Reginald Wilson its director. This resulted in Warter and Wilson disavowing the colour bar as early as 8ᵗʰ May. Laurence Lindo accepted that the Transport Holding Company had issued a general policy directive of no discrimination but that this had been ignored in Bristol. Instead of issuing a written directive the Transport Holding Company sent senior men to Bristol to negotiate between the Bristol Bus Company and the TGWU. For the next few months the company and union were locked in secret negotiations.

We had not until the Bristol Bus Boycott campaign focused on civil rights or discrimination against Black people and this is what influenced Tony Benn and Harold Wilson to address the issue. Fenner Brockway MP who it was once said of 'That man frightens me he is too much like Jesus Christ', also played his part by asking questions in Parliament about the Bristol Bus Company's ban on Black labour. We were also supported by the Campaign Against Racial Discrimination (CARD) which was in the process of being formed at this time.

Our victory was swift and came on 28th August 1963. The number of various strategies we used and public opinion helped. The role of Sir Philip Warter too was also crucial. As Chairman of the Transport Holding Company in London, he played an important role in the whole process of getting the ban reversed.

Sir Philip gave instructions to Ian Patey that he should reverse the policy on racial discrimination. I have no doubt that Laurence Lindo and Sir Learie Constantine were very much part of those negotiations in London working behind the scenes.

At the same time, the fact that Sir Learie was very high profile helped. He stood out as a public figure, well loved by the cricket fraternity all around the country. He brought us a lot of support from the public and swelled the tide of public opinion in our favour.

I think this illustrates how influential the new Commonwealth High Commissioners were and how well they played their part in protecting the rights of their country men and women. It also shows the international nature of this campaign. It was initiated locally in Bristol, supported nationally by key Labour MPs, discussed in the media, inspired by a strategy used by an American civil rights campaigner and finally aided by High commissioners from the Caribbean.

The High Commissioners evoked the voice of our international allies and we were able to utilise these transnational connections to add weight to our protest and this strongly influenced the nature of our campaign, and choice of tactics. This certainly helped its successful outcome and the effect it had on British society.

All these factors produced a multi-pronged attack that secured us a victory after only a few months, six in fact, from the beginning of the campaign until Ian Patey came back and said he would be lifting the ban on Black employees on the buses. Of course, at the time I was attacked by racists and had my life threatened and all the usual things one would expect.

Auspiciously, there was a strange but fortuitous coincidence on the day Martin Luther King made his *'I had a dream'* speech in Washington and addressed his followers saying, *'We will hew hope out of despair. Let freedom ring!'* and the 200,000 crowd at the Lincoln Memorial responded to every pause in his speech with *'Yes oh Lord let freedom ring!'.* This was the day when the Bristol Omnibus Company announced the end of the 'colour bar' on the buses. The first person employed was a Punjabi sikh called Raghbir Singh who started work as a conductor on 17th September, 1963.

Raghbir was a very principled person who took a cut in wages *'to see if white people kept their promises'.* He had been employed as a fitter at £14 a week but took the job as a bus conductor for £10 a week. It was also on this day that President Kennedy called on the American people to *'accelerate our effort to achieve equal rights for all our citizens'.* This plea was due to be given out at the Labour Day the next Monday, but the US White House released it to coincide with the civil rights demonstration in Washington led by Martin Luther King on the 28th August. I think this coincidence illustrates the zeitgeist of the times and shows the interconnection and international elements at play in the Bristol Boycott campaign.

A few days later Norris Edwards from Jamaica and Muhammad Raschid and Abbas Ali from Pakistan joined Raghbir Singh as Black conductors on the Bristol buses.

The first Black bus driver was Norman Samuels who lived in St Paul's. Norman had arrived in Britain from Jamaica in 1960. The day he took his driving test, people lined the streets to see the first Black person in Bristol driving a bus. He started work as a bus driver on October 15th , 1964, the same day that his son Vernon was born. Vernon went on to become a world-class triple jumper and represented Great Britain at the 1988 Olympics and the 1990 Commonwealth Games.

Guy Bailey and I felt we had won the battle; it was a moral victory as well as a political one. It was I believe the first successful

Black-led national protest against racial discrimination and the promotion of equal opportunities that this country had seen.

Overall the press was quite supportive. I felt they connected with what I was saying; that Martin Luther King was fighting for civil rights in America and we should be doing the same thing here. I knew that would strike a chord with sections of the British press. The American factor was also causing a surge in international Black consciousness and that helped at the grassroots as the support of Labour MPs and Caribbean High Commissioners helped in the corridors of power.

On a local level the following all supported the boycott campaign, students, minority churchgoers, sportsmen and women, Tony Benn, Julia Gaitskell, Anthony Lester Q.C., Bristol University lecturers Ronald Sampson, Prof. H. Dickinson, John Malos, Michael Banton. Local left wingers Alderman St John Reade, Cllr. J. Boss, Don McLaren, the Reverend Vivian Thomas and TGWU member and long-time activist J.E. Flowers and the local Communist Party also helped. There was as well a youth worker in Hartcliffe who circulated a petition, which several busmen signed, and numerous letters supporting the boycott.[33]

During the campaign I was in touch with all sorts of people from the liberal left such as Julia Gaitskell, from the Institute of Race Relations, who was also Hugh Gaitskell's daughter and very active against racism. Another supporter was Paul Foot, a distinguished left-wing journalist. He was the son of Hugh Foot, former Governor General of Jamaica. Paul was also the nephew of Michael Foot, leader of the Labour Party from 1980 to 1983.

Paul was an investigative journalist who was very supportive of me. He used to tell me the story about when he did his National Service. He went before his brigadier and was asked which

33   Dresser, 1986

regiment he wanted to go in and he of course requested a Jamaican regiment. The brigadier looked at him with astonishment and asked why he wanted to go to Jamaica. Paul explained that his father worked in Jamaica that's why he wanted to go there. The brigadier asked him what his father did, and Paul replied, 'He's the Governor General of Jamaica' Well that changed things and Paul actually went into the Jamaican regiment as a young officer.

An amusing incident occurred after our victory. I took a taxi to the station and the driver recognised me. He said, 'That boycott of yours was great.' I replied, 'Thank you' and he added, 'Oh we did more business at that time than we've ever done.'

The impact of the campaign was to have repercussions on the civil rights of Black people in Britain because it influenced the introduction of the 1965 Race Relations Act. It did not break the unholy alliance between management and unions, however, as can be seen from the immigrant strikes at Courtaulds Red Scar Mill in Preston in May 1965 and the Imperial Typewriters strike in Leicester in 1974 where there was a large National Front presence.[34]

What that short campaign over buses in Bristol did was bring about anti-discrimination laws in this country. The substance of that experience was around the impact it had and the beginning of Black people of Britain taking on a role inspired by the civil

34   The immigrant strike at Courtalds Red Scar Mill in Preston in May 1965. The management there tried to force Asian workers to work more machines for proportionately less pay. Journalist Paul Foot covered the story. An agreement between the TGWU and management meant the strike failed. This episode exposed the trade union and management collaboration against immigrant workers.

We can see the same forces at work in 1974 at the Imperial Typewriters strike in Leicester where there was a large National Front presence. Central command had set up 'grievance meetings', which were mass meetings, where strikers expressed their grievances that were then typed up and co-ordinated into a series of demands. This forged close bonds between strikers and their local leadership. The Race Relations Board intervened, and the company closed the factory. The TGWU refused to make the strike official and so the multi-national company was able to win against a workforce not supported by its union. The only positive outcome was the militancy demonstrated by the Asian women. (**Ramdin 1987 p270-271**)

rights campaign in America. Before all this the issues were about Teddy Boy violence against Black immigrants in areas such as Notting Hill.

The 1965 Race Relations Act split and ultimately transformed the existing grassroots movement for equality. The moderate Black leaders made efforts to work within the new structure of 'community relations' established by the Act, while more radical Black leaders followed a different path. The radical British-born Black population took their parent's place and the UK became a centre of the world-wide Black Power movement.[35]

I was sceptical too, as many Black people were, as we saw that the Government wanted to take the sting out of the protest we had started. Black leadership should have come from the community, as it had done in America where it was generated from the churches and the street. We also wanted to dictate the agenda of how race relations would develop in England. By introducing a law as early as they did, they took on the agenda. We were left with a lot of community liaison officers instead of real change. It can be argued that the campaign, while it focused on civil rights, at the same time, in many regards, derailed an emerging civil rights movement in Britain. The Campaign Against Racial Discrimination (CARD) collapsed after the bringing in of laws against racial discrimination.

The Bristol Bus Boycott campaign was to change the social history of Britain and the relationship of Britain with its own Black British. It is becoming clearer now that it has historical roots. Mike and Trevor Phillips in their book 'Windrush' state that the Bristol Bus Boycott set up a standard that the law underpinned and considered the campaign a bold step into territory which had traditionally been the exclusive property of white workers.

35   Juravich, 2008

Encouraged by the success of the Bristol Bus Boycott campaign, in 1964 I took on the Bay Horse pub. I was now being told by several Black people that they couldn't get into public houses because the bar staff would say they were not welcome there. Black people were unwelcome not just in pubs but in dance halls, clubs, hotels and swimming pools. So I was receiving quite a lot of complaints from Black people who found it difficult to get into these places because they were being barred and they particularly referred me to the Bay Horse pub in Broadmead where they wouldn't be served.

I decided that I would then test that out to see if what they were saying was actually true or was an exaggeration. Subsequently I went into the bar and I was initially served half a pint but then told to get out because they didn't serve Black people. I said I hadn't done anything wrong. It was the manager who then said, 'We don't want you Black people in here because you are a nuisance.' I refused to leave, and he said he would call the police, so I replied, 'Well call the police.'

Eight police officers came with an inspector in a Land Rover. I was surprised by the number of police officers who arrived just to ask me to leave, which I duly did. I was then told that I would be arrested and charged for refusing to leave licensed premises. So I was taken to the Central police Station, Bridewell at about 8 or 9 O'clock in the evening and I was released from the cell at midnight. Later in life I was to muse on how this experience was to make me the first freemen of the city to have been locked up in the city's central police cells.

I didn't realise at the time that there was an Irish man in the pub who saw everything and was outraged at the publican's and the police's behaviour. He could see I had done nothing wrong. He then went to the police station to try to tell them that I hadn't done anything that warranted me being removed and they told him to 'F*ck off'.

It was front page news in the local press at the time. It highlighted the fact that there was no protection in law for Black people. There was no law to protect Black people from such humiliation. Again members of CARD in London told me that in the forthcoming Act of Parliament they would highlight this kind discrimination which should be unlawful.

The first and only Chair of CARD was David Pitt. He was originally from Grenada, but considered himself an Englishman. He was the second Black person to become a peer in the House of Lords. He lived in London and had set up CARD having been inspired by Martin Luther King's visit to London when King was on his way to receive the Nobel Prize in Stockholm for leadership. King preached at St Paul's Cathedral and afterwards met thirty Commonwealth immigrants and a few white sympathisers at the Hilton Hotel. All kinds of radicals, communists, anarchists, liberals, labour and conservatives were involved but its executive was middle class, intellectuals and professionals. It failed to amend the 1965 Race Relations Bill and turned its attention to the proposed tightening of immigration control.

In 1967 CARD approached Jack Jones, General Secretary of the TGWU, to ask if the Union would put out a pamphlet in conjunction with CARD on discrimination in employment and affiliate formally with CARD. The answer was no. CARD had failed to co-ordinate the efforts of other groups active in anti-discrimination work, or to involve existing immigrant organisations due to lack of time, money and personnel.

During the Bay Horse campaign CARD didn't have a cohesive structure and was falling apart but the struggle in Bristol had given them a cause to gather round. Among the people involved were Dame Jocelyn Barrow, Julia Gaitskell, and Anthony Lester. It gave them an opportunity to revisit how they were going to involve CARD in the civil rights movement in Britain.

However CARD was supportive when I went into court a few weeks after the Bay Horse incident, charged with refusing to quit licensed premises. I had an excellent solicitor, David Roberts, who had been recommended by Anne Hewer, the chair of my steering group committee. He was very concerned about what had happened. And I spent the whole time in court arguing with the different versions of what the police were saying. There were eight different accounts of the situation according to the police. Some said I was trying to rush back into the pub to cause a nuisance, others said I was being disorderly inside, all of which were pure fabrication. The landlord said I wasn't being polite enough and did not say please. The Press enjoyed a headline with that one.

The story had now gone national. The last day, on the Friday when the case was coming to a close, the front page of the Evening Post read 'Caribbean leader made a fool of himself'. This was a quote from the prosecutor who tried to tell the magistrates that I wasn't the victim of racial discrimination but had provoked the situation by my behaviour.

The same Irish man who tried to defend me on the night of my arrest turned up at court and made himself known to me. He made it clear he wanted to speak on my behalf. He told the magistrates exactly what happened to him at the police station and how he was told in no uncertain manner that they didn't want to listen to what he had to say. So when I was leaving the court the headlines 'Caribbean leader made a fool of himself' appeared rather ironic as the magistrates by that time had dismissed the charges against me and censured the police by fining them £25 for bringing the case in the first place. To top it all I was awarded costs and the pub manager lost his job.

Harold Wilson kept his promise but the victory over the Bay Horse public house had a powerful effect in London and Bristol as the first Race Relations Act of 1965 wasn't about the right to fair treatment in employment or housing. It was to do with the right of people of different races to have access to public places. It was limited to making it unlawful to discriminate against Black people based on their colour in public places. Of course I thought this did not go far enough but was nevertheless pleased by this first step.

The 1965 Act also set up the Race Relation Board with three commissioners acting in a judicial capacity. The Board was responsible for setting up local conciliation committees whose duty it was to try and deal with problems of racial discrimination and community relations. The Board was supposed to enforce the Act, but the Board could only take civil action, not criminal ones, against an individual who refused to comply with its judgement. It didn't really have any powers as it could not impose penalties and relied on a means of conciliation with offending parties. This complex system of conciliation effectively took the teeth out of the legislation. The Government was worried about the backlash of the white working class and wanted to bring equality in by stealth. Those of us who didn't go along with that, and I was one of those, felt that the Government should confront racism rather than treat it as a problem of welfare. They however saw the issue as not about colour but about welfare and culture.

Nevertheless the Act fell short of addressing the more serious and fundamental issues of discrimination against Black people even though I had received support and encouragement from senior Labour MPs. It appeared to me that management and unions were not above opposing the rights of Black people and the labour Government, which had been returned with a small majority in 1964, was very aware of the potential danger of the struggle over widespread discrimination in employment. It was also clear that the Government had to be careful with the unions who at this time were their main financial backers.

There were demands for tougher measures and it was that twin force of union and management that in the form of the Trades Union Congress and the Confederation of British Industry opposed that demand. Here we see the influence of employers and unions and the fear of public opinion on the Government.

I wrote to the papers in my capacity as secretary to the West Indian Development Council questioning to what extent the new law would change or affect conditions for the Black immigrants in Bristol. I stated that from the onset we thought the law a bad one conceived out of muddled thinking and political expediency with an eye on the next general election.

I made it clear at the time that we thought it a great failing of that particular legislation that it did not protect a Black person from racial discrimination in employment where racial discrimination existed more widely than in any other section of our society. Large numbers of Black people with good qualifications, as well as their children who were studying hard at school, were not protected against discrimination despite hard-earned academic qualifications. We were concerned whether the second generation of young Black people was going to be accepted by their British contemporaries or pegged forever as semi-educated unskilled labour.

Despite the new law there was still no means by which young Black people could be spared the indignity of being refused suitable employment on account of the colour of their skins.

The Home Secretary's about turn in taking the criminality out of the Bill and substituting it with conciliation committees clearly indicated that not enough time and serious thought were given to the Bill at the time it was presented to Parliament.

I also expressed our disappointment that it did not remove racial discrimination from housing as well. It was no use blaming Black people for herding themselves together when estate agents and building societies would refuse them mortgages to buy a suitable home for their families.

I stated that until the law dealt with the two important issues of employment and housing, we would have the same situation as the northern cities of America. No law can change a person's heart, but it can go a long way to influencing social behaviour.

I made it clear that it was the intention of Black people in Bristol to report to the committee set up by the Act cases of racial discrimination in employment and housing in spite of the fact that the committee had no statutory power to deal with it. We believed that if this policy was carried out throughout the country the Race Relations Board would seek to persuade the Home Secretary to review the law as it stood then.

To be fair to the Labour Party however, later with a bigger majority in 1968 the Labour Government did deal with the crucial issues of employment and housing, but more of that later.

My young fellow evacuee and I at Dunmow. I've always liked this picture. We used it on the cover of the first edition of 'Memoirs of A Black Englishman.'

My mother Olive Stephenson in her Women's Royal Army Corps uniform.

My grandmother Edie Johnson was a West End actress.

This is me aged 4.

One of the care workers and I at Dunmow. I was evacuated there in 1940 and put in the care of Essex County Council.

I remember Miss Martin was a care worker at the children's home in Dunmow.

On the beach at Mundesley-on-Sea while working at Mundesley Holiday Youth Camp in Norfolk.

I passed out in 1954 and my first posting was to RAF Waterbeach near Cambridge.

I was the only Black cadet at RAF Cosford in Staffordshire. The seven years in the RAF from 1953-1960 were to change my life. I saw another world travelling round Europe.

Enjoying a pint with RAF colleagues.

While I was stationed in Germany I joined the Rover Scouts to work with the children of RAF families who were at military schools. This inspired a change in my career.

Rudyard Kipling's The Jungle Book was used as a motivational book for the Scouts. The adult leaders were named after characters from the novel. I was Baloo.

I bought a Mercedes car while I was stationed in Germany which gave me the freedom to explore the country and meet ordinary Germans and their families.

Our wedding day at Christ Church, Clifton in October 1965. From left: Roy Hackett's daughter Dawn, Roy, myself and Joyce, Duffus, Pearl and Sherrie.

Cutting the cake at our wedding reception.

Joyce was from Clarendon in Jamaica and lived in Manchester with her godmother when she arrived in the UK. She then moved to Bristol.

Raising a glass to the happy couple. Roy Hackett was best man at our wedding.

Muhammad Ali became a friend of the family. Here he is with my son Junior and I.

The boys couldn't believe it when Muhammad Ali, Heavywright Champion Of The World, turned up at assembly at Tulse Hill School and shadow boxed on stage.

Muhammad Ali addressing the boys at Tulse Hill.

Joyce collecting a nursing award at Manor Park Hospital, Bristol in 1966.

In 1965, I invited Millie Small, the Jamaican singer who had a hit with My Boy Lollipop, to Bristol to meet young Black teenagers.

I became close frinds with the actor Norman Beaton who was well-known for his eponymous role in the TV series Desmond.

My sister Josie and I. As children, we were separated by the war and only really got to know each other when we were adults.

Tony and Lalel Bullimore threw a great leaving party for Joyce and I at the Bamboo Club in St Paul's when we moved from Bristol to Coventry in 1968. Pictured at the Club (from left): Bristol's Lady Mayoress and Lord Mayor, Joyce and Denis Howell (Minister for Sport), two unknown dancers, Wally Jenkins, leader of Bristol City Council, and Lalel.

My family and I with Cleo Laine and Johnny Dankworth.

General Garba chair of the Anti-Apartheid Committeem of the United Nations was a first-class campaigner. I met him on several occasions – here with Junior, Fumi and Joyce.

Joyce, baby Fumi, Junior and I.

Meeting the Mayor of Lambeth with Daley Thompson and John Conteh.

I got to know Jack Charlton when I was on the Sports Council. Here he is signing autographs on a visit to Tulse Hill school.

At an event with Sam Ramsamy (left) of the anti-apartheid pressure group South African Non-Racial Olympic Committee (SANROC).

I introduced John Fashanu to Kenneth Kuanda when the former President of Zambia was living in London.

Mr. Paul Stephenson, secretary of the Bristol West Indian Development Council, and Miss Joyclin Annikie, who is on the nursing staff of Manor Park Hospital, Fishponds, were married at Christ Church, Clifton. Among the guests were the Postmaster General, Mr. Anthony Wedgwood Benn, and Mrs, Benn, pictured here with the happy couple at the reception.

Tony and Caroline Benn were among the guests at our wedding.

The Bus Boycott in the Western Daily Press.

Sir Learie Constantine visiting the Beau Street Youth Centre in Baptist Mills, Bristol.

Sir Learie Constantine and Roy Hackett at Bristol Temple Meads station.

Here I am with Mr Douglas, Mr Geoff and Sir Learie Constantine discussing the Bus Boycott in Roy Hackett's front room in Belle Vue Road, Easton.

I accompanied Sir Learie to meet the Lord Mayor of Bristol at the Council House in 1963.

Students parade across The Centre with placards in support of the employment of coloured labour on Bristol buses.

The Bus Boycott campaign received a major boost when students from the University of Bristol marched in solidarity from Clifton to the centre of town.

He takes pay cut to test promise

TURBANNED Raghbir Singh became a bus conductor yesterday—to see if white people kept their promises. And last night 37-year-old Raghbir said: "It was a very beautiful day. There was nothing to worry about."

Raghbir, the first coloured crew man on Bristol's buses since the city's bus colour bar was scrapped nearly three weeks ago, added: "I applied for the job to see if the bus company kept to its word."

He gave up a better paid job as an engineer fitter to make the test. And he said after his first day's stint on a No. 9 bus: "The other busmen have all been very kind and friendly.

"Before I started the chief came up to me and said: 'If there's any difficulty, come to me and talk it over.'

LUCK

" My driver was a beautiful chap. We had a cup of tea together afterwards. And he asked if I'd enjoyed the journey. People all day have been wishing me all the luck in the world.

"My wife won't mind the cut in the pay packet. She says the principle of what I'm doing is more important."

As a fitter Raghbir got a regular £14 a week. As a conductor he will get nearly £10 basic.

He must be the only college-educated busman in Bristol — and probably England. In the Punjab he studied English, art, history, geography and maths.

FREEDOM

Before going to his home in Meridian-place, Clifton, where his wife and three children, aged one to fourteen, were waiting for him, bearded Raghbir added: "I enjoy this life more than my old job.

"You're meeting all sorts of people all the time instead of being tied to a bench. You know, it isn't hard work ... it's freedom."

Raghbir: It isn't hard work... it's freedom

COLOURED MAN ON PUB CHARGES

Western Daily Press Reporter

Paul Stephenson, secretary of Bristol's West Indian Development Council, was arrested after an incident in a Bristol public house on Saturday. He will appear in court today on two summonses.

PAUL STEPHENSON
In court today

They are: Failing to leave licensed premises when requested; and behaving in a disorderly manner.

The incident occurred in the Bay Horse, Lewin's Mead.

Police were called there by the licensee, Mr. Douglas Bowden, and helped to eject him from the building.

Freed on bail

Following a further incident outside, Mr. Stephenson was arrested. Later he was charged, and released on bail.

Two years ago, Mr. Stephenson, aged 27, of Waverley Road, Redland, organised a West Indian boycott of Bristol buses.

How the local press reported Raghbir Singh becoming the first non-white bus conductor in Bristol and my court appearance after I was arrested for refusing to leave the Bay Horse pub.

From Left: Roy Hackett, Tony Benn, the Lord Mayor of Bristol, myself and Guy Reid-Bailey in 2003 on the 40th anniversary of the Bus Boycott victory.

I attended the awards ceremony at Bristol Cathedral in 2009 to receive my honorary degree from the University of the West of England.

I was joined by Fumi, Joyce and Junior to receive an honorary Open University degree in November 2009.

A proud day for myself and the family when we visited Windsor Castle to receive my OBE in 2009,

2014: Rob Mitchell, Dr Madge Dresser, Lilleith Morrison and the late Mike Baker at Wards in Barton Hill where Mike made the commemorative plaque for the bus station.

I was joined by Guy Reid-Bailey (left) and Roy Hackett for the unveiling of Mike Baker's plaque at Bristol Bus Station on August 28th, 2014. (Picture: CB Bristol Design)

The Aftermath Of The Bristol Bus Boycott
1963-1972

I was still employed by the Joseph Rowntree Trust (administrated by Bristol City Council Education Department) on my three-year contract as a Youth Worker. After winning the fight with the Bristol Bus Company Anne Hewer was very keen that I carried on and stayed in Bristol, so they extended my contract. However, during this period I felt there was pressure being put on my employers to stop having me around.

My relationship with colleagues from the Youth Service staff was satisfactory, probably because I was by this time very high profile because of the Boycott campaign. It had its negative effects though because the head teacher, who had previously been very supportive of my work and shown genuine concern for the education of immigrant children, banned me from the school. After I became a public and controversial figure, he said it wasn't necessary for me to keep teaching at the school. Because I was a supply teacher, he was able to do this, but I think that he was under pressure from the local political establishment.

During the campaign the Youth Committee tried to bar me from working at the Youth Centre. After the campaign was successful they let me carry on at the Youth Centre and I was once again given work in school.

Because of the success of the campaign I was invited to America by Mr Banks of the National Association for the Advancement of Coloured People. They wanted me to talk about racism in Britain and about the campaign in 1963. A Bristol City Council Education Committee made funds available for me through the Rowntree

Trust to visit America and Jamaica from August 1964 to February 1965. The idea of the visit to Jamaica was to get an understanding of the culture and lifestyle there.

I left Bristol for New York in August and was welcomed by Mr Banks when I arrived. I stayed at the famous hotel Theresa in Harlem on 125th Street and 7th Avenue. President Castro had stayed there when he was at the United Nations in September 1960. It was fascinating to learn that Castro insisted that the chickens were live because he felt at risk from the Americans, in case they poisoned his food.

It was at this time that the Beatles had journeyed to American for their first highly successful tour. I remember asking a young Black Harlem youth if he would like to meet the Beatles and he replied he would love to meet them. I said I'm sure they must be feeling fed up stuck in their luxury hotel in New York. Surely, they would have loved to have mingled and seen live Black stars, Black singers and heard Black music at the Apollo theatre which was almost opposite their hotel.

I had been invited to visit the Black Muslim mosque and for the first time felt the enormous power of a young Muslim preacher who went by the name of Louis X but later was to be better known as Louis Farrakhan.[36] I was welcomed to his mosque where I saw for the first time in my life the impressive sight of a congregation of disciplined rows of Black women in wraps and Black men in suits. It was a magnificent and breath-taking vision.

I was welcomed by Louis X and he made a serious attack on Malcolm X who he said had betrayed the Muslim cause because he had criticised Elijah Muhammad the leader of the Black Muslims.

---

36   Louis Farrakhan, who became leader in 1978 of the Nation of Islam (An American movement that combined Black nationalism with elements of Islam), is a controversial figure who has denied accusations that he is anti-Semitic, homophobic and racist.

I was to meet Louis Farrakhan later in Jamaica in the 1970s. I was most impressed by his eloquence but felt his spiritual intolerance to various groups was a major flaw. Later ,he requested that I helped him come to England, but it was during the time of the Thatcher government and there was no way that someone like Louis X would have been given a visa. His fluency was impressive; I had never heard anyone speak so articulately.

During my stay in New York I visited a young offender's prison, holding mainly young Black teenagers who were there on drug charges, anti-social charges, rape and other serious charges. I felt that somehow many were victims of a social system that didn't give them much hope. They were more victims of the system than the system were victims of them.

I was struck by the ratio of Black Americans and white Americans on the staff as much of the staff at junior level were Black and at senior level white. This was like what was happening in England with our criminal justice system at the time.

Although we have by no means arrived at a state of real equality in our institutions, we have made some in-roads. At a visit in 2009 to Ashfield Young Offenders Institution I was happy to see attitudes were slowly changing and a Black director had been appointed and was soon to take up his post. At the same time we must be alert to the fact that a disproportionate number of young Black men are in jail. This illustrates the fact that despite the improvements made there is still a long way to go.

Back in 1964 I went on to Washington, Philadelphia, and Richmond, Virginia. It was when I was in Richmond, the capital of the Confederacy, that I was told to book into the John Marshall Hotel, previously an all-white luxury hotel named after one of the generals who fought to save the South and slavery.

I arrived early in the morning on a Sunday to confirm my

booking and when I got to the hotel it was packed with white Americans with ten-gallon hats. It was clear that there was some conference or convention on. Everyone was glaring and staring at me. The only Black people I saw were two bellboys by the lift who were also staring at me. I went to the reception desk and spoke to the receptionist and asked if she had a reservation for Mr Stephenson. She said, 'A reservation for Mr. Stephenson – hold on'. The whole of the hotel foyer was reduced to silence and everyone was listening to my voice, which did not sound American. The hotel receptionist turned to me and said, 'We have a reservation for Mr Stephenson from England, but he hasn't arrived yet' so I said, 'Well I am Mr Stephenson from England' and she said, 'Are you the Englishman.' I said 'Yes', and she went back to where the keys were and came back with them and said, 'We hope you have an enjoyable stay here Mr. Stephenson.' The Black bellboys then came running to collect my bags and took me up to the first floor to a luxury suite. I was surprised that the National Association for Advancement of Coloured People (NAACP) was willing to pay out so much for my accommodation.

That evening when I met up with a regional group from Richmond for dinner, they asked how I liked my accommodation. I told them it was first class but said they shouldn't have put themselves to the expense of paying for it. They then informed me the hotel was named after a Confederate general who fought against Lincoln during the American Civil War and it was the most prestigious hotel in the southern states of America. Indeed, it had been a lynchpin of racism. A few weeks ago they had a letter in response to their campaigns against discrimination from the management of the John Marshall Hotel saying that they would allow Black people for the first time in history to come and stay there. Since they knew I was coming from England they thought it would be nice to let me stay in the best hotel in town. I joked saying, 'I thought I'd come to give talks about racism in Britain not to desegregate the South!'

I left America after Thanksgiving Day to fly to Jamaica where I was to spend six to eight weeks looking at the life and culture of that country. The minister of Youth and Social Services, Eddie Seaga, of the Jamaica Labour Party (JLP) looked after me. He was later to become Prime Minister of Jamaica. It was fascinating arriving in Jamaica late in the evening. As I was being driven from the airport, I saw notices that said keep to the left which reminded me of England and it also reminded me of the enormous colonial hold that Britain still had on this island of Jamaica. I was late for where I was supposed to be staying so they put me up in the YMCA in St Andrews, a middle-class part of town.

I woke up to the splashes of people swimming in the pool at six or seven in the morning. I had a meeting with the Permanent Secretary of the Department of Youth and Social Services at ten o'clock and after breakfast I thought it was so sunny and warm with blue skies, I'd walk into town it was such a lovely day. Well after about half an hour I was completely drained with the heat.

I was looking for any taxis that may be passing by but couldn't find one. I did come across a guy selling coconut water however and asked him for a ride on his donkey in exchange for money for his coconuts. He agreed and I spent an hour sitting on this donkey while he stopped often to sell his coconuts as I got hotter and hotter wondering what time I was going to get to see the Permanent Secretary of the Ministry. It was quite a raw deal. I arrived at the Ministry very hot very bothered and very sweaty.

I was to stay in Worthington Avenue in Kingston, a predominantly middle-class area. My landlady was a dual heritage Jamaican who had married a white Englishman who was very racist. I discovered that in Jamaica there was a very strong class system, not so much colour, though this was still important as the blacker you were the lower down the class system you were, but it was really class that mattered to the Jamaican identity at that time.

While I was there, I went into the countryside to visit Chestervale Youth Camp. The Norman Manley government had established these training centres or youth camps after his election in 1954. Manley had appointed George Cadbury (of the famous chocolate family) as his Senior Economic Advisor. Cadbury had found the truancy rate of eligible boys in school was fifty per cent; there was illiteracy, crime and an abundance of educational dropouts. He advised Manley that he could not build a country on this basis.

The Manley government addressed this problem through the Youth Camps. Fifteen to nineteen-year-old dropouts were recruited into a manageable residential community. The residential part was to avoid the 'unlearning' processes after school. The discipline was moderate but responsible, applying some of the concepts of the gang, but where their leadership skills were developed and harnessed positively and constructively. In fact, giving them a better gang to join!

A Board of Management was established chaired by Father Sherlock and offices were set up in Kingston with Vin Lawrence as director and Owen Bachelor as deputy. The whole nation united to support the idea. Alcan Jamaica Limited provided 47 acres of land at a nominal rent at Cobbla, Manchester as the site of the camp and doctors did the medical examination of the recruits free of charge. Volunteers from the British, Canadian and UN Peace Corps also helped.

At first the boys were under tents on empty land and the growth and development of their institution was entirely in their hands. Leadership skills were encouraged, and boys would be appointed as Welfare Leaders, Project Leaders and elected Dorm Leaders. Project Leaders under the guidance of Project staff would deal with everything. The six hundred boys grew the crops, built the camps and workshops, made the roads and provided the meals. Illiterate boys were trained by their colleagues after a course at JAMAL (a national programme in literacy training). Others attended classes in English, Maths and related subjects while the brightest attended local schools in the evenings for extra lessons.

The first two camps were Cobbla and Chestervale and another for five hundred girls was established in Cape Clear, Highgate, St Mary. Later many of the young people went on to achieve successful careers. One of the Youth Camp graduates became mayor of Kingston and many are involved in executive positions all over the world.

A Government car took me to Chestervale Youth Camp in the Blue Mountains. It was incredibly beautiful in those mountains, breathtakingly so. We got stuck because we didn't know where the Centre was. My driver stopped a guy on a donkey carrying food from his plot of land and he described how to get to the camp by way of chains (one eighth of a mile). The use of this antiquated measurement demonstrated to me that rural Jamaica was still economically behind.

When we got to the camp, I met Vin Lawrence the director. Later I was to visit a second camp and meet Owen Batchelor, the deputy director, who oversaw Cobbla Youth Camp, teaching youngsters.

"It is one of the tenets of psychology that children, who, for whatever reason missed their early childhood training, could with love and proper guidance and discipline in adolescence, recapture much of what they lost earlier. Their habitat should not be far removed from what they were accustomed to so that all improvements would be visibly seen as coming from their initiative and innovative skills."[37]

I stayed at the project for a week or two and saw what the youngsters were doing and went down on the truck into Kingston on the daily ride there and back.

I think it was a great shame that these camps were closed by the Bustamante government. It gave these youngsters hope. They didn't need firearms they were looking for ploughshares, how they could farm, how they could mend cars. It was very unfortunate, a mistake I think, that the Jamaican Labour Party (JLP) made closing these training schools.

In Jamaica I found myself welcomed by both classes. One of the things they were all struck by was the way I spoke, the accent I spoke with. I also found this in America. When I did an interview on a show in America about racism people phoning in couldn't believe it was a Black man they were speaking to over the radio. This episode shows there were some deep fundamental cultural identity problems. It had an effect on those I spoke to and became friends with.

When Harold Wilson became Prime Minister in 1964, I was still in Jamaica, but I wrote a letter congratulating him because he had been supportive during the Bristol Bus Boycott campaign.

Race had very much been at the forefront of that election, with racist groups deliberately mis-representing the Labour Party's policy on immigration and coining the slogan, *'If you want a nigger for a neighbour – vote Labour'.* Harold Wilson was faced with a paradox. On becoming leader of the Labour Party he championed the interests of the English working classes and

37 Batchelor, 2018

at the same time was prepared to defend the rights of the Black immigrants who were often exposed to racial discrimination at the hands of white workers.

The 'white backlash' with its seeds firmly planted during the stormy debate on the Commonwealth Immigration Act in the summer of 1962 took sufficient enough root to oust Patrick Gordon Walker from the traditional Labour seat of Smethwick in the 1964 general election. The Conservative Party candidate lost no time in exploiting the racial fears of the white community, and right-wing forces stirred up false race propaganda in a deliberate attempt to appeal to the worst instincts of human nature. Thankfully Labour won the election and Harold Wilson was able to address the race issue as he had promised.

I was delighted to receive a reply personally to the letter of congratulations I had sent him. This had quite an impact on the Jamaican media. They were interested in the British Prime Minister's letter to me which indicated his support for a multi-cultural and multi-racial Britain.

While in Jamaica I was invited to Manchester Boys School in Mandeville, whose headmaster at the time was Gerry German, a Welsh radical teacher who cared enormously about the political and social concerns of Jamaica. I spent a week at the school and was warmly and affectionately received there. They had great successes in exams, and it was a first-class grammar school.

Gerry German was later to be sacked by the Jamaican Prime Minister Bustamante because he made clear his political alliance with the more left wing People's National Party (PNP). He was also a close friend of Norman Manley, the leader of the PNP. Gerry was a very charismatic person, so much so that Bustamante feared his influence on the student's parents. That's why he was given the push despite being a talented Head. He eventually left

Jamaica and became a senior education officer in the Commission for Racial Equality where I was also a senior liaison officer in London and there, I had the pleasure of working with him. He attended my inauguration as a freeman of the City of Bristol in 2008. I must say I felt closer to Norman Manley politically than I did to Bustamante, so felt sympathetic to some of Gerry's political views.

On 24th January in 1965 Churchill died and there was an enormous outpouring by the white and Black middle classes for the loss of a great hero. He was widely remembered in Jamaica. He had stayed in Jamaica with the owner of the Daily Express, Lord Beaverbrook, and was fondly remembered by some people there.

I got from the trip to America and Jamaica a sense that the negative things I'd been told about Black people were wrong and that the Black people of America were a very attractive group who were more sinned against than sinning. I was there at the time of the civil rights revolution and at the beginning of the pride in African roots and the slogan, 'Black is Beautiful'. It was an exciting time and really wonderful to see a group of people who had been so severely repressed coming out and saying we are not going to be repressed any more.

Back in England things were changing; the phrase 'Black is Beautiful' was on many people's lips and Black American music was very much centre stage in the music world. The first live Motown tour of England was taking place and it had been booked for the Colston Hall in March 1965. The artists featured were Stevie Wonder (who was only fourteen years old), Diana Ross and the Supremes, Martha and the Vandellas, Smokey Robinson and the Miracles, the Temptations, the Four Tops, and the Jackson Five. While this amazing line up had been sold out in other cities, here in Bristol there had been a problem with ticket sales so I had been given several hundred to hand out. Three hundred members of Bristol's Black community attended that concert and I certainly had a good evening. I spent some time backstage where I saw a lovely young woman I wanted to impress and asked her if she was Martha from the Vandellas. I received a very stern reply informing me that I was speaking to Diana Ross. I vowed never to make the mistake of confusing two different divas again!

I engaged with the music world on another occasion when I invited Millie Small the Jamaican singer who had a hit with 'My Boy Lollipop' to Bristol to meet young Black teenagers here. It was a great event for the newly arrived Caribbean immigrants and for Millie who seemed to truly enjoy herself.

It was later that year that I met and married Joyce, a Jamaican nurse. I found her surprisingly militant – she came from a rural background, as did most Jamaicans who I found were usually very conservative. Joyce was different though; she was emphatic in insisting on dignity for Black people. I met her in May 1965 and by October we were married. She was young, attractive and very keen to identify with my struggle. She had already heard about me when she lived in Manchester because of the Bristol Bus Boycott so imagine her surprise when she opened the door to me one evening. I stood there asking for a signature on a housing petition that I intended to take to the House of Commons; that is how we met.

The housing campaign was one against the council, who were placing Black people in houses which were totally unfit and unsuitable. We were campaigning for more housing from Bristol City Council. They were then sending Black people out to Knowle West and Southmead making them more vulnerable to extreme forms of racism from poor whites in those predominantly white but deprived areas. Hence their children were being subjected to the most extreme forms of racism.

Black people were being forced to live in terrible conditions and therefore we marched against this. It was blatant racial discrimination because people letting out houses were saying 'No Blacks, no Irish, no dogs, no children' so they were squeezed terribly getting accommodation wherever they could, and this of course was sub- standard. While they were being forced to live in these awful conditions because of their colour they were at the same time blamed for the housing shortage. People would sometimes share beds on shifts. The housing shortage and urban decay mainly caused by Government policy was still being blamed on the Black presence here.[38]

My campaign was to get Bristol City Council to provide more housing. Joyce took my petition to work and gathered some signatures from the other nurses. It turned out that Sherrie Eugene's[39] uncle was a mutual friend, so she sent me a message to say that the petition was ready and I went round to Joyce's home in Montpelier to collect it and I asked her out.

Joyce was from Clarendon in Jamaica and had lived in Manchester with her godmother when she first arrived but had recently moved to Bristol. I used to go round and leave messages for her, as there weren't so many phones in those days. I would ask her out to various functions, such as dinner and dances. On one occasion I took her to see Stevie Wonder when he came to Bristol. It was on a visit to Joyce while we were listening to Mahalia Jackson Sings on Joyce's radiogram that I asked her to marry me. I think we still have this LP. When Joyce accepted my

38   Owusu, 2000
39   Sherrie Eugene Hart is a popular, award-winning TV presenter first known for her ability to sign for the deaf.

proposal, I wrote to her parents to ask for her hand in marriage. They wrote back giving us their blessing. Not long after, we married, and she has been a great support to me ever since. Tony Benn came to our wedding with his wife Caroline. She too was a lovely woman, who like him was a warm and genuine person.

In 1964 Denis Howell, who I had first met when I was a student at Westhill, was the Under Secretary of State for Education and Science now that Labour had won the election. One day on the terraces of the House of Commons overlooking the Thames on a lovely summer evening where MPs would gather with their spouses Denis introduced me to Bessie Braddock.[40] She invited me to Liverpool to see the work she was doing in the dual heritage community in Toxteth, Liverpool. Many there were descended from Irish women and African seamen.

Bessie Braddock was a larger than life character who had a blunt and commanding but likeable manner. She was to my mind extremely popular with the people of Liverpool. We were walking in the centre of the city together and were stopped numerous times by Liverpudlians eager to speak to her about their concerns. Her popularity was such that it took us ages to walk from the centre to Parliament Street.

She showed me Stanley House in Liverpool where she supported youngsters who were developing boxing skills. I found the young people there challenging but friendly and generous. They were an isolated community from the rest of Liverpool, and many had been the victim of racism but they were united in their community values and sought better educational opportunities, an end to racism and the right to be treated equally as Liverpudlians.

40   Bessie Braddock was a fiery female MP who used extraordinary tactics to draw attention to causes such as the under privileged in Liverpool, mental health reform, barrow girls and prison conditions.

I loved the period I spent there when I also met (Adina) Dorothy Kuya who was the city's first Community Development Officer. She was to develop her own training agency 'Affirmata' which was the first to offer training in all aspects of equal opportunities and management. She was also a member of the committee that set up the award winning 'Transatlantic Slavery Gallery' at Merseyside Maritime Museum in 1994.

I was then asked by Denis Howell to sit on the Youth Service Development Council with Sir John Hunt and Professor Stuart Hall the academic[41]. This was my first government appointment by a minister. Sir John Hunt, of Everest fame, was then director of the Duke of Edinburgh Award, and on the Youth Service Development Council. John was nothing like me, we had such different backgrounds, he was an honorary brigadier from the British Army, but he was so easy going that we struck up a very strong relationship

We got on so well that Dennis Howell suggested that we set up a special commission to do some research about young immigrants in

the Youth Service. John and I went around the country giving talks about it, along with Stuart Hall, from the Centre for Contemporary Cultural Studies at Birmingham University. Stuart Hall was a visionary race theorist, and made important contributions to the field of cultural studies allowing useful dialogues around questions of culture, race and ethnicity.

We chose to look at what I was doing in Bristol with young immigrants and we realised we were striding ahead with these youngsters. I took the youngsters out on all kinds of expeditions,

41   Stuart Hall suggests that British Cultural Studies do not follow fully the logic of a structuralist paradigm – hence the Black population are not active and creative agents in their own history and culture as these are not conditions of their own making. (**Roxy 2000)**

to Somerset and other places. I wanted to share the kind of happy childhood experiences I had had, enjoying the beauty of nature and the self-sufficient discipline of camping, with them. I felt it would be a formative experience for them. The Black youngsters were particularly enthusiastic about going to the countryside. Some of the children had never seen the English countryside before, which was very different to tropical Jamaica where most of them came from.

One farm we stayed on in Somerset was Rookery Farm in Edingworth. It was owned by fairly liberal Methodists, the Clapp family, who wanted to do their bit for race relations and accommodated us there at weekends. It had an enormous impact on the children. The youngsters really enjoyed themselves there even though I would make them climb up Brent Knoll, which was quite a hike for them. John Hunt and I worked together doing a lot of work with the British-born children of migrants that came from the Caribbean and India getting them to form integrated, cohesive forms of community relationships – this had never been done before.

The Youth Service Development Council produced a report called 'Young Immigrants and the Youth Service' in July 1967. Lord Hunt was the chair and our brief was *"To consider the part which the Youth Service might play in meeting the needs of young immigrants in England and Wales and make recommendations".* Our recommendations called for discussion at local level among all concerned with encouraging new attitudes to the problem; improvements in the Youth Service itself (including training); and community-based approach work with young immigrants. Local authorities and voluntary organisations were urged to review their broad strategy and policy in this respect and to assess their Youth Service provision in terms of these particular people.

Clearly stated was the need to involve the help of a wide range of social agencies, and in particular the schools, colleges of further education, the Youth Employment Services and employers, the churches, social workers and the local voluntary liaison committees and the National Committee for Commonwealth Immigrants.

As part of this initiative John Hunt had invited me to talk to public schools about the need for an understanding of diversity and integration and I was a guest at Eton College at Eton Chapel. Eton in those days, even today, is the crème de la crème of education. There I met Ralph Sadleir, a great guy who was very helpful to me. He had arranged my visit and looked after me while I was there. He was the senior chaplain and a descendant of his namesake who was falconer to Queen Elizabeth I a post that went back to the time of Henry VIII.

At Eton the house captains and games captains were elected by their peers and if they did exceptionally well at the internal exams there, they could be elected as Library Scholars (prefects). They had special powers and privileges. This status gave them powers to discipline other students. They wore grey trousers and coloured waistcoats and had the power to fine other boys. They had junior boys (fags) running errands for them. On arriving at Eton I heard one of these boys calling down the corridor and a lot of thirteen-year olds came dashing into the corridor to see what the senior boy wanted. The reason they responded so quickly was that the last boy to arrive would have to do an errand for the senior boy. I understand this system has changed in recent years. There were two types of entrants to Eton: King's Scholars who had won a place there with a scholarship; and others called Oppidans who went through the normal route.

If you were in a comprehensive school, you might just make

it to Oxford. On the other hand if you were an Etonian public-school boy you didn't do the 11 Plus you did an exam called an Election at thirteen. These were elite academic boys waiting to get into Oxford or Cambridge University and they were ready for Oxbridge by the time they were sixteen. In my opinion this system made a place like Eton very difficult to radicalise. The price of privilege however, sometimes exacted a deadly cost, as these boys at sixteen were under such pressure that a few would attempt suicide.

Here I was given an insight into the highest level of British education. I was made very welcomed and most of the young people were very happy to listen to what I had to say at Evensong on Sunday evening.

It did not come as a great surprise, however, that one or two were very anti what I was saying and felt that having a Black man preach at Eton Chapel was going too far. In later years there was a book published of what Eton boys put in their diaries and one of the entries said, *'This evening we had this black guy preaching to us from the pulpit – black power – really the establishment has lost its nerve.'*

Nevertheless it still remains one of the most interesting and significant times for me, teaching diversity and community relations to Eton College. I also went to talk to schoolboys at Marlborough School, Sir John's old school. I was talking about integration, diversity and race relations to the British establishment's children who came from aristocratic, historic families and who were highly privileged. At the same time I was working at the grassroots in the heart of one of most deprived areas of England in St Paul's Bristol putting it into practice. Through this experience I was getting an insight into the contrasts of the British education system. Yet strangely enough both groups of young people seemed to have more in common than not. They were just youngsters who loved pop songs and the Beatles.

After the ordeal of preaching to a packed church on Sunday at Eton Chapel, I was invited by two senior Library Students (prefects) to have a beer at their school club called Pop. This club is an elite within an elite and carries a great deal of prestige in the world as it is made up of senior boys who have excelled in academia or sports and who go on to high office. One member of this elite club was Boris Johnson and another Old Etonian who failed to get into Pop but still managed to become Prime Minister was David Cameron.

I was treated with utmost respect by the senior boys with several of them jokingly telling me that I should become a member of Pop! I drank their watered-down beer and proceeded to talk to the boys about the need to welcome diversity in English society. Looking back at that experience, I could not help feeling that, in comparison to what I had experienced in the state education system, there was a serious gulf in promoting educational equality in this country. My experience at Eton alerted me to inequality and the need for greater social mobility in order to become a more cohesive society.

I emerged from the state education system designated as Grade One D to find myself speaking in front of hundreds of boys at the most elite school in the country, indeed the world.

As part of the same initiative I had a whole week at Clifton College, Bristol taking assembly with several hundred young people. Some people were very hostile when I said what a racist situation there was in Bristol. I challenged them. I said to the senior chaplain 'Come with me to an estate agent while I try to find accommodation today and tomorrow, I'll come back and tell you in assembly what happened.' The Clifton College students keenly accepted the challenge and the senior chaplain, and I went to an estate agent in Park Street. The young woman there said they have got a place but when she went to arrange a viewing she returned and said they don't take 'coloureds', so I was refused openly. The senior chaplain was aghast and of course at assembly the next morning I told the school what had happened. It shook the school. That was the power of my links with the public schools, bringing racism out into the open and allowing the young people there to really see what was happening.

It was during this period that I was asked to address the Oxford Union, which I duly did but was given the distinct impression that the people hosting me were ever so slightly disappointed that I was not as radical as Malcolm X.

I was now being targeted by the establishment as someone who could talk about migrants especially with respect to young people. Nadine Peppard, the general secretary of the National Committee of Commonwealth Immigrants (NCCI), knew about me because of the Bristol Bus Boycott campaign and was keen to get me involved in the NCCI. This body had been set up to 'co-ordinate on a national basis effort directed towards the integration of Commonwealth citizens into the community'.

It was the Archbishop of Canterbury, Dr. Michael Ramsey, who wrote to invite me to go on the Education Committee, a subcommittee of the NCCI. I worked on Dr Ramsey's Committee looking at the difficulties faced by young Black people.

The NCCI met from 1965 to 1968 and was replaced by the Community Relations Commission (CRC). This was later renamed Racial Equality Commission. The CRC, which worked alongside the Race Relations Board and the NCCI, progressed from dealing with specific immigrant problems to the larger concept of Community Relations. The change in its title reflected the change in its role. This was an important and significant acknowledgement of the need for community relations.

The CRC had been set up in 1968 by the Race Relations Act that replaced the extremely tame Act of 1965. Because the 1965 Act was highly criticised, there was pressure for something better. Lord Anthony Lester of Herne Hill QC[42] had helped Roy Jenkins to write a memorable speech on racial equality in Britain, in May 1966, in which Jenkins defined integration *'not as a flattening process of assimilation but as equal opportunity, accompanied by cultural diversity, in an atmosphere of mutual tolerance'*. He thought it was important to accept Black people's culture and not try to assimilate them into an English one.

In 1967, Jenkins intended to extend the legislation. Unfortunately, he was fated not to implement it because he was soon succeeded at the Home Office by James Callaghan who was responsible for the 1968 Race Relations Act and he was not as sympathetic to cultural diversity as Jenkins. At a parliamentary Labour Party executive meeting in 1971 an argument about the Kenyan Asians resolution broke out with Tony Benn supporting Joan Lester against Jim Callaghan. At that meeting Jim Callaghan said, 'We don't want any more Blacks in Britain'.[43]

The 1968 Race Relations Act, which was wide in scope but weak in enforcement, made it illegal to refuse housing, employment or public services to people because of their ethnic background. One of the most controversial areas of the Act however was the exclusion of government services, such as the police, from legal proceedings.

While civil rights for Black people in Britain was making very

---

42 Lord Lester of Herne QC along with Dr David Pitt and others founded the Campaign against Racial Discrimination (CARD).
43 Benn, 1988

slow progress there were also more restrictions on immigration. In 1967 when African Asians, fearing discrimination from their own national governments, began to arrive in Britain this prompted the Government to rush through the 1968 Commonwealth Immigration Act. Asians from Kenya and Uganda had retained their British citizenship following independence, and therefore were not subject to the 1962 Immigration Act. The Conservative Enoch Powell and his associates set about campaigning for tighter controls, and an outcome of this scaremongering was that the Labour Government responded with the Commonwealth Immigration Act of 1968. It extended control to those without a parent or grandparent who was born in or was a citizen of the UK.[44]

Being British and Black was, and to a large extent still remains, a complex matter. I was aware of this and I was trying to make improvements for the young Black immigrants. Father Peter Berry, a canon of Coventry Cathedral and a very skilled communicator, had heard of what we were doing in Bristol. He was very keen to have me working in Coventry. My chair Anne Hewer was very anxious to keep me in Bristol, but my contract had come to an end and I had done my job in Bristol. The move to a new city proved to be an interesting part of my life.

Before I left Bristol for Coventry in 1968, I had a big rousing party in the Bamboo Club[45] thrown by Tony and Lalel Bullimore. I had the honour of opening the club a few years before. Joyce and I were always welcomed there and would often go there for a night out and when we had guests, I would enjoy taking them there. At my farewell party people like Dennis Howell came and

---

44   www.nationalarchives.gov.uk (Themes, Commonwealth immigration control legislation) Retrieved 30/11/2020
45   The Bamboo Club opened in 1966.

the guest list also sparkled with veterans of the campaign. Even some of my opponents such as Oliver Tomkins, the Bishop of Bristol with whom I was now reconciled attended. Wally Jenkins, Leader of City council, who was vehemently opposed to the Bristol Bus Boycott campaign also turned up. I welcomed this feeling of unity, this coming together of friends and ex- foes. It was a hell of a do, a great send-off which gave me a tremendous feeling of affability as well as achievement.

When Tony Bullimore was applying for a licence to open the Bamboo Club the then chief constable George Twist came to see me about it and asked my opinion. I supported the application and George Twist said, 'If you support it, we won't oppose it'. The club, which provided the first truly integrated club in Bristol's entertainment scene, has its own history and a unique place in Bristol's African and Caribbean community. Joyce and I were invited to the club's official opening and Tony, Lalel, Joyce and I have been friends for many years. When I lived in Coventry and visited Bristol, they would put me up.

When I left for Coventry, the Race Relation Acts of 1965 and 1968 had been passed and the situation was looking brighter, but it was then that Enoch Powell made his sickening 'Rivers of Blood' speech, which turned on a time bomb. It was to have an ominous effect on large sections of the country who thought he was right, particularly amongst the police force, which practically made a saint of him. Again this was to have an impact on my own life over the next few years.

I was appointed to the Coventry Community Relations Council (CRC) as an executive officer. This was a voluntary organisation made up of white liberals, Africans, Caribbeans, Asians, Punjabis and various ethnic groups. Before I went for the interview, I rang the chief executive of Coventry City Council and questioned whether I'd be the best person to be appointed as I was of African British origin and it was mainly Asians in Coventry. He advised me to come for the interview, as it was a job across the board for all ethnic groups. If he had told me on the phone that there might be language and culture issues that made the post inappropriate for me, I wouldn't have gone.

The Council was headed by the Vice Chancellor of Warwick University, Jack Butterworth. I found him quite amenable although at times I felt as if I was having an audience with him on matters relating to race relations in Coventry. He was also someone who I felt had a slightly different agenda to mine.

On one occasion I was asked to invite Dick Crossman, a Coventry MP and Government minister, to our AGM. When I met him at the train station he asked me what he was expected to do and I said perhaps talk about the passing of the Race Relations Act and what the government might do to strengthen it all. He said he didn't know anything about the Race Relations Act and couldn't speak on just that. When I spoke to Jack Butterworth after he said, 'Well we've got a meeting with Crossman after the AGM, so we'll take him out to dinner.' I understood from what Butterworth said that he wanted Crossman to back his proposal that Warwick developed a medical facility at the University. I felt, though amenable, Jack's main interests lay elsewhere. He eventually became Lord Butterworth.

After a year, because of the problems Jack Butterworth was having with students, he wanted to step down and Rev. Peter Berry suggested Mr Walter Chin, Coventry's Chief Education Officer should become the next chair of Coventry Community Relations Council which he did in due course.

I discovered that I had some powerful allies in my campaign against racism in Coventry, which included the Right Rev

Cuthbert Bardsley, the Bishop of Coventry from 1956 to 1976. He was a former bishop to the armed forces. He was very supportive of my campaigns in Coventry because of my high-profile activities in Bristol and so I would imagine that his approval of what I was trying to do in Coventry was relayed around the establishment there.

At first, I felt hesitant about going to what was a Sikh community as I had been working with an African Caribbean, Jamaican community. Coventry was mainly Sikhs. But I needn't have worried because I was able to get through to the Sikhs. They gave me an enormous amount of support in my fight against racism particularly with the police. There was a lot of confusion among the small group of Africans and Caribbeans who wondered what on earth I was doing. They hadn't seen a Black English guy having such a rapport with immigrants from the Punjab before.

I was invited to many Sikh weddings and became well known in the city. I felt I had enormous support from the Punjabi community, who would invite Joyce and I into their homes for meals. I only had to say I wanted to do something, and they would back me. We even went to London on anti-apartheid marches.

On one occasion in order to raise funds for camping trips I organised a variety performance at the town hall where I sang Frank Sinatra's 'My Way'. I had practised for weeks miming the song first. People were coming up with notes to donate money in support while I mimed. The Asian community enthusiastically backed this event. The hall was packed. It was a wonderful evening and one of its highlights was when I saw this beautiful woman arriving in a majestic Nigerian costume looking like an African queen. To my surprise and delight it turned out to be Joyce, my wife, who hadn't told me what she was going to wear that evening.

I used to take both the Asian and African Caribbean

youngsters out on various events and projects. We went camping in Wales and the Norfolk Broads. We also went to Germany for the Olympic Games in Munich and other trips to Europe through links I had established during my National Service in Germany. John Naumann, an English lecturer who taught English at the Folk House in Park Street, Bristol had taken us across to Europe to meet up with students. Some I also took in a small group to Scotland. I was helping to train the older Asian and African Caribbean teenagers of fifteen or so to work with the younger children of about seven or eight.

I also took them on trips to Lord Hunt's house at Henley-on-Thames. I was at the time promoting the 'Immigrants Youth Service' report and John invited me to stay at his home for a while. Later he was to entertain, mainly a group of young Asians at his home. He was keen to see how young Asians integrated into English communities.

I brought the children of the Asian and Caribbean communities together. If left separated there might well have been discrimination between them but working together being Black and English neutralised the sense that they were different to each other. They shared a common experience.

Joyce was very supportive of my work and our house was sometimes used as a cooling off space for young people who were having problems with their parents. We used to liaise between the parents and teenagers and help facilitate good relations between them.

Courtenay Griffiths, who came from a large Jamaican family, was the only Black youngster in a direct grant grammar school. I met him when I went to speak at his school, and I got to know him and his family when he was a young sixth former. He went camping with us and looked after the younger ones. I was, more or less, his mentor and assisted him getting into to the London School of Economics (LSE). He felt disillusioned there and left but after some encouragement returned and became president of the Black Students Association at LSE, eventually becoming a QC.

He has been a counsel in some very high-profile trials such as the Damilola Taylor murder trial, the Blakelock murder trial, the Broadwater Farm riot, the Brighton bombing, the Harrods bombing, the Canary Wharf bombing and the M25 appeal. I am very proud of him. He used to accuse me of being an Uncle Tom, so I have to smile now he is so much part of the establishment. I am sure he will laugh at me too now I am an OBE.

Many of the migrants in Coventry at that time were Punjabis and a few Africans and Caribbeans. I managed to meet them quite a lot and help to support marches against racial discrimination in working men's clubs. At the time the white working men's clubs would not allow membership to Asian and Black people. Fose Hill Working Men's Club was one such.

In 1970 I was invited as a guest of the Episcopalian Church in North America. I well remember arriving at Buffalo Airport in New York State being greeted by Anglican Black nuns and being referred to as the Rev. Paul Stephenson. After that I met the man who was probably the first Black bishop of the Episcopalian Church in New York State. He welcomed me and offered greetings to Coventry Cathedral, which they had good relations with. After a while of being called the Reverend I decided to tell everyone that I wasn't a Reverend, which by the look on the faces of the nuns had come as very disappointing news. While I still received their curtsies and respect, I sensed their strong feelings of disappointment that I wasn't a man of the cloth.

My first engagement was a television interview where I spoke quite openly about racism in the US. Later that evening a leader of the local Black Panthers' unit, who had seen my television interview, rang to invite me to speak at one of their meetings. I preferred a non-violent approach to change so declined this offer. I nevertheless felt sympathy for and an understanding of their militancy against racism. At the same time the Bishop felt that my television interview was rather too radical for his congregation who were mainly Black and white middle-class Americans so he cancelled my speaking engagement with his church. That left me I think somewhere between the two perspectives.

I was in New York State for about a week to ten days and met with Black civil servants of the state who took me to a labour farm of migrant workers who were exploited for their labour and lived in harsh conditions. They were unable to buy their way out because of the system that kept vulnerable Black labourers constantly in debt to their employers. A large number of Black people there lived by picking fruit for owners of the land who did not pay them fairly. I was taken around and shown the terrible conditions in which those Black families lived. You could call it slavery – like sharecroppers. It had a profound effect on me at the time. It was a depressing picture and I knew I could never work under such harsh conditions.

Later I took the bus from Buffalo to see Niagara Falls, which is a tremendous and spectacular display of the raw power of nature. The sight and sound of it, while magnificent, makes you feel the frailty of the human condition. It is a truly awesome display. I was grateful to Coventry Cathedral and Father Peter Berry who instigated the visit.

When I returned to Coventry I returned too to the problem between the police and the Black community. Once a superintendent told me that his officers couldn't arrest Black youths. I asked him why not and he said because they keep saying they are going to report the police to you. I told him I couldn't stop police officers arresting someone who lawfully needs to be arrested. If an arrest is unlawful, unfair and it's coming from a racist attitude and they come to me, then I will try to help them and see if we can resolve it. But to say that police officers are too frightened to arrest these youngsters because they are going to take it to the Race Relations Officer is nonsense. This is the sort of attitude I had to put up with at the time.

There was a lot of hostility from the police to the Black community and there was a time when the Police Federation passed a no confidence vote in me as a Community Relations Officer of the city. I enquired what they meant by no confidence since I was quite a high-profile public figure in Coventry at that time. They said I didn't co-operate with them enough. This was ludicrous, as I was very much involved in trying to promote a different attitude by the police towards the ethnic minorities. There was a very hard-line attitude by certain sections of the Police force towards the Black and Asian community. The Police thought I was too active in my support of that community in Coventry and disliked me. They would sometimes put their two fingers up at me as they passed in their Panda cars. I of course ignored them when they did this.

Against the backdrop, serious crimes were being committed against Black people. In Leeds in 1969, homeless Nigerian vagrant David Oluwale, who had previously been subjected to a series of violent and vicious attacks by two policemen – including being urinated on and violently kicked – was last seen being chased by those officers near a river in which his body was found.[46] This is a crime all the more hideous when you realise it is perpetuated

46   Fryer, 1984

by people supposedly there to uphold the law. The judge directed the jury to acquit the policemen of manslaughter, so they were only found guilty of ABH and given sentences of 27 months and three years.

There were times when my home was attacked by the National Front. Of course, I reported it to the police and in fact went to the Chief Constable of Warwickshire to get my wife and I some sort of protection against bricks being thrown through our windows which happened on six or seven occasions. What they did was put Panda cars in my drive so I couldn't get my car out at times. They had to do something but did it in a way that inconvenienced me.

In 1972 I took up a post in London and several police told me that when it was announced that I was leaving Coventry, a big roar of cheers went up from police stations around the city. Of course, not all the police were against what I was doing, but there was a substantial hard-line core of police officers who had hatefully opposed me. This was before the Macpherson report condemned the Metropolitan police as institutionally racist.

My Return To London
And Then To Bristol
1972-2013

I left Coventry for a post in London I saw advertised in the *Caribbean World* and in the *Guardian*. It was as a National Youth Officer for the Community Relations Commission (CRC). The CRC (a non-Government agency) was set up to encourage greater integration and better relations between people from different ethnic groups. The idea was to use its legal powers to help eradicate racial discrimination and harassment, to work with Government and public authorities and to promote racial equality in all public services. It was also to support local and regional organisations, and employers in all sectors, in their efforts to ensure equality of opportunity and good race relations and to raise public awareness of racial discrimination and injustice, and to win support for efforts to create a fairer and more equal society.

Unfortunately, the 1968 Race Relations Act's effectiveness in championing the cause of equality was curtailed by certain factors. The Act itself did not have enough power to make an impact on the services of state, such as the immigration service, which was outside the scope of the Act, so outside the Commission's remit. We couldn't touch any of the Crown's activities.

My post in London involved promoting the Youth Service around the country and I felt it was a natural progression of what I had been doing in Bristol and Coventry. I found out later that there was some opposition to my appointment however from Mark Bonham-Carter, the chair of the Race Relations Board who was hostile to me taking up the post because he thought I was too radical and that I might destabilise the work of the Commission.

His view was that I shouldn't address the issues of racism, but I should concentrate on poverty and social dialogue – he was one of those people who saw the problem as a welfare problem, not one of race. I had stated that we should take the working men's clubs to the Race Relations Board for racial discrimination, which was now unlawful because of the 1965 Race Relations Act. He had seen all the press reports about this from Coventry, which he found alarming. It was literally through the influence of David Pitt, the former chair of CARD, who persuaded Bonham-Carter to allow my appointed, that I was able to take up the post.

My line manager at that time was Gavton Shepherd who was Guyanese and the Senior Officer for the Commission. He was well regarded in Brixton for the work he was doing in the local church. We got on extremely well. He allowed me discretion on all the issues I was confronting. As well as running conferences for the young people across the country, I was also taking Black youth workers to Amsterdam to learn about Anne Frank and the Nazi atrocities of the last World War. He never interfered with anything I was trying to do but was always supportive.

Soon after taking up my post I went with Joyce to meet her family in Jamaica, so that was my second visit there. Joyce's father had passed on, but I met her mother and the rest of her family. Our children weren't born then. Her brother nicknamed me the 'chief' because I would take the initiative in any plans being made. This was a time when reggae was a world-wide phenomenon thanks to Bob Marley, and I said to my brother in law, 'Jamaica will never be the same again, the people have found a voice.'

Returning to Jamaica after eight years was like witnessing a whole new nationhood of people. It seemed like a cultural revolution had taken place among the youth population. I wrote to the papers saying how a rhythmic pulsating rhythm had entered the consciousness of this new generation of young people. The way in which the new young people of Jamaica walked, talked, lived and danced, I said needed to be understood if the traditional English institutional and educational processes are to be successful in tapping the energies, talents and intelligence which resided in this new awakening.

I could see that already there were signs of a serious breakdown within the existing educational system regarding the education and training of qualified teachers. It is estimated that approximately 90,000 Jamaican school children were illiterate. The newly elected government launched as one of its major priorities a national literacy campaign to reverse the tide of illiteracy on the island. I thought the high social intelligence that existed among the young illiterates is evidence that the existing educational system, particularly in rural Jamaica, was not reaching the young in a way that engaged their new emerging consciousness.

It was significant that when I first visited Jamaica Marcus Garvey's body had been returned from England for burial there and a special service was given in his honour by the Government of the time. This was something to which Jamaican youth could relate.

While I was there, I was privileged to attend a large international seminar, held at the University of the West Indies on the life and philosophy of Marcus Garvey. The seminar, which was opened by the Prime Minister, Michael Manley, was attended by distinguished Black intellectuals and academics from Africa and America. They paid tribute to Garvey as one of the greatest Black men that had ever lived. What emerged from that conference was a call to the Black people of Jamaica to regard Africa as their Motherland and those with a deep and passionate love for Africa should go there and assist in its development.

I felt Jamaica was faced with new influences regarding Africa. On the one hand the Black nationalistic voice of the Garveyites calling for a full-scale repatriation to Africa and on the other hand the more religious voice of the Ras Tafari wanting a return to Ethiopia.

There was an African consciousness sweeping through Jamaica at this time and this was not confined to the masses of the poor Black youth for it was being articulated and developed by youths in the island's leading secondary schools, colleges and among students at the University. I felt we should analyse the historical processes possibly beginning with the Maroons[47] who were the first freed African slaves, having freed themselves by escaping the plantations. They had a long and protracted period of warfare with the British plantation owners until emancipation.

I felt at the time that Jamaica stood at the crossroads of its destiny. Its youth were feeling a great attraction towards Black African nationalism whereas the Jamaican Government was committed to a policy of Jamaican nationalism. The Government had introduced plans to encourage an ambitious youth and community programme in which thousands of Jamaica's under-privileged Black youth could be trained in craft, agriculture and forestry farming and be encouraged to involve themselves more in the development of the communities from which they came. The scheme had been welcomed by all sections of Jamaican society for its success largely depended on the self-reliance, confidence and commitment of all participants in the scheme including the politicians, leaders, instructors and the youth themselves.

---

47   Maroons were escaped slaves who lived in the Mountains of Jamaica and were so successful in their opposition to the establishment that the British Government was forced to sign treaties with them.

I felt that the warmth and beauty of the people, their determination to live a proud and honourable life was surely the nation's greatest asset. Sometimes I saw the poverty that people had to deal with, and this reminded me of old Nellie Bright in Bardfield, England and showed me in graphic terms how poverty could claim anyone whatever their race or country.

I would sometimes sit in the rum shops there enjoying sitting and talking to the men (women seldom came inside) and we would have all sorts of discussions putting the world to rights. Sometimes people from England would recognise me and so come and say hello. I used to spend time in conversation with local people and after my excursions I would often return to a family concerned for my welfare.

I would often be out for hours and my brother and sister-in-law would worry because in those days there were no mobile phones, and they were surprised that Joyce didn't worry too. She of course knew I loved to go and talk to people. On one occasion I brought back two gentlemen who knew the real history of Jamaica and told us about people like Marcus Garvey and Paul Bogle.[48] I liked to wander round and meet people and get a view of how they lived and what they thought. On another occasion in the mountains I was offered a smoke with some people, I stayed to talk but declined the smoke.

In later years when I returned with our children, they enjoyed themselves too, as I would take them to places like King's House to meet the Governor General and once, we were also invited by Michael Manley's physician to come for dinner. We sometimes stayed in Jamaican hotels, which the children particularly enjoyed.

---

48   Marcus Garvey was the first of Jamaica's national heroes and a proponent of the Back to Africa movement. He is a prophet of the Rastafarian movement. Paul Bogle was hung along with George William Gordon for his part in the Morant Bay rebellion in 1865. This rebellion paved the way for better practices in court and some social and economic improvements for the people.

On returning to London it was not difficult to settle in as I had been brought up there after the war, so I was used to it. I felt London was my base. I stayed in West London when I first came back. After we sold our house in Coventry, we moved into a maisonette in Tulse Hill in West Norwood in 1974. I got to know various individuals who were working with young Caribbeans in Brixton and contacted a number of Caribbean leaders of the local community, and generally got to know various individuals who were working at the time in Brixton. I found myself setting up conferences all over the country and helping young Asians and African Caribbeans to get a better feel of what the countryside was like. This was building on the work I'd already done on the Hunt report.

By one of those strange coincidences in life, as a child in Dunmow, I had met Michael Denison who was living there with his wife Dulcie Gray. He and his wife had starred in the film 'My Brother Jonathan' and Michael was later to have the lead role in the popular television series 'Boyd QC'. Michael Denison had also been in a film called 'Black Joy' with Norman Beaton, who became a close friend of mine when I moved to London. Norman was a successful Black actor best known for the eponymous role of 'Desmond', in the popular television series. He also had the distinction of being the first Black teacher to be employed by Liverpool Education Authority.

Norman would come over to visit the family. One night we invited him to stay because it was late, but he had to share with our young son who was already asleep. Soon after he had retired our son came running in to us saying that he could hear a monster in his room. It turned out to be Norman's snoring that had alarmed him. Norman was a natural character actor and a generous person who displayed an intelligent and considerable wit. Though good for a laugh he could also be very serious and earned the respect of some of the great Shakespearean actors such as Judi Dench, Glenda Jackson, Vanessa Redgrave and Peter Hall. He was a described as 'one of England's leading actors'. Harold Pinter's comment on his performance as the lead in 'The Caretaker' at the National Theatre in 1981 was that his performance was memorable and that he was a brilliant actor – one of the most remarkable talents in the country. Bob Hoskins said of him he had a unique talent with a mixture of heart-breaking honesty and a devastating sense of the ridiculous'. He was versatile in many fields and had also been a singer and a playwright.

After his untimely death in 1994 I helped organise Norman's memorial service at Southwark Cathedral. This memorial service, which was arranged by the Dean and Cannons of Southwark Cathedral, was a way of acknowledging his professional talent. I invited Frank Bruno to this occasion, and he was keen to come and acknowledge his respect for Norman. Frank Bruno was highly conscious of the way the media portrayed him and was eager to show his independence as a young Black boxing champion.

In 1974 John Fraser, MP for Norwood, invited me to go on the board of governors for Tulse Hill School, a large multi-racial comprehensive boys' school in Brixton. The school was famous for educating Ken Livingstone, Mayor of London, and the Jamaican poet Linton Kwesi Johnson.[49] The school has now been redeveloped as affordable housing and it was in this block that Jean Charles de Menezes was resident when police in July 2005 mistakenly thought he was a terrorist and killed him.

At that time in the early 1970s, I noticed that large sections of the staff had low opinions of the Black children in terms of their academic performance. I saw there was an obvious need for a role

49   Linton Kwesi Johnson is known and revered as the world's first dub poet.

model for these young boys who found it difficult to identify with the white teachers. The school was in a bit of a turmoil. More than fifty per cent of its 1,300 students were Black and I felt they needed positive Black role models. That possibility came in the shape of Muhammad Ali when he visited London in 1974.

Muhammad Ali was on his way back to Chicago from Zaire after his 'Rumble in the Jungle' fight with George Foreman. I jokingly said I'd try and bring him to the school so when he arrived in London I went to the Hilton where he was staying and met him in the foyer. I said, 'Muhammad Ali, it's great to see you. Congratulations on your win.' Then I asked, 'I wonder if you'd like to come down to our school and see my pupils?'

He replied with a question, 'Go down to your school?'

'Yes,' I said, 'they'd love to see you.'

By the look on his face he seemed quite interested but he hesitated, 'Well, I'm a busy man. I gotta go to Chicago.'

I said, 'I know but just a few hours would be great if you could.'

We continued to chat then he wanted to know how much I'd pay him. I looked him straight in the eye and said 'Muhammad, I haven't got a dollar.'

He responded, 'Not even a dime?'

Then said, 'You have more nerve than Frazier' but he agreed to come and from then Muhammad and I just hit it off. We got on well, our vibrations were good. He asked that the press wasn't told in advance about his visit, because he didn't want it turning into a media circus at the school.

I met some of the children on their way to school and told them I had a big surprise for them. When they asked what it was, I said I was bringing Muhammad Ali to the school and they laughed thinking I was still joking and said, 'Yes we know'.

Joyce, who was pregnant at the time, and I collected

Muhammad in the morning from the Hilton Hotel. I'd hired a car of course and we drove over to Tulse Hill School. When we arrived, he met the headmaster and some of the senior staff and I brought along Rudi Walker who I saw quite a lot of at the time. Rudi's family would spend time with us as he and his wife had a son and daughter about the same age as my children. They are a lovely couple and Rudi is very amusing and entertaining. They also came to see us in Bristol when he was appearing at the Old Vic. He played in 'EastEnders' for eighteen years, but at the time he was in the hit sitcom 'Love thy Neighbour'.

The whole school of one thousand three hundred boys were wondering what on Earth they had been assembled for as we had managed to get Muhammad into the headmaster's study without them seeing him. We had never had the school out in full at one time before, but we knew we couldn't have half of them in class and the other half in the assembly hall. That would have been hard to manage given the excitement we were expecting.

The Head got them all hushed and quiet; I then started to introduce Muhammad Ali to the boys at school. I told them I wanted them to greet a young man who was just returning from Africa who was on his way back to Chicago in the United States and to give him a big warm hand. It remained really quiet so I said, 'Give a big hand to Muhammad Ali' and everything stayed hushed and silent. The boys seemed remarkably unresponsive. Ali looked at me and I looked at him and then he walked out on stage into a wall of silence until the children recognised him and then the hall erupted into wild thunderous applause, cat calls, noisy screams and cheers of amazement. They brought the roof down!

They knew him as Cassius Clay, not as Muhammad Ali so hadn't realised who it was when I introduced him. There was a strange irony in this because he had accepted my invitation to come partly because I had addressed him as Muhammad Ali when a lot of people were still calling him Cassius Clay (his original name which he changed in the 1960s). It was a good thing that I had shown him that respect. It was because of this that he rewarded the school and me with a visit, which was to have a long-reaching effect on the school and the pupils there.

Once on stage he announced, 'I've got a poem for you Mr Stephenson.'

> *I like your school Mr Stephenson*
> *I admire your style*
> *but your pay is so cheap*
> *I won't be back for a while'*

The boys loved him, and he invited one of them to spar with him. Another amusing thing happened when some children asked Joyce for her autograph because they thought that she was Muhammad Ali's wife. The occasion was a tremendous success. To this very day I get recognised by ex-pupils who remember it. He served as a role model for some of the boys as it was really something to have had Muhammad Ali at their school.

On our way back to his hotel, when we were passing Buckingham Palace, he asked with a twinkle in his eye if the Queen was in and seemed quite interested in visiting. I told him she wasn't in because the flag was not flying – she prefers to be in Windsor. I said, 'Don't worry too much about that Muhammad as you are a king.' So that took his mind of it. I had momentarily considered stopping at the Commons so Denis Howell could meet him, as I knew Denis was a great fan but felt daunted by the security risk and the frenzied media circus that such an impromptu visit would have caused.

When I returned him to his hotel I asked if we could channel his known interest in sport for young people into something in Britain. That is how we came to set up the Muhammad Ali Sports Development Association (MASDA). It was set up two years later in 1976. Its aim was to promote sports development, principally among ethnic minority young people in the inner city, as a means, to develop self-confidence and social interaction between young people of different racial groups living in disadvantaged and deprived economic circumstances. Muhammad used to come over once a year to the prize giving and he would sign the certificates for the children. I also influenced him into opening the Muhammad Ali centre in Birmingham, getting the person behind it to come and meet him with the plans.

We had hundreds of young people who were encouraged to take up sports that Black youngsters hadn't been involved with such as pony trekking, tennis and angling. We had Asian and Caribbean youngsters flocking to join the various sporting groups we held. The youngsters didn't just stay in Brixton, they were taken on trips to the Norfolk Broads as well. MASDA was based at Tulse Hill School but other schools also participated and girls who lived in the area were involved as well.

I asked Herman Ouseley, who I first met when he was the first Black chief executive of Lambeth Borough Council, to become the deputy Chair of MASDA. He is now Baron Ouseley of Peckham Rye in Southwark.

The athlete Daley Thompson and footballer Garth Crooks were among others involved. We met annually with a lot of the Black emerging sportsmen, football stars such as John Fashanu and John Barnes, the boxer John Conteh, cricketer Clive Lloyd and the Wimbledon tennis champion Arthur Ashe. They were all involved in promoting MASDA. Many other sports personalities also supported MASDA over the years

We had support from a wide range of people including the late Cardinal Basil Hume, head of the English Catholic Church. I went to see him at Westminster House and asked for his support, which he was delighted to give. He was very keen to promote the work of MASDA and attended the annual prize giving at Brixton Town Hall and met with the instructors. He was a very pleasant and easy-going person.

I stayed in touch with Muhammad down the years, even visiting his home in Los Angeles and remaining in touch with him even after he was afflicted with Parkinson's disease. Strangely enough we never discussed boxing.

Meeting him was like a spiritual event because I was meeting him on a level where we were working together. We were trying to influence each other's thoughts and thinking. He was very much his own man; someone who possessed the ability to seemingly know what you were going to say before you said it, always anticipating you one step ahead. It must have been an enormous thing for him to get Parkinson's disease at such a young age when he was on the threshold of another career. He is still a great role model for countless young people throughout the world. It is a great privilege to have known him and to have worked with him. He was truly the greatest!

It was also in 1974 that Roy Jenkins became home secretary again, developing new anti-discrimination legislation on gender as well as race. In the White Paper 'Racial Discrimination' it states:

"Racial discrimination, and the remediable disadvantages experienced by sections of the community because of their colour or ethnic origins, are not only morally unacceptable but also a form of economic and social waste which we as a society cannot afford."[50]

50   Lester, 2006

The White Paper suggested using government contracts as a tool for securing compliance with the law. Had this been done it would have been a very effective method of ensuring the law had some bite. The concept of unlawful discrimination was extended to include not only direct discrimination such as notices that say 'No Blacks' but also indirect discrimination such as advertising jobs in places where it is unlikely to be seen by minority groups. For the first time, alleged victims were to be given direct right of access to courts and tribunals. The Commission for Racial Equality, which would have 'a major strategic role in enforcing the law in the public interest', was created.

The new strategy was not implemented as originally envisaged. Jenkins left the Home Office in September 1976 and the Callaghan administration did not make use of government contracts to secure equal opportunity practices.

The 1976 Race Relations Act did create the Commission for Racial Equality (CRE) which replaced the CRC, so I was now employed in the same capacity as before but by the CRE. The areas in its legal remit were Education, Housing, Industry, the Civil Services and Goods and Services but budgeting constraints restricted the cases it could take on. The Act also imposed compensation limits on race discrimination awards. This did not change until the 'Race Relations Remedies Act' in 1994, when MP Keith Vaz introduced a private member's bill to correct this.

The 1976 Race Relations Act remained unchanged for more than twenty years. The CRE recommended repeatedly and unsuccessfully that the Act should be amended to require public authorities to promote racial equality. Meanwhile, the racist murder of Stephen Lawrence and the subsequent report of the Macpherson Inquiry persuaded Home Secretary Jack Straw to strengthen the 1976 Act by extending the prohibition against direct and indirect racial discrimination to public service providers, and by imposing a statutory duty on the public sector to promote racial equality. The way in which the duty has been implemented is excessively mechanical and bureaucratic, and the CRE was not given the resources to carry out the necessary monitoring.[51]

In private sector housing, conditions meant there was severe overcrowding and in the public sector there were moves to disperse the Caribbean community. This could have unfortunate repercussions for individuals who would find themselves isolated and surrounded by racist neighbours. In the 1970s after the Runnymede Report on housing it was clear the situation was worse. This led to the development of Black-led housing associations but the Black community had had its back to the wall long before this started to happen.

It was also in the 1970s that the British Government was to find itself in breach of international law because of immigration. They were to extend 1968 immigration controls even further.

This situation was further compounded when in 1969 new laws in Kenya forced Asian traders out of business and it was estimated that 20,000 British passport holders would come to Britain. In February 1971 the Conservative Government now in power enacted further legislation limiting immigration from Commonwealth countries. The Act replaced employment vouchers with work permits, allowing only temporary residence. It also tightened the immigration control administration and made some provision for assisting voluntary repatriation.

This Act also introduced the concept of 'patriality'; those with close UK associations were exempted from the act. This rule was introduced to allow white Africans in similar circumstances to

51   Lester, 2006

have the right to live in the UK, clearly reinforcing the 'colour bar' already in place. This particularly affected the newly independent Commonwealth countries of East Africa when African Asians found their British Overseas passports were effectively worthless. It was not until 2002 that the 1968 and 1971 immigration legislation was successfully challenged under the European Convention on Human Rights.

The United Kingdom had signed but did not ratify Protocol Four to the European Convention on Human Rights because of its position toward British nationals who were denied the right to freely enter and live in their country of nationality. Article 3 of Protocol Four states that, *'No one shall be expelled, by means either of an individual or of a collective measure, from the territory of the state of which he is a national.'* It also says that *'no one shall be deprived of the right to enter the territory of the state of which he is a national.'*

The government, because of the 1968 and 1971 Immigration Acts, was also in defiance of other international laws as the United Nations Convention on the Rights of the Child, Article 7 states. *'The child shall be registered immediately after birth and shall have the right from birth to a name, to acquire a nationality and as far as possible, the right to know and be cared for by his or her parents.'* It also states that *'Parties shall ensure the implementation of these rights in accordance with their national law and their obligations under the relevant international instruments in this field, in particular where the child would otherwise be stateless.'*

The changes in immigration Law from 1962 onwards were to eventually lead to a hierarchy in the different types of British citizenships. The British Nationality Act 1981 abolished the Commonwealth and United Kingdom citizenship status and replaced it with three categories of citizenship from 1st January 1983. They were British Citizenship, British Dependent

Territories Citizenship (which was renamed British Overseas Territories Citizenship by the British Overseas Territories Act 2002) and British Overseas Citizenship.

During this period I continued to concentrate on improving things for the children of Black immigrants. While I was in London there were two celebrities, Cleo Laine and the late Johnny Dankworth, who I invited to set up a music award, known as 'The Cleo Laine Award'. This was at the local girls' school, the Dick Shepherd School, and although it was mainly centred there children from schools all around could also participate. John was very helpful with all that and the children given the award could attend the music school set up in Cleo and John's house at the famous 'Stables' in Wavendon, Buckinghamshire. All youngsters were welcomed, and white youngsters also benefited from what they did.

That went on for about five years and I chaired the awards from 1977 to 1982. Both Cleo and Johnny were very enthusiastic, and the awards proved very popular. Cleo is very outgoing and great fun. Johnny was very easy going, encouraging and generous. John was a great humanist and strove to identify with the causes of anti-racism. Cleo and her children can be proud of having had such a wonderful husband and father. My last meeting with them both was at St. George's concert hall in Bristol where they were performing in aid of charity.

It was also in London that both my children were born at King's College Hospital. The two most important days of my life were their births. First, I witnessed my son, Paul Marcus's birth. He had kept us waiting as Joyce had a long labour and I was there helping. When he finally arrived, I felt that was the most joyous moment in my life. After the birth Joyce blossomed into a picture of serenity as she held our son. Two years later Funmilayo followed in the same hospital but her arrival was so swift that she got there before I did. Her arrival also presented me with a unique and tremendous feeling of joy.

They grew up initially in West Norwood where they went to school. Later they went to a private primary school in West Dulwich. The decision to put them into a private school was partly because Joyce and I wanted to give them the best educational opportunity but also because they, particularly my son, were experiencing racial abuse in the playground at the local infant school. Junior was quite young at the time and I didn't want him subjected to the kind of pressures I had been under at my primary school. They had a much better experience at private school where there were other Black children in the school. In fact, after returning to Bristol they found themselves among the few Black children in Westbury School.

The decision to move them I believe was to lead to the Lambeth Labour Party having me fired from my governorship at Tulse Hill School. I was perceived as too much to the right so when my three years came up when I would have automatically been re-appointed, they said they weren't appointing me. They could do this as I was the Labour nominee.

Ted Knight, Leader of Lambeth Council, was very hard left and a very engaging person. He wanted me to use MASDA to influence the Labour vote in London among the ethnic minorities, which I refused to do. I had been taken to Ken Livingstone's flat in Brixton and I got the impression, it was to see if I would make a Labour councillor. I think he decided I wouldn't because I was not sufficiently left wing in my politics. They also saw I was very independent and would not necessarily follow the party line.

It was at this time that the Liberal Democratic Party was being formed and through my work with the Sports Council I met Dr David Owen in Holland in the Dutch parliament where we discussed sports and apartheid. He subsequently invited me to be a member of the Liberal Democrats. Owen kept sending his political agents to ask me to join the Liberal Democrats, which I never did. A Labour minister had made my appointment on the Sports Council and I didn't feel I could walk out on that type of loyalty. I always voted Labour. I only stopped voting labour because of Tony Blair when I saw how his policies were taking the Labour Party away from its white working class roots and so leaving a power vacuum for the right to fill.

In 1976 Denis Howell invited me to join the Sports Council when he saw what I had done with Muhammad Ali at Tulse Hill School. I was the only Black person on the Sports Council as it was all white and made up of and included the 'great and the good'. Its chair was an ex-rugby Lions captain Dickie Jeeps. He was a small guy and a no-nonsense type of person. We were to clash over South Africa, and I remember telling him at a dinner my wife and I were attending that if he were to make racist jokes we would walk out.

Also on the Council were, amongst others, Lieutenant General Sir James Wilson, an Oxford blue, who invited me to Aldershot as his guest, Jack Charlton the footballer and Mary Rand, a track and field athlete and Olympic gold medallist for the long jump in 1964.

I was warmly welcomed on to the Sports Council by Jack Charlton, a former England player, who was in the World Cup-winning English football team of 1966. This was the most glorious moment in English football history. I invited Jack to Tulse Hill School to meet the students, where the Head, the staff and pupils warmly received him. The youngsters were especially pleased, as he and his brother Bobby were the football heroes of the day.

He also visited Joyce and me at our home in Tulse Hill for lunch. He was very friendly and went out of his way to make me feel comfortable on the Sports Council. On trips we made as part of our duties on the Council we would sometimes go to a bar for a late-night drink. On one of these trips we drove to Wales to visit a climbing Centre in the Snowdonia National Park and it was during that time he told me of his love for the outdoors and that if he hadn't been a footballer he would have been a forester. If he had made that decision, who knows, England may never have won the 1966 World Cup!

It was also at this time that I was to strike up a strong relationship with Britain's and America's world boxing champions, which would include Frank Bruno, John Conteh, Lloyd Honeyghan and this all stemmed from meeting the master of them all, Muhammad Ali.

Lloyd Honeyghan had adopted the nickname Ragamuffin Man when his opponent called him that before a fight. He was a welterweight world champion, who dumped his welterweight belt in a bin soon after winning it because he disagreed with the WBA rules that allowed matches in apartheid South Africa. Shortly after that the WBA stopped sanctioning fights in South Africa.[52]

I got on well with Lloyd's mother and father and they would visit us at our home in Bristol and they in turn would invite me to watch some of Lloyd's fights. I took them and Lloyd once to the House of Commons and introduced them to Denis Howell and Lloyd was delighted to see the enormous interest MPs in the house had in his achievement. The Prime Minister of Jamaica also proclaimed Lloyd a people's hero after he won the world

---

52   https://peoplepill.com/people/Loyd-Honeyghan (Retrieved 28/11/2020)

title. Interestingly enough, he had a close relationship with Mike Tyson.

There was a time in the Sports Council when we visited Belfast as a guest of the Lord Mayor. I spent a short time off the official programme and had a beer on the Falls Road. The pub was similar in atmosphere to Irish pubs in Coventry where there was a large Irish immigrant group. I also visited Stourmont and was surprised by how small the parliamentary chamber was.

My main mission on the Sports Council was to help the Council to understand the position of the young immigrants and to promote sporting activities for them. Sports' governing bodies in Britain will remember my strong opposition to Apartheid. While I was on the Sports Council, I was involved in the protest movement with Sam Ramsamy who was a South African in exile. He formed an organisation promoting no sports contact with South Africa, known as SAN-ROC. Sam was a formidable character who talked me into supporting SAN-ROC. We got on well and campaigned together for three or four years. Sam was a deeply loyal person who was very dedicated and paid a lot of attention to detail. He was highly professional and when apartheid ended Nelson Mandela made him president of the South African Olympic Committee.

In 1977 , Commonwealth Presidents and Prime Ministers agreed, as part of their support for the international campaign against apartheid, to discourage contact and competition between their sportsmen and sporting organisations, teams or individuals from South Africa. The agreement was unanimously approved by the Commonwealth of Nations at a meeting at the Gleneagles Hotel in Perthshire, Scotland. It became known as the Gleneagle Agreement.

Michael Manley was instrumental in pushing this through. It

promised to discourage contact and competition between their sportsmen and sporting organisations, teams or individuals from South Africa. In other words a boycott by Commonwealth countries of South African sporting events until Mandela was free. I campaigned against all contact with South African sports until the ending of apartheid.

At the time I was also doing a lot of grass roots community development sports work, so I was on the one hand being politically active in the anti–apartheid campaign while in my voluntary time running MASDA. With MASDA I was bringing Black role models such as diplomats, footballers and boxers into the Brixton community and giving opportunities to young Black youngsters to become coaches, amongst other things. We trained both boys and girls to become coaches.

In 1982 MASDA held a reception at the House of Commons banqueting suite to inaugurate the Black British Standing Conference Against Apartheid Sports under the chairmanship of Lord David Pitt and Lord Chitnis. Early in the year MASDA had begun its support for the United Nations Year of Sanctions against South Africa. The aims of the Standing Conference were to mobilise British African Caribbean and British Asian citizens to support the principles of the 1977 Gleneagles Agreement and to form a parliamentary lobby made up of MPs of both Houses and sporting interests within the Black community. It also wanted to ensure that the British Government's commitment to the Gleneagles Agreement was consistent with their policy against racial discrimination and to educate, stimulate and propagate the principles enshrined in the Gleneagles Agreement.

When I was working with Sam Ramsamy, I spent quite a lot of time doing interviews for the World Service and eventually went over to the United States as guest of General Garba, the chair of the Anti-Apartheid Committee of the United Nations. I was able to meet General Garba on several occasions. He was a first-class campaigner and was dedicated to ending apartheid in South Africa. I was told by some of the ambassadors to the United Nations from Barbados and Jamaica that they often heard me on the news campaigning for the Gleneagles Agreement. In 1979 I was greatly touched by an award given to me by the United Nations for my work against apartheid.

I went to America with John Conteh, Clive Lloyd and Sam Ramsamy. John Conteh was very outgoing and a lovely guy. He was getting over alcoholism when we met up. He wanted to be identified as a role model for young Black men. When we were in New York as guests of the Anti-Apartheid Committee, in the evening John, who was not drinking, would sit in a bar in New York central station with him drinking juices while I was having beer. He was highly popular, always ready with a joke and a good conversationalist. He came to visit us in Bristol when he was playing in Blood Brothers at the Theatre Royal in Bath. We once went to a restaurant for a meal in London and people were queuing up for his autograph. We got on very well and he attended a number of events I put on in Brixton, where he was enthusiastically applauded and loved.

Clive Lloyd was a real contrast to John Conteh as he was very reserved. He was also someone who paid a lot of attention to detail. Daley Thompson was someone else I met through the Sports Council. He was an up-and-coming star athlete when I first met him, but he was very poor and didn't have much help at all. In spite of the fact that I asked the Sports Council to help him they turned him down. I said to him at one time, if you win a gold medal in Canada at the Commonwealth games, you will never look back, and that is exactly what happened.

We had lunch together and I introduced Daley Thompson to John Conteh and they decided to train together at Crystal Palace. I don't know if that ever happened. Daley had a very supportive aunt, Doreen Raymond, who gave him a great deal of help. I tried to persuade him not to go to South Africa. I was very critical about him for that but looking back I think he was probably right as he established himself as a first-rate world athlete and that was his way out of poverty. He did eventually come out against South Africa. He was a determined person, very much his own man but he certainly has a soft spot.

Another sporting personality I worked with was footballer Garth Crooks. He was playing for Stoke when I invited him to speak at Lambeth Town Hall at a MASDA event. Garth made a brilliant speech. He was very shrewd, highly intelligent and a natural communicator who was very supportive of what I was doing. John Barnes, who played for Watford at the time, accompanied him. I asked John if he too wanted to say something but although he supported the event with his presence, he preferred not to give a speech.

John Fashanu was another sporting personality I encountered during my term on the Sports Council. I took John to some schools where he spoke to the children and he was very popular and impressed the youngsters in his Mercedes. He was very much a showman and the youngsters loved him as he was doing 'Gladiators'[53] at the time. He was a presenter par excellence, a great communicator and a very smooth character who took risks when perhaps he shouldn't have done. I spoke on his behalf in court when he was accused of match fixing. He was acquitted but it was a lot of stress for him at the time. He had been a good role

---

53   Gladiators was one of the defining game-shows of the 1990s where members of the public competed on an assault course with professionals.

model up to the time of the trial.

I had introduced John Fashanu to the former President of Zambia Ken Kaunda,[54] who was living in London. We had an informal lunch with Ken Kaunda, who told us about his political differences with Mrs Thatcher particularly about sanctions against apartheid South Africa. Mrs Thatcher took the rather unreasonable view that anyone who supported the ANC was a 'terrorist sympathiser'. I have a great deal of respect for Ken Kaunda, who did a lot for human rights in Africa.

Eventually my work on the Sports Council led to an invitation from various Black sports organisations to visit South Africa. On hearing that I was likely to go to South Africa, P.W. Botha's Government wanted me to be part of a programme they were doing about sports opportunities for the Black South Africans in their townships but I said I wasn't going to be used in that way. That is how I came to be banned from there in 1980. I still have the letter telling of my ban. I fact I have it framed and on displayed on my wall. I was surprised when the ban came and Thatcher's Government didn't lift a finger to protest against it, even though by the terms of the Gleneagles Agreement, Commonwealth countries were supposed to boycott South African sports. I was told that Mrs Thatcher was very upset with what I was doing, and it was rumoured that she thought I was a terrorist sympathiser.

Apartheid South Africa and sports was very much a problem when I was on the Sports Council. In 1981 the tour of the South African rugby team the Springboks was an explosive issue. I felt it was a mischievous tour to test South Africa's political acceptability on apartheid.

When the English rebel cricket team under the leadership of Graham Gooch and Geoff Boycott decided to tour South Africa,

54   Ken Kaunda was the first president of Zambia from 1964 to 1991.

I naturally opposed the event. Jack Straw, who was more radical then, called on Margaret Thatcher to condemn the rebel tour[55] but she refused.

Apart from breaking the Gleneagles Agreement, it was clear that with twelve English cricket rebels doing a renegade test series in South Africa this would ruin the Commonwealth Games that September in Australia. I said at the time that South Africa was out to kill the Brisbane games – and they were going to pay whatever money was necessary. For a few thousand pounds Boycott and Company very likely tarnished international cricket in this country. It was a reckless tour in my opinion. I felt that if the Test and County Cricket Board (TCCB) left the way open for the 'unofficial' England team to play against the visiting Indian and Pakistani teams that summer, a split in world cricket might come about. I had been critical of the TCCB because they seemed anxious to get South Africa back into test cricket.

The argument that the tour was building bridges for Blacks was nonsense. They had already banned me from going to South Africa. The South African regime would go to any lengths to get international sporting recognition. Sport was a number one religion for them. Without it, it would have very serious psychic repercussions on their confidence to maintain the apartheid regime. It could have been a death blow to the South African regime if the TCCB had banned the rebels, thus allowing the visits of the Indian and Pakistani teams to go ahead that summer.

The twelve rebels, or the 'dirty dozen' as they were referred to at the time, had been banned from ever playing again in Jamaica. Sam Ramsamy had said that he was shocked to think that players

---

55   The series of seven cricket tours staged between 1982 and 1990 were known as the rebel tours because South Africa was banned during this period from international cricket due to the apartheid regime.

could accept blood money which had been accumulated by the exploitation of Black labour.

I couldn't get the open support of the Conservative Sports Minister, Neil Macfarlane, for the Gleneagles Agreement, so in the end I resigned over Mrs Thatcher's failure to condemn the rebel tours of South Africa. In fact, I knew they weren't going to re-employ me and I had only three months to go.

I had asked Dickie Jeeps if the Sports Council could hold a special meeting to consider the tour's implication, but this was also refused. They should have met on such a grave issue. I think the Test and County Cricket Board should have barred those playing in South Africa from county cricket as well as Test matches.

I wrote to the Neil McFarlane, who re-appointed me to the Sports Council when the Conservatives won the 1979 election and told him that the Prime Minister's reaction to the rebel tour was morally indefensible and deeply humiliating. I felt that Thatcher's attitude regrettably gave the impression to the country's Black and Asian communities that she had little regard or understanding of their feelings over the matter.

Mrs Thatcher had been very outspoken about her condemnation of the British athletes going to the Olympic Games in Moscow but did not condemn the South African tour. This I felt she should have done for moral reasons over and above any political considerations. Other Black people who had been asked to serve on various sporting bodies also felt badly let down and betrayed. My resignation caused quite a stir in the press but I'm sure that certain people in Downing Street were pleased to see me go and were in no way going to persuade me to stay.

I found it amusing when I finally went to South Africa after the ending of apartheid. Sam Ramsamy invited me to lunch at a South African sports centre in Johannesburg. Now that was something else because everyone was coming up to us, all these white secretaries of various sports and shaking us by the hand and saying, 'Welcome to the club'. I said, 'Sam eight years ago if you and I were ever in South Africa we would have been locked up on Robben island!'

During the time I was still campaigning against apartheid I was also still in contact with Denis Howell. I used to see Denis Howell at the House of Commons and visit his home in Birmingham. The only thing I didn't manage to do was get Denis and Muhammad Ali together. He would have loved that. Denis had a strong personality and he spoke with panache and leadership.

He had been a mentor for me, as Tony Benn had been mentoring me too, but Denis was from the Right and Tony was from the Left, so I had to keep a balance between them. And I did! I kept my relationship with Tony Benn intact, as I would see him in Holland Park when I was in London and in the House of Commons. Tony was always keen to see me. His wife Caroline was very active in education at the time and was involved in writing books on the subject, so she was interested in me being one of the governors of Tulse Hill School. We would often sit and chat. I invited Tony Benn to meet up with Black councillors such as Phil Seely who was councillor for Brent. Tony and I remained life-long friends.

I consider Tony Benn a monumental hero of the left who despite his privileged background served his country well and who, during the Bristol Bus Boycott, was an essential lynch pin between the local Black community and the Houses of Parliament. His support of the Bristol Bus Boycott gave that campaign legs and made possible the first law against racial discrimination. His tremendous contribution of life in service to the people has made him popular and well-loved in Bristol as well as a national treasure.

It was in 1981 that an opportunity came for me to go to Israel. Professor Hammond from the University of California invited me to meet up with a young group of African American nationals who were living in Dimona on the edge of the Negev desert. They were devout Christians and I spent some time with them and their priest. It seemed to me that they were uncomfortable living next to the Israelis. They took me to Jericho, which was full of flies, and arranged for me to stay in Jerusalem where I visited a mosque.

I also washed my feet in the River Jordan as a symbolic gesture and took a taxi from Jerusalem to Bethlehem where I met up with a Palestinian family who were very kind and invited me to have a meal with them. Their son was a shepherd, and it made me smile to think that whilst in Bethlehem I met a shepherd!

I questioned an Israeli shopkeeper and challenged her because she was selling pictures of Jesus as a blue eyed European and he would have had the darker complexion of a Middle Eastern man. She replied that they did this because of the British and American tourists.

Before returning to London I spent a couple of comfortable days in Tel Aviv where I found the Israelis very friendly. They were interested in the fact that I was born in England as they had assumed, I was part of the American community at Dimona.

In London I had the pleasure of working with Darcus Howe, the well-known Black writer and television presenter, on developing the Notting Hill Carnival. Darcus was very able and communicative. He could communicate with anyone. He would always know what side of the bed you got out of and know how to exploit it. We became quite friendly and remained so. The carnival event had begun as one of the more significant responses to the Notting Hill riots of 1958. A Caribbean carnival was Claudia Jones' idea[56] and it was first held at St Pancras Town Hall in January 1959 and reincarnated in the 1970s as the largest street festival in Europe, the Notting Hill Carnival. I was to play my part in that reincarnation.

The situation was slightly tense as the police were making objections to the Notting Hill Gate Carnival, which was upsetting the Black youngsters as they saw it as their carnival and did not want any police interference. Owning it gave them a sense of power and identity, which of course annoyed the police. I worked directly with a Trinidadian organiser they used to call Teacher, his name was Leslie Palmer and we would sit in George Berry's pub The Coach and Horses in Brixton with Darcus Howe and discuss the Carnival.

The Carnival organisers had produced a proposal to extend it with floats to drive through Notting Hill. The idea was resisted by the police who thought it might be hazardous to have lorries with sound systems, drums and steel bands driving through the streets. To top it all Teacher was under threat of being fired if they didn't raise enough funds.

It fell on me to recommend whether we gave them a grant to extend the Carnival. I was convinced when I sat down and spoke to the Carnival committee that it was worth commissioning and at the time, I had the power to grant up to £500 to small groups so I authorised the maximum of £500. It was a lot when you consider that the Trinidadian High Commission gave them only £25. I often wonder if the CRE hadn't given the Carnival that £500 how it would have developed. Before that the Carnival had been a children's local community event under the flyway. What

56   vogue.co.uk-and-lifestyle/article/claudia-jones-notting-hill-carnival (Retrieved 27/12/20)

was proposed was a far wider event which would combine other groups and their music in a way that brought them dramatically to the public's attention. It was a bold initiative.

The grant had a profound effect on the Carnival. It gave the organisers confidence and saved Teacher's job. The day they were thinking of firing him, the money came through. It was the biggest donation they had. Large floats were introduced, and part of its popularity was due to the live radio broadcasts from the Carnival by Alex Pascall, now an OBE, on his daily Black Londoners programme.

I was also involved with Darcus Howe through the protest marches about the New Cross Road fire in Deptford where thirteen young people died in what was suspected to be a racist attack. I marched with my wife and Darcus Howe on the 15,000 strong protest march. This fire took place in January 1981 and the inquest in May, which returned an open verdict, merely produced widespread concern about the authority's unwillingness to produce answers for the bereaved. The incident is believed to be one of the triggers of the Brixton riots.

I had seen those riots of the 1980s coming and had even predicted them. I felt they posed a major threat and challenge to the future social stability and fabric of post-war British society as we had known and understood it. I stated at the time that no major English city with a sizeable Black ethnic population could afford to be complacent about the dangers and lessons to be learnt from such a threat and if they were, they did so at their peril. The vast majority of Britain's Blacks were trapped in the inner city by an invisible wall of racism that denied them equal job opportunities, or promotions. Many were daily faced with having to live in poor housing with no future hope or job prospects, leading lives of despair, frustration and hopelessness.

My own experience of being Black and English, of having been a vice chair of the board of governors at Tulse Hill school in Lambeth, having founded the Muhammad Ali Sports Development Association in Brixton and worked there for what was then twelve years gave me certain insights. I had observed over the years, that the vast majority of white British people had no understanding of the deep psychological impact their racism had on Black British-born young people. Racism was rampant in British society. It was institutional as expressed in our immigration and nationality laws, educational institutions, churches, media, trade unions and political parties.

I warned then that Britain's inner cities with their poverty, bad housing and unemployment were fast becoming Black English townships policed by insensitive, white law officers. Black British youths were beginning to identify with the dispossessed African youths they saw daily on television fighting apartheid in the Black townships of South Africa. Many were then allying themselves with the aspirations and the struggle against racial oppression of the Black revolutionary movement of South Africa. I felt if England was to avoid the permanent establishment of Black townships within its own cities as a feature of British society, then the Government and people of Britain must be jolted out of their complacency to the horrendous future it may face. I wrote to the papers to ask 'At the turn of the century, apartheid in South Africa will have been assigned to the rubbish bin of history. Will England have Black townships still burning?'

The riots here at the beginning of the 1980s looked as if the troubles in South Africa may well happen here. Happily, there was some damage limitation in places and by April 1981 all Bristol defendants accused of riotous assembly had, with the help of Paul Boateng, been acquitted of any charges. An enquiry was set up under Lord Scarman to investigate the inner-city disturbances, but more disturbing was the fact that the government sanctioned the use of CS gas and plastic bullets in riotous situations.[57]

It was also in 1981 that I was surprised by an invitation to join the Press Council, especially after the way I left the Sports Council. My resignation from that body had been a rather stormy one. I had thought I was the kind of person the Press Council would not want to touch.

The chair of the Press council was the Governor General of Australia. I was recommended by Lord Hunt who felt I was not being treated fairly in respect to my campaign against sporting ties with South Africa. He felt I should have been given more support with the anti-apartheid campaign and tried to redress the balance by recommending me for the Press Council. The chair was very friendly and had connections with Oxford University. I felt I was in very prestigious company as many of my colleagues on the Council had been given knighthoods and peerages.

It was a good twenty years after the Bristol Bus Boycott and admittedly there were some improvements in race relations. Changes in the law had made overt racism illegal but underlying attitudes were less affected. There was also complacency. Employers could not openly discriminate but that did not mean that they took any action to make things better.

I wanted to see a policy of positive action followed. Editors should go out of their way to bring more minorities into newspapers. The changes since I first started campaigning in Bristol included an awareness of what racism was. When I first confronted the authorities, they didn't understand what I meant because it was so ingrained in the culture. But now public consciousness is beginning to realise that racism is an evil thing,

57   Benn, 1992

but we still had a long way to go. It was not a question of whether they liked Black people or not but of how we were perceived, and who had positions of power over us and if they used those positions to keep us at a disadvantage.

It soon became obvious to me that the Press Council, though peopled by' the good and the great', lacked any teeth when it came to deal with the general public's concerns about press stories that affected them.

We had several journalists and trade unionist appearing before the Press Council for what they perceived as inaccurate reporting. On several occasions Arthur Scargill appeared before the council and proved to be a very convincing witness. He was very articulate and communicative and did brilliant presentations and several times when I questioned him, we all felt he had a point. He was not being treated fairly by the press. Paul Foot also appeared before the Press Council. He was able to account for his journalistic conduct as being fair and appropriate and defended his conduct well so was exonerated.

Fleet Street was not happy with the Press Council. It lost the confidence of the Fleet Street editors and the Prime Minister Margaret Thatcher was particularly disturbed by the way the Press Council had supported the rights of a journalist to investigate her husband's bank account.

The demise of the Press Council was swift and it was soon replaced by the Press Complaints Commission in which the public had no rights to apply on behalf of other complainants. This loss of the right of the public to be represented by a third party meant the editors of Fleet Street were to have much more powerful influence on adjudications. This is why Fleet Street is now self-regulated, yet ironically and one of the things the Press Council was trying to achieve was an independent regulator.

While I was still on the Press Council, I decided to move from London to Bristol in 1982. I had always wanted to live in the country, but my children preferred the city, so I moved my family to Bristol which was a compromise. It was a city but very close to the countryside I loved and was easier to get out of than London. I had fallen in love with the English countryside during my days as an evacuee during the war and I was so enchanted with it I wanted my wife and children to have the easy access to it that Bristol provided. For the next ten years I commuted to Manchester and London as I was the senior officer for race and community development for the north of England. My house in Bristol was my base though I stayed in London or Manchester from time to time.

It was in Manchester that I met Ron Phillips when he was providing training and housing for Black homeless youths there. Mike Phillips was also doing similar work in Brixton in the 1980s and Trevor Phillips, also based in South London, was a journalist and television presenter at the time. These brothers were very supportive of MASDA and in the 1990s Trevor Phillips organised a reception in honour of the successful Bristol Bus Boycott campaign in 1963. He did this because he felt that people of his generation owed much to those that had paved the way for them. I believe those brothers come from a unique family on a par with the Dimblebys.

In 1986 Alfred Fagon, a Jamaican playwright, who had lived and written plays based in Bristol, was found dead outside his London flat. He had died of natural causes after his morning jog. The police, despite looking round his flat which had on his desk a union card, letters, a passport, a diary with phone numbers and a BBC script lying on his bed, found no indication of friends or family. This was gross negligence by a young policeman who made assumptions that this man was a loner who nobody would miss. After two weeks Alfred's body was cremated in a pauper's ceremony and his ashes scattered over a hedge marked T91 and it was two weeks before his family and friends knew he was dead.

Naturally this upset a lot of people and I organised a petition demanding an enquiry into how the police handled his death and set up Friends of Fagon in Bristol. There was a memorial service for him in London and David Mutusa was commissioned to do the sculpture of Alfred Fagon which now stands at the green on Grosvenor Road, Bristol, which Alfred always called the heart of St Paul's. As a result of the investigation into how Alfred Fagon's death was treated they found there was negligence, but no disciplinary action was taken. I was disgusted at the police attitude. What happened was appalling and I wrote to the Police Complaints Authority to press for disciplinary action, which failed.

By 1992 commuting from Bristol to London and Manchester became onerous especially after an injury to my foot so I bid farewell to the CRE and was given a warm and generous farewell party by my colleagues.

Once back in Bristol I realised a dream I had had for a long time. Joyce and I extended our family by fostering. It was a rewarding experience. I had thought about fostering children but there had been difficulties, Joyce wanted to continue her nursing career and I respected that, especially as I had been commuting to London and back to Bristol which was very stressful period. When I left the CRE however we agreed to do some emergency fostering. Our own children were great about it and happy to share us with other children.

First, we had a youngster whose mother had deserted him and then we took on two young brothers and instead of having them for three months we had them for two and half years. One child we had was very difficult and both Social Services and the school did not know what to do with him. He was quite disturbed and was seeing a psychologist. He also had to be individually supervised during breaks but after only six weeks with us he had adjusted well enough to be able to play with the other children without supervision. The psychologist asked me how I did it!

In all we fostered eight children. They were very resilient, and it proved an insight into the social care of young ethnic minority children by the local authority. There were many positive aspects of fostering for us, but it was very stressful especially for my wife, so we finally gave it up, but we would see some of the youngsters from time to time.

I was also a consultant to Focus Consultancy in Wiltshire where I worked with Professor Chris Mullard who had a contract with the MOD to recruit ethnic minorities into the army. I later worked with Chris as a Community Race Relations Development Officer in assisting Gloucester Council to set up a Community Relations Council and a race relations network in the county and the city which would serve Gloucester and Gloucestershire and bring in Stroud and Cheltenham. Having worked with Asian and Caribbean families there I felt that Gloucester was more at ease with integrating Asian and African Caribbean communities than Bristol. The city council there was particularly keen to engage with these groups.

I was also very keen to have Bristol as a city acknowledge its role in the slave trade and campaigned to have the new bridge across St. Augustine's Reach dedicated to the memory of an enslaved man called Pero. He had been brought to Bristol from Nevis by the Pinney family who owned a plantation on that island. On the 16th March 1999 I was very pleased to attend the dedication of the new bridge along with Paul Boateng, who was then Home Office minister and who named the bridge after Pero and stated that it did not merely cross a stretch of water but helped us to span time and understand and perhaps confront a shared past. A past which needed telling, not only about exploitation but about the coming of freedom through struggle. I made it clear I thought Colston[58] a racist slave trader and slave owner who had been paid homage as a benefactor of the city for too long and that with the naming of the bridge we paid honour and respect to the victims of that atrocity.

In Bristol there were so many Black people in the professions I met that had a story to tell that I felt they should have their stories preserved by the Bristol Record Office where I had already stored a lot of photographic material about my life. I found that the Record Office was very interested in taking my archives and using them as a starting point to bring in other Africans and Caribbeans who had contributed to Bristol life.

This was a way of recognising their achievement. That is how Bristol Black Archives Partnership (BBAP) was first engendered. Preserving the records of all communities is essential to people everywhere so everyone can see the contribution made by all groups everywhere, not just in Bristol. This can enhance the work of the curriculum in Citizen Studies. It would also provide positive Black role models for school children and promote self-esteem and pride in the Black community. I also felt that once an archive for the African and Caribbean communities had been established that it was important to extend it to other BAME communities. The year 2007 marked the two hundredth anniversary of the Act of Parliament abolishing the slave trade in England. This seemed an opportune year for the inception of BBAP.

58   Edward Colston a Bristol born slave trader and wealthy merchant who died in 1721

I had the generous support all the time I was working on this of John Williams, Karen Garvey and Lilleith Morrison. The inspiration for this came from the need of Bristol to know the entire history of its Black citizens from before slavery and not just from the Bristol Bus Boycott. The 'Me We' calendar was a route to that. I saw its potential, as once people saw themselves in the calendar, they would feel they had been recognised. After the BBAP project ended the 'Me We' calendars continued for another two years with Lilleith Morrison, Angus Brown, Hyacinth Hall (Bristol's first Black headteacher) and Caroline Baker-Bennet working voluntarily to produce them.

In 2007 we launched BBAP with Rob Mitchell as its chair and Tony Benn attended this event as the guest speaker. BBAP also produced biographies of the Black Bristolians in the first calendar which were made into learning material for schools in Bristol. An amusing fall out of this was an incident one day when I saw two schoolgirls walking home from school and one asked me if I was Paul Stephenson. I said 'Yes' to which she replied, 'I thought so – we done you in our history lesson in school this afternoon.'

Jay Tidmarsh, the Lord Lieutenant at the time, was also very supportive with this and used his office to promote racial tolerance and harmony. I believe he genuinely wished to convey this message and was the first Lord Lieutenant to openly pursue racial harmony in this country. I think the fact that he spent some time in Jamaica when doing his National Service meant he became endeared to the island and its people. He used community cohesion as a strategy for developing tolerance and this gained him appreciation from BAME communities.

I think I may have met him through Tony Benn but my first memory of him was at the celebration for Tony Bullimore's safe return after Tony survived getting lost in the Atlantic. I developed a close relationship with Jay as he used his influence as a former Master of the Merchant Venturers to seek a dialogue with and an understanding of the African and Caribbean communities. We are in a dialogue which I believe can have a positive outcome for the future between the Merchant Venturers and the African and Caribbean communities.

I also worked voluntarily with the Empire and Commonwealth Museum to commemorate the abolition of slavery. They had their initial grant to the Heritage Lottery fund turned down, so they asked me to help with renewing their application to that fund. I gladly gave my time and energy and advice in doing this, which subsequently proved to be successful as they were awarded over £800,000.

It was also at this time that Bristol City Council's commemoration in 2007 of the abolition of the slave trade in 1807 drew criticism from some radical Black groups who were angered and infuriated by the way they set about the process and what was felt to be a lack of consultation with the Black community. The perception was that the City Council was not listening to what the Black community wanted and some groups wanted to boycott the meetings. I felt however that we had to recognise it and not throw the baby out with the bath water.

I felt it was important to acknowledge in Bristol the significance of the year 1807 so the party leaders and officers would meet at the Council House in partnership with the Empire and Commonwealth Museum. We set out to win the attention of the Bristol population both Black and white of what went on at that time between 1698 and 1807 and to educate the public to realise that Bristol alone took half a million Africans and enslaved and sold them in the Americas.

The Bristol Legacy Commission came out of work done

during 2007, the commemoration of Abolition year. The idea of bringing a continuing focus on slavery and its devastating legacy which we find ourselves with today was engendered. It compelled me to use some of my time in helping to establish and chairing the Bristol Legacy Commission. It was set up by Paul Barnet, Head of Leisure and Culture, and those of us who helped to run events during Abolition year stayed on and formed ourselves into the Commission.

The following year held a special event for me. It was on December 4th, 2008 that Bristol had its first Black Freeman. Being made a freeman of the city I feel was a great and exciting honour. It meant much to me, as when I first came to Bristol things were very different. Now I felt able to accept this honour in the name of all those people who, like myself, had been subjected to prejudice and discrimination. This was a way for Bristol to say things are changing. I was very moved after the ceremony when I arrived home to find a message from Tony Benn, who had been there, congratulating me.

I was also delighted to be involved in the Bristol Legacy Commission's funding of the African and Caribbean Chamber of Commerce and Enterprise (ACCCE). This is the foremost business and enterprise support organisation dedicated to African and Caribbean led businesses in the west of England. In November 2009 the African and Caribbean Young Enterprise (ACYE) was also launched.

I had always had a close affinity with Black Caribbeans, Americans and Africans with whom I shared a common ancestry. Our forefathers had land and people taken from them to be economically exploited, the consequences of which we still live with today, in the form of racism.

Many people assume I am Jamaican. Once I was giving a talk

and I emphasised that I was born here, my mother was born here and so was my grandmother. Afterwards a girl came up to me and asked if it was true that I was born here. I replied 'Yes. I was born here'. To which she commented 'You must be the oldest immigrant I've ever seen'.

She can be forgiven for such an error because of her youth but in the past even adults found it hard to believe I was English. I told one Headmaster who asked where I was born, that I was born here. His response was, 'No I mean before that.'

The assumption that if you're Black you can't also be British is at last receding into a grey past, as the young Black second-generation Caribbeans are unmistakably Black and British. 'This precious stone set in a silver sea' is their home and my home. You can imagine my surprise nevertheless when I received a letter from the Prime Minister's Cabinet Office asking me if I would accept an OBE if it were offered to me.

I thought someone was pulling my leg, but as I read the letter again it began to dawn on me that it was genuine and my surprise turned to astonishment. I had always considerd myself to be a thorn in the side of the establishment and here they were rewarding me for it!

I felt heartened by the OBE as I felt the local establishment who had at first not appreciated what I was doing at last saw that racism was a destructive force and that combating it was essential for a fair and equitable society.

On 7th April 2009 my wife and two grown up children ,Paul Junior and Fumi, came with me to Windsor Castle to see the investiture. The Queen spoke to me about the work I had done over the last forty-five years in addressing inequality and promoting good community relations.

Not long after, In June 2009, I visited Montgomery, Alabama

to see the place that inspired the Bristol Bus Boycott campaign. It had been Rosa Parks and Martin Luther King's inspirational struggle for civil rights that had galvanised me into action in 1963 and I wanted to see the place it all began. It struck me that Rosa Park's tremendously brave act of defiance had put her in danger of being beaten up, even possibly losing her life. She connected to history in an important way and acted with great courage. She wanted to see how far she could push it. Jesse Jackson said of her 'She sat down in order that we all might stand up and the walls of segregation came down.'

Rosa Parks's action was to flash across America, across the Atlantic and across the world. Her refusal to move to the back of the bus in Montgomery, Alabama in 1955 sparked off the Montgomery Bus Boycott. This campaign ignited the social explosion that was the civil rights movement in the USA and propelled Martin Luther King to prominence as a civil rights leader. Its consequence was the civil rights legislation implemented by President Johnson in 1964 without which Barack Obama would not have become the first Black president of the USA.

That movement also sparked off repercussions in Bristol because Rosa Parks rebellion on that bus inspired our strategy in Bristol and began a change in Britain that would start to address the rights of Black British citizens. This reiterated for me the belief that one person can make a difference, but she was part of an organisation where each person made a difference by standing together. How much more powerful that is.

On Thursday 26th November 2009 I was awarded an honorary degree from The University of the West of England and have received another from The Open University. These honours I am happy to accept on behalf of all those who have worked for equality and social justice.

Appendix to the First Edition

In the 1960s I addressed the racial issue in a way that it had rarely been addressed during the post war years. I was inspired by Rosa Parks, Martin Luther King and the Black Americans who fought for human justice by opposing the evil of discrimination and segregation. I had similar aims and wanted to achieve similar results in Britain non- violently and to give the new immigrants from the Caribbean and Africa a sense of hope and equality in all walks of their lives, in Bristol, nationally and internationally.

The outcome of both the Bristol Bus Boycott campaign and the Bay Horse court case was to highlight racism in Britain. Though I never became embroiled in party politics, these incidences not only brought racism to the eye of the general public but were also to have an impact on the more political path my life would take. More importantly it had repercussions outside my own personal life.

The Bristol Bus Boycott and Bay Horse court case need to be seen in the light of future legislation. They sparked the first of many laws that dealt with equality, but the ensuing legislation cannot be viewed in isolation; the immigration and nationality laws that sprang up at the same time show another perspective.

As we have seen, in 1914 the British Nationality and Status of Aliens Act declared that any person born within the British Empire was a British subject. Then in 1948 new immigrants arrived in Britain encouraged by the 1948 Nationality Act, which gave Commonwealth citizens unqualified rights to enter and remain in Britain. Alarmed by the newcomers, the Conservative Government later retracted this right when they passed the 1962 Immigration Act, which applied controls for the first time to Commonwealth citizens.

Why weren't the Commonwealth citizens welcomed with open arms? After all they had been invited here. It seems there was a failure of Government which meant the newcomers were in competition with the host population for housing, employment and education. MacMillan who was housing minister in 1951 promised to build 300,000 house a year but reversed this policy in1954 after discussing the social and economic problems caused by immigration. A further cut of twenty-five to thirty million pounds in the social investment budget had a further impact on housing, education and hospitals.

The newcomers also had their skills downgraded and had to accept jobs for which they were overqualified. Schools too were unprepared for the children of the Commonwealth citizens as they were not given any support or training to cope with children of other cultural backgrounds. This often led to children being erroneously categorised as SEN.

The new immigrants of the Windrush generation would demand equity and justice in the workplace, but both management and unions would oppose them as they did in Bristol in 1963, at Courtaulds Red Scar Mill in Preston in May 1965, and in 1974 at the Imperial Typewriters strike in Leicester. Without the union behind them, working Black people had little chance of success which prompts the question, why was the Bristol campaign successful?

Something different happened in 1963 to make the campaign a success. Management and Union collusion were the primary feature of a few strikes and campaigns involving Black people's demands for equity and justice. Without Union support working Black people could not hope to succeed. Our campaign however marshalled the support of prominent Labour MPs, Caribbean High Commissioners as well as the groundswell of popular opinion through the press. The use of a strategy associated with the high-profile civil rights movement in America also brought the press on board. Moreover, I felt that discrimination was a non-runner and had no place in a civilised community.

Ian Patey's remarks in defence of the ban were so offensive that they made me feel confident of victory. Once he went public with his opinions, it was clear his arguments were unsustainable. I had no shadow of doubt but that we would win when people saw how unreasonable a thing it was. For most people the idea of discrimination was after all odious. In retrospect, there was more to it than that and the campaign was also to have repercussions which came as an unforeseen bonus.

Previously there had been no civil rights campaign in Britain that focused on discrimination against Black people, and this is what attracted prominent Labour MPs such as Tony Benn and the leader of the Labour Party Harold Wilson. Our style of campaign too caught the public imagination as we could be perceived as part of a wider international movement taking our cue from the American civil rights movement. The press picked up on this and were in the main supportive of the boycott. Other international influences were at play too. The involvement behind the scene of the Caribbean High Commissioners Laurence Lindo and Sir Learie Constantine was crucial to our victory and it was their negotiations with the Transport Holding Company in London that ensured our rapid success.

Our victory against the Bristol Omnibus Company was only the beginning. When I made that phone call for Guy Bailey to the Bristol Bus Company neither of us really knew how far this thing would go. I found my political legs in Bristol when I realised the injustices that were going on here, but the campaign gave me my political wings. My personal contribution was to be in the field of Race Relations but the legacy of the Bristol Bus Boycott and the Bay Horse incident was to be the start of civil rights for Black people in Britain as it led to the introduction of the first Race Relations Act.

That short battle of only a few months with the Bristol Omnibus Company was to bring about anti-discrimination laws in this country and lead to a change in the social history of Britain and the relationship of Britain with its new immigrants. It was an exciting and extraordinary feeling to be part of the process that brought about the first anti-discriminatory law in Britain.

It was not going to be a smooth ride however as the 1965 Race Relations Act gave people of different races the right to have access to public places but was not about the right to fair treatment in employment or housing. Furthermore, instead of imposing penalties it set up a complex system of conciliation, which made it ineffective. It also set up a Race Relations Board, but one which could only take civil action, not criminal proceedings, against non-compliance.

A few years later the 1968 Race Relations Act made some improvements. It addressed the issue of housing and employment and set up a new body, the Community Relations Commission, with extended powers. Government services, such as the police however, were still exempt from legal proceedings.

A look at other legislation shows that the British Government was prepared to address the civil rights of Black people while erecting barriers to further immigration. The crisis of the East African Asians who left East Africa as a result of the increasing process of Africanisation meant the Labour Government rushed through the 1968 Immigration Act in March. This Act restricted the number of African Asians with British passports who could enter the country, by allowing in only those with a parent or grandparent who was born in or was a citizen of the UK.

Further restrictions by a Conservative Government in 1971 also introduced the concept of 'Patrials' (those with close UK associations) who were exempted from the Act, ensuring that white African British passport holders were not kept out. This, like the 1968 Act, contravened Protocol Four of the European Convention on Human Rights which guarantees right of abode for nationals, a right recognized in international law. These legislations also contravened the United Nations Convention on the Rights of the Child. This was not to change until the Amendment to the 1976 Race Relations Act in 2002.

The changes in immigration Law that had started in 1962 were to eventually lead to a hierarchy in the different types of British citizenships. There are now (in 2021) six different types of British citizenship. Some of these were defined in the British Nationality Act 1981, which came into force on 1 January 1983 and initially created three types of British citizens.

As changes were made to immigration laws, many changes were also made to the race relations legislation and anti-discrimination laws grew up for other groups such as women and the disabled. The 1976 Race Relations Act had further strengthened the law against discrimination and extended the prohibition against direct and indirect racial discrimination to public service providers and imposed a statutory duty on the public sector to promote racial equality. The Commission for Racial Equality was also set up, but it was not until 2000 after the Macpherson Report into the racist murder of Stephen Lawrence that the 1976 Act was amended to include the police for the first time.

Forty-six years after the Bristol Bus Boycott campaign the Single Equality Bill was published in April 2009 and came into force in the autumn of 2010. The Bill harmonised and in some cases extended existing discrimination law covering the 'protected characteristics' of age, disability, gender reassignment, marriage and civil partnership, pregnancy and maternity, race, religion or belief, sex, and sexual orientation. It addressed the impact of recent case law which was generally seen as having weakened discrimination protection, and harmonised provisions defining indirect discrimination.

There were fears, at the time that some minority rights may be weakened by being included with others. What is certain is that there has been a long slow climb from a time when notices said 'No Blacks, no Irish, no dogs' to a time when new legislation tries to create a unified public sector duty, intended to promote equality in public policy and decision-making, existing provisions being extended to the protected characteristics of sexual orientation, age and religion or belief, and proposes a new public sector duty related to socio-economic inequalities.

The journey from a Race Relations Act that prevents Black people being discriminated against in public places to a law that gives equal rights to all is the legacy of the Bristol Bus Boycott. 1963 was both a moment in time that defined Black British civil rights here in England and it is a living legacy, one that in a world of poverty and prejudice must be constantly fought for and improved.I believe that Britain stands at the crossroads of its willingness to forge a truly multi-ethnic, multi-racial and multi-faith society. Failure to face this challenge could bring about community chaos and political disaster. Non-discrimination legislation can lead to respect for human rights and social justice. It is within our grasp to build a global world recognizing the human rights of others for future generations scandal. It is time that the laws that are supposed to protect us are enforced.

Afterword To The Second Edition

50 Years After The Bus Boycott
2013-Onwards

By Lilleith Morrison

I first met Paul Stephenson in 2007 when I became a project officer for the Bristol Record Office. I was a late comer to my own history, and though part of the Windrush generation, I didn't really know much about the history of the Caribbean until my 'awakening' when I came to Bristol in the early 1980s and subsequently started teaching Caribbean History in colleges and community centres.

It was when employed by the Bristol Black Archive Partnership that I first came to realise the impact and importance that Paul Stephenson's working life had had on British history and on many individuals' lives too. He held a torch of inspiration for other Black achievers whom he had supported and inspired over the years. He also commanded the respect and admiration of colleagues and friends irrespective of their race.

In 2008, Paul Stephenson was approached by the Bristol Radical History Group to support The Seven Stars Project. This was in honour of Thomas Clarkson who helped found 'The Society for Effecting the Abolition of the Slave Trade' in 1787. Clarkson visited Bristol to gather evidence against this abominable trade. While engaged in this project he was based at the Seven Stars, where the landlord, Thompson, was also an abolitionist.

Clarkson interviewed sailors returning from slave ships as they came ashore in Bristol and was able to compile a dossier of the horrors of the trade and the unscrupulous dealings of the slavers. His research, which he presented to MP William Wilberforce was a vital contribution to the abolition movement and gave force to Wilberforce's arguments when presenting an abolition bill to parliament, which became the Slave Trade Act and received Royal Ascent on March 25, 1807.

The Seven Stars pub in Thomas Lane, St Thomas, Bristol played a crucial role in the history of the abolitionist movement but there was only a small outdated Blue Plaque there to commemorate its importance, while in contrast Edward Colston's statue stood prominently at the heart of the City Centre. A city built on the blood and wasted lives of the people Colston had exploited for his monetary again. While Bristol City Council dithered about removing this offensive statue, they barely recognised the role of the abolitionist Thomas Clarkson. The accomplished Jamaican Historian, political activist, trade unionist and lawyer Richard Hart helped Paul Stephenson to raise £3000 to commission a more suitable plaque for the pub. Paul Stephenson hosted talks at the pub to raise money and the plaque made by Mike Baker was unveiled on May 1, 2009.

Richard Hart who had made Bristol his home in later years was a Jamaican who had been a founder member of the People's National Party (PNP) of Jamaica formed in 1938. In 1942 he was arrested, and without a trial, imprisoned by the British Colonial Government for his political activities. He was "an unrepentant Marxist who never denied what he believed in, even when he was arrested and imprisoned"[59]

He was famously expelled from the PNP as one of the four H's (Ken Hill, Frank Hill, Arthur Henry and Richard Hart) in a purge of the leftist radicals by Norman Manley in 1952. Richard Hart

59 www.jamaicaobserver.com/columns/Richard-Hart--Marxist-and-historian_15746408 (Retrieved 20/2/2021)

was also a lawyer, and served as Legal Consultant and, briefly, as Attorney General in the People's Revolutionary Government of Maurice Bishop in Grenada.

Maurice Bishop's New Jewel Movement of Grenada sought to prioritise socio-economic development, education, and Black liberation but Bishop was killed in a coup in 1979 which the Regan administration in the USA used as an excuse to invade the island and replace the Government with one they found more acceptable.

After the American invasion of Grenada, Richard Hart went to live in London before finally settling in Bristol. His historical publications were as pioneering as his life because he wrote history 'from the ground up' as reflected in some of his major works such as 'Slaves Who Abolished Slavery', much in the same vein as CLR James author of 'The Black Jacobins'.

'It was Hart's view, meticulously documented in his historical writings, that the end of slavery in the British Empire was not bought about by a magnanimous gesture 'from above' inspired by Christian charity, but by the realisation of the British ruling class and government that if they did not take the initiative to emancipate the slaves, they would be faced with increasing and increasingly successful, slave rebellions which would eventually lead to the loss of their colonies.' [60]

He contributed significantly to the telling of Caribbean history and it is said of him that his long life allowed him to put the missing pieces of Jamaica's political history together. He passed away at the age of 96 in 2013 and is interred in Arnos Vale cemetery, Bristol.

60 peoplesworld.org/article/richhard-hart-jamaican-marxist-historian-dies (Retrieved 20/2/2021)

On the 50th anniversary of the boycott we formed the Bristol Bus Boycott (BBB50) group. The launch of the group was hosted by Rob Mitchell at the M Shed beside the vintage bus and featured Bristol Black poets including Ros Martin and Miles Chambers.

Other events involved a debate '50 years on from the Bristol Bus Boycott, are race and class still powerful forces shaping life in our city?', also held at the M Shed hosted and by Roger Griffith. I wrote a radio documentary using archival material about the Bristol Bus Boycott which was performed by Rob Mitchell, Angus Brown and others and broadcast in June 2013 on the local community radio.

Two of the objectives of the BBB50 Group were to erect a plaque at Bristol Bus Station to commemorate the Bristol Bus Boycott and to produce learning materials about the Boycott for use in local schools. With regard to the learning materials, our group secured the funding from the Council to produce a pamphlet.

Thanks to the support of Bristol's elected Mayor George Ferguson, First Bus and the University of Bristol, the Bristol Bus Boycott 50 group was awarded £5,000 and commissioned the late Mike Baker to create a plaque commemorating the protest. I was happy to write the text for it.

Mike Baker told Richard Jones how pleased he was to be given the opportunity to produce the Bus Boycott plaque. This is how Richard describes Mike and his work. "He was a socialist and a committed opponent of racism in all its forms. He visited Paul and Joyce on a couple of occasions to gather information about the Bus Boycott for his preliminary sketches. He was very precise and wanted details of the sort of clothes worn by the activists in 1963. He even asked Paul about the colour and shape of the ties he wore at the time. His attention to detail was remarkable.

Along with Paul Stephenson, Madge Dresser, Rob Mitchell and Lilleith Morrison from the BBB50 group, I visited Mike's workshop at Wards Of Bristol sign makers in Barton Hill and was fascinated to see the plaque take shape. It was a painstaking process with everything done by hand. Mike was a great craftsman and a radical thinker. I was saddened to hear he had passed away in March 2020.

The plaque was unveiled at Bristol Bus Station on August 28, 2014 on the 51st anniversary of the Bristol Bus Boycott victory. Paul was very grateful to all the people who contributed to this lasting memorial. Paul was also delighted when the historian and broadcaster David Olusoga included the site of the bus station plaque in his top 10 places in Britain signifying the history of power, protest and progress."

During this project Rob Mitchell previewed his documentary 'New Black' at the Watershed which looked at local Black political leadership 50 years after the Bristol Bus Boycott through Bristol's first Somali councillor, Hibaq Jama and the campaign by Marvin Rees to become mayor. This finally led to the film 'The Mayor's Race' directed by Loraine Blumenthal. This film followed Marvin Rees, whose Jamaican father wouldn't have been allowed to work on the Bristol Buses when he first came to England, but now his son, Marvin Rees was on a journey to become the first Black mayor in Bristol thus making him also the first Black mayor in Europe.

As part of our 50th anniversary celebration in Oct 2013 Unite and South West TUC and Unite Against Fascism relaunched Madge Dresser's 2nd edition of 'Black and White On The Buses: The 1963 Colour Bar Dispute In Bristol'.

Madge Dresser is a Jewish American who has made Bristol her home. As she will tell you herself, she was taught by Angela

Davis and the fact that she also comes from a minority ethnicity may have inspired her interest in Black History. She was the first person to publish a well-researched pamphlet on the Bristol Bus Boycott in 1986 which was also informed by her use of eye-witness accounts of that campaign.

Her major works concern the Transatlantic slave trade and immigration communities based in Bristol. They include 'Slavery Obscured: The Social History Of The Slave Trade In An English Provincial Town' which firmly proves Edward Colston's involvement in that despicable trade and the role it played in Bristol's prosperity. 'Trade And Bristol Ethnic Minorities And The City c. 1000-2001' which she co-wrote with Peter Fleming tells the stories and shows the contributions that immigrants have made to Bristol life for centuries.

She is an academic and an activist, involved with the 'Journey To Justice' charity and was proactive in its launch in 2013. This organisation aims to 'Through their stories and arts – to galvanise people to take action in their own journeys to justice.' Her contribution to our understanding of how the dynamics of race and culture have played a major part in Bristol's history has been significant.

In the Autumn of 2018 Jeremy Corbyn, who was then Leader of the Opposition had coffee and a filmed discussion with Paul Stephenson in a coffee shop in Bristol. Jeremy then accepted an invitation to visit Paul's home and meet his wife Joyce. Paul at the time was in the early stages of Parkinson's disease but you would never have known it as they had a warm-hearted discussion in which Jeremy talked about setting up an Emancipation Educational Trust if Labour won the election.

In March 2019 Paul lost his wife Joyce who was a great support to him. She encouraged him in his campaigns against apartheid, attending demonstrations and backing him when he went on conferences all over the country. When in Coventry he did a lot of work with the Punjabi community and she attended weddings and cultural activities with him.

When they moved to London and MASDA had weekend sports events at different venues, Joyce would sometimes find herself cooking for 40 people. She did a lot of entertaining with many of the people Paul associated with, such as Cleo Laine and Johnny Dankworth.

When they returned to Bristol and started fostering, Joyce, who had done voluntary work supporting families, knew some of the foster children's mothers, so she couldn't continue the support she was giving them as they weren't allowed to know where their children were. Joyce was radical in her approach to politics and someone who backed Paul's political endeavours one hundred per cent.

In 2020 Paul was very moved by the honour of having an engine named after him by Great Western Railway Company. Even more pleasurable for him was the knowledge that he was chosen for this honour by popular public vote. This he told me meant a great deal to him.

Working on this book with Paul was another paradigm shift in my understanding of how racism works, as my research revealed the power plays behind the scenes that had such a destructive effect on individual lives and society as a whole. I have been aware of Black children incorrectly categorised as having special educational needs and so not provided with the educational opportunities that would have enhanced their life choices. If some of these children, as adults, seem to have a chip on their shoulders it is because the system put it there.

Without understanding how racism is built into our

institutions and culture we cannot change it. The fact that both Paul and I both experienced being put into lower streams before working our way up to the 'A' stream in our secondary schools could have been a case of discrimination.

Consider the following leak from a confidential report by Alderman Alfred Doulton, Headmaster of Highgate School.

"On a rough calculation about half the immigrants will be West Indians at 7 of the 11 schools, the significance of this being the general recognition that their I.Q.s work out below their English contemporaries. Thus academic standards will be lower in schools where they form a large group". [61]

Where did this idea that Black people were less intelligent than white people spring from? And more importantly why does it sometimes feel as if it is still with us? The answer to the first question is transparent. The Transatlantic slave trade which transported more than 14 million Africans (the exact number is in dispute because records were not always kept) to the New World to use as free labour had, to justify this atrocity, categorise us as heathens or people considered being of a lower order who were not entitled to the same rights and consideration as their enslavers. How else could they justify this exploitation?

This particular type of slavery lasted for about 300 years and proved so profitable that when it was eventually abolished it was the plantation owners that were compensated not the enslaved. This kind of slavery is now illegal. Yet the descendants of the enslaved are often ghettoised in cities today often living in poor conditions.

Is this because the system has been tweaked rather than changed? It is the labour of the slaves that enriched and allowed

---

61   https://www.georgepadmoreinstitute.org/collection/black-education-movement ('Haringey Comprehensive Schools' Section 5 (c) 13 Jan 1969). See BEM/1/2/5. (Retrieved 16/2/21)

cities such as London, Liverpool and Bristol to grow. Let's look at the nature of labour.

Marx says "Political economy confuses on principle two very different kinds of private property, of which one rests on the producers' own labour, the other on the employment of the labour of others. It forgets that the latter not only is the direct antithesis of the former, but absolutely grows on its tomb only." [62]

Our economy which is based on capital has large companies and global monopolies owning the land, resources and means of production, forcing workers to become 'wage slaves'. The arrival of Europeans to the Americas literally used slave labour which kick started the industrial revolution in Europe. This allowed the European Governments and companies acting as their agents to conquer and exploit the resources and people of most of the world between them.

Hence Capitalism is based on exploiting the labour of others which necessitates keeping a class of people as workers who produce goods and services of all kinds to enrich others. BAME and white working-class communities have been the 'workers' in this production and it is in the interest of the wealthy who own the media and have powerful influences on governments to ensure that individuals may be able to get through the glass ceiling, but 'workers' find it difficult to successfully challenge this situation because the system depends on the majority remaining where they are.

In addition a lack of opportunity in education, good housing and well-paid jobs puts 'workers' in competition with each other and misdirects their opposition from their exploiters to fighting among themselves as we have seen with the lack of union support for BAME workers by unions in the UK during the 1960s and

62   Marx, Karl Das Kapital 2019 Benediction Classics, Oxford

1970s. By 1962, as we have seen, barriers are being constructed against immigrants with further immigration legislation which the 'Windrush Lessons Learned Review' by Wendy Williams states were sometimes racially motivated. [63]

That report goes on to state that the 1971 Immigration Act entitled people who had arrived from Commonwealth countries before January 1973 to "the right of abode" in the UK but gave them no documents to prove this. Nor did it keep records, so this effectively set a trap for the Windrush generation. [64]

The subsequent Home Office policy of creating a 'hostile environment' for illegal immigrants was to spring that trap for the Windrush generation. Under the Conservative-Liberal Democrat Coalition Government in 2012 the Home office's hostile environmental policy was set up by Theresa May whose target was to reduce immigration to less than 100,000. She failed to achieve this target but did bring in a set of administrative and legislative measures designed to make staying in the UK as difficult and painful as possible for people without leave to remain.

Among these were new restrictions to reduce non-European immigrants was one that allowed only British citizens earning more that £18,600 a year to bring their spouses or children to the UK. This effectively separated families of British citizens by wealth rather than rights. In October 2013 Theresa May said: "We will extend the number of non-suspensive appeals so that, where there is no risk of serious and irreversible harm, we can deport first and hear appeals later."

How were the 'workers' of the Windrush generation coming

---

63   https://www.gov.uk/government/publications/windrush-lessons-learned-review p9
(Retrieved 19/2/2021)
64   Ibid

to the UK between 1948 to 1973, treated by the host nation? It is estimated that of the 550,000 Caribbeans who migrated to the UK between 1948 and 1973 approximately 50,000 had not regularised their residency status. This meant the latter were vulnerable to being illegally subjected to the Home Office's hostile environmental policy and hundreds were wrongly targeted by immigration enforcement.

These policies led to people being threatened with deportation and many were illegally deported. Thousands of people also lost their jobs as they were deemed not having the right to work in the UK. Others were prevented from access to health care or made to pay exorbitant amounts for that healthcare. Many were exiled and prevented from returning to the UK. Elderly people were barred from working, refused access to Government services and lost access to welfare benefits.

The police would report both perpetrators and victims of crime to the immigration enforcement and use coercive tactics to enter homes. Many lost their jobs or their homes when they were deemed illegal immigrants and some died in custody.

"In 2001 Nathaniel went on holiday to Jamaica with his daughter Veronica. Little did either of them know that Nathaniel would never see the UK again. When they set off to come home to the UK, immigration authorities told him he would not be allowed back into the country.

"The type of passport he had had for 45 years, which declared him a citizen of the UK and Colonies, was no longer good enough, though it had been in 1985, when he last made the trip. And it had been in the mid-1950s, when he arrived in the UK as a young man, in common with thousands of other men and women and children, members of what we now know as the Windrush generation.

"Nine years after his holiday, Nathaniel died in Jamaica, unable to afford treatment for prostate cancer." [65]

The Windrush Scandal first surfaced in 2018 at a meeting of the Jamaican High Commission in London. Diplomats and campaigners demanded a remedy to the changes in the immigration system that deemed Caribbean immigrants illegal. And despite the media coverage and the thousands of heart-breaking stories that have come to light very little has been done to date, 2021, to compensate the victims of this tragedy.

Ken Morgan a former teacher moved to the UK aged 10 in 1960 and worked and lived here for more than 30 years until 1994 when he went to a relative's funeral in Jamaica. On his way back he had his passport confiscated and remained in Jamaica for a quarter of a century until the Windrush Scandal broke in 2018 and then suddenly British diplomats called to offer him a temporary visa to allow him to travel to the UK. He then applied for British citizenship when he got back but was refused after a delay of almost two years on the grounds that he was out of the country on a date five years before he made the application. At the time he was barred from being in the UK because they had wrongly confiscated his passport. [66]

It appears that not very much has changed since the scandal has come to light. The recommendations of the 'Windrush Lessons Learned Review' by Wendy Williams March 2020 were: " The Home Office must acknowledge the wrong that has been done; it must open itself up to greater scrutiny; and it must change its culture to recognise that migration and the wider Home office policy is about people and, whatever its objective, should be

---

65   https://www.gov.uk/government/publications/windrush-lessons-learned-review p8
(Retrieved 19/2/2021)
66   Guardian 22/11/2020

rooted in humanity." [67]

Yet Priti Patel has shelved promises to end the 'hostile environment' for immigrants, an 'improvement plan' suggesting it will remain in place until at least 2022. [68]

On 30 the April 2020 the Guardian revealed that the backlog of Windrush cases reached 3,720 and Priti Patel had admitted there were 1,111 cases yet to be considered with 150 people waiting for longer than six months and 35 people having spent more than a year waiting for a response. And in addition to this 24 people who were wrongly deported or detained have died. The Guardian also revealed that only 35 people at the time had been granted 'urgent and exceptional support'. [69]

The Windrush Scandal has clearly shown that the workers invited here after the war to help Britain rebuild were not always treated as citizens with rights.

It is also true from the examples of history that people will always struggle to make the world a fairer and more equitable place. From Toussaint L' Overture who ended slavery in Haiti to the Tolpuddle Martyrs who started the Trade Union movement in Dorset, people will continue to oppose injustices as they did in 1963 in Bristol.

The COVID-19 pandemic has also demonstrated the reliance that society has on its essential workers and the important and vital role they play in all our lives. It has also highlighted how BAME communities play a significant role in this contribution to the workforce.

It is not in fact stockbrokers and banks or highly paid company executives who have kept us safe and supplied our necessities during this pandemic but working people and some have shown their power.

In 2020 Black Lives Matter (BLM) protesters tore down Edward Colston's statue on Bristol City Centre and threw it into the Floating Harbour. Edward Colston was a major figure in the Transatlantic slave trade but Bristol respected him as a generous benefactor of this city. This was totally inappropriate. The continued use of his name showed racism is alive and kicking. He is not a suitable role model for future generations. The Black community, and others had long been objecting to the memorialisation of Colston through the statue, the Colston Hall, Colston Tower, Colston School and many street names, as an insult to the memory of the enslaved people whose stolen lives has made Bristol wealthy.

The video footage of the removal of the statue went global and resulted in a world-wide discussion about the memorialisation of historical figures, particularly those who had made their fortunes from the slave trade and has inspired the removal of other inappropriate statues across the world.

Eight days after Colston's statue was removed, his name was taken down from the Colston Hall and a long-term project to re-name the building came to fruition three months later. It is now called the Bristol Beacon, a name that pays no tribute to the enslaved people those exploited labour helped make Bristol a large thriving city.

I know Paul felt disappointed that Bristol City Council had not listened to us, but the matter was taken out of their hands by the Black Lives Matter protesters. The incident shows that change will come one way or another and as history has shown us it comes from people willing to make a stand. Paul Stephenson has been someone willing to make such a stand. He is a fierce fighter for equality whose charm and amiable disposition shows the calibre of the man and why so many of his old opponents are now praising him.

NATIONALITY & EQUALITY ACTS AND IMMIGRATION ACTS

NATIONALITY & EQUALITY ACTS	IMMIGRATION ACTS
1914 British Nationality and Status of Aliens Act *(Person born in the British Empire is British subject)*	
1948 Nationality Act *(Gave Commonwealth citizens unqualified rights to enter and remain in Britain)*	
	1962 Immigration Act *(Applied controls to Commonwealth citizens entering Britain)*
1965 Race Relations Act *(Gave people of different races the right to access public places)*	
1968 Race Relations Act *(Addressed issues of housing and employment and set up CRC, Community Relations Commission, but Government services and the Police were exempt)*	**1968 Immigration Act** *(Restricted the number of Asians and Africans with British passports entering Britain)*
	1971 Amended 1968 Immigration Act *(Introduced concept of 'patrials' those with close UK associations exempt from the Act. Ensuring white African passport holders were not kept out.*
1976 Race Relations Act *(Extended the law to service providers and the public sector and created the CRE, Commission for Racial Equality)*	
	1981 British Nationality Act *(Created 3 types of British Citizenship. There are now in 2021, 6 different levels of British nationality)*
2000 *(The 1976 Act extended to include the Police.}*	
2010 The Single Equality Act *(Covered age, disability, gender reassignment, marriage & civil partnership, Pregnancy and & maternity, race, religion or belief, sex & sexual orientation)*	

AWARDS

1979 **United Nations Special Committee Against Apartheid**
awarded with great appreciation by General Joseph Garba
chair of the award and Nigerian ambassador to The United
Nations.

1988 **West Indian World Publishers Community Award**
For services and achievement to the Black community

1988 **Bristol City Council Community Award**
for achievement and services rendered to the Black
community in Bristol

1996 **Bristol South West African And Caribbean Council
Community Achievers Award**

2006 **Bristol City Council – One Person Makes A Difference Award**

2008 The first Black person to be placed on the Roll of Honorary
Freemen of the City and County of Bristol.

2009 Order of the British Empire (OBE) for services to equal
opportunities and to community relations in Bristol

2009 'Honorary Masters' from the University of the West of
England

2010 'Honorary Masters' of the University' from the Open
University

2014 Honorary Doctorate' of the University of Bristol

2015 Bristol University names a transport hub in his honour

2016 Diversity UK LifeTime Achievement Award for work on
diversity and inclusion

2017 Pride of Britain Award for LifeTime Achievement presented
by Lennie Henry

2020 GWR (Great Western Railway) names a train in his honour

BIBLIOGRAPHY

Araeen, Rasheed (2000) Black Art; A discussion with Eddie Chambers' in Kwesi Owusu (ed) 'Black British Culture & Society' Routledge

Batchelor, Owen (2018) 'Youth Development – a Jamaican Experience' Pelican Publishers

Benn, Tony (1987) 'Out of the Wilderness Diaries 1963-67' Hutchinson

Benn, Tony (1988) 'Office Without Power Diaries 1968-1972' Hutchinson

Benn, Tony (1992) 'The End of an Era Diaries 1980-1990' Hutchinson

Carter, Harris & Joshi (2000) 'The 1951-1955 Conservative Govt. & the racialization of Black Immigration' in Kwesi Owusu (ed) 'Black British Culture & Society' Routledge

Dresser, Madge (1986) 'Black & White on the Buses' Madge Dresser & Bristol Broadsides

Dresser, Madge & Fleming, Peter (2007) 'Bristol: Ethnic Minorities and the City 1000-2001' Phillimore

Fanon, Frantz (1986) 'Black Skin, White Masks' translated from the French by Charles Lam Markman (1967) first UK edition (1986) Pluto Press

Fryer, Peter (1984) 'Staying Power: the History of Black people in Britain' Pluto Press

Gilroy, Paul (2000) 'Between Camps Nations, Cultures and the Allure of Race'(Allen Lane/ reissued by Routledge 2004 with new introduction)

Harris, Roxy (1981) 'Being Black: Selections from Soledad Brother & Soul on Ice' New Beacon Books

Harris, Roxy (1996) 'Openings, Absences & Omissions Aspects of the treatment of 'race', culture & ethnicity in British cultural studies' in Kwesi Owusu (ed) 'Black British Culture & Society' (2000) Routledge

Jones, Claudia (2000) 'The Caribbean Community in Britain' in Owusu,

Kwesi (ed) 'Black British Culture & Society' Routledge

Juravich, Nicholas A. (2008) 'Your Fight is Our Fight' Dissertation submitted for the degree of Master of Philosophy in Economic and Social History April 2008 Christ Church Oxford

Marx, Karl (2019) Benedict Classicals, Oxford

Owusu, Kwesi (ed) (2000) 'Black British Culture & Society' Routledge

Owusu, Kwesi (2000) 'The Commission for Racial Equality & the Politics of Race Relations interview with Sir Herman Ouseley' in Owusu, Kwesi (ed) 'Black British Culture & Society' Routledge

Paul, Kathleen 1997 'Whitewashing Britain: Race & Citizenship in the post-war era' Cornell University Press

Phillips, Mike & Trevor (1998) 'Windrush The Irresistible Rise of Multi-racial Britain' Harper Collins

Ramdin, Ron (1987) 'The Making of the Black Working Class' Gower Publishing Ltd

Samuel, Raphael (1989) 'Patriotism: The Making and Unmaking of British National Identity Minorities and Outsiders Vol 2' Routledge

WEBSITES

Caribbean Air Crew WW2 www.caribbeanaircrew-ww2.com Retrieved 18/2/2010

Citizenship Review (Lord Goldsmith QC) Http://www.guardian.co.uk/society/2001/feb/22/equality.raceequality Retrieved 2/3/2010

Citizenship Review (Lord Goldsmith QC 2007) http://www.justice.gov.uk/docs/citizenship-report-full.pdf Retrieved 18/2/2010

Claudia Jones www.vogue.co.uk-and-lifestyle/article/claudia-jones-notting-hill-carnival Retrieved 30/11/2020

Commonwealth Immigration Act 1962 https://www.nationalarchives.gov.uk/cabinetpapers/themes/commonwealth-immigration-control-legislation.htm Retrieved 27/12/20

Constantine, Sir Learie www.nalis.gov.tt/biographylearieconstantinebybridgetbrereton.htm Retrieved 11/4/2009

Farrakhan, Louis http://www.biography.com/articles/Louis-Farrakhan-929 1850 Retrieved 16/10/2010

https://www.georgepadmoreinstitutue.org/collection/black-education-movement (Haringey Comprehensive Schools' section 13 Jan 1969) Black Education Movement 1/2/5) Retrieved 16/2/21

https://www.gov.uk/government/publicatiuon/windrush-lessons-learned-review (Retrieved 19/2/2021)

Hart, Richard www.jamaicaobserver.com/columns/Richard-Hart-and-historian-15746408 Retrieved 20/2/21

Hart, Richard www.Peoplesworld.org/article/Richard-hart=Jamaica-marxist-historian-dies (Retrieved (20/2/2021)

Honeyghan, Lloyd (Ragamuffin Man) http://www.boxrec.com/media/index,php/Lloyd_Honeyghan Retrieved 17/7/2009

International Slavery Museum www.Liverpoolmuseums.org.uk/about/trustees/asscoiates.aspx (Adina Dorothy Kuya) Retrieved 24/2/2010 www.journeytojustice.org.uk

Lord Lester of Herne www.83.137.212.42/sitearchive/cre/anthology_04.html (Lord Lester of Herne) Retrieved 2/3/2010

Race Relations Act 1965 and 1968 http://news.bbc.co.uk/onthisday/hi/dates/stories/december/8/newsid_4457000/4457112.stm Retrieved 27/12/20

http:news.bbc.co.uk/onthisday/hi/dates/stories/november/26/newsid_3220000/3220635.stm Retrieved 27/12/20

Race Relations (Amendment) 2000https://www.legislation.gov.uk/ukpga/2000/34/contents

Robeson, Paul: Here I Stand (1999) https://www.pbs.org/wnet/
americanmasters/paul-robeson-career-timeline/67/Retrieved 27/12/20

NEWSPAPER ARTICLES

Bristol Evening Post September 27th 1962 (Bristol Record Office (BRO)
42840/pm/1)

Bristol Evening Post April 30th1963 "What are trade Union leaders doing to
get the race virus out of the systems of their rank and file?"

Bristol Evening Post May 2nd 1963 "Bristol Bus Crews back the boss" by
Keith Jefferies

Bristol Evening Post May 2nd 1963 Students march

Daily Herald May 4th 1963 (Bristol Record Office 428040/pm/3)

The Times May 7th 1963

Western Daily Press May 14th 1963

Bristol Evening Post March 4th 2005 (BRO 42840/pm/41) Black soldiers
billeted in Drill Hall - Old Market

The Guardian 22/11/2020 Windrush victim refused British Citizenship
despite wrongful passport confiscation

The Guardian 30/4/2020 Windrush backlog reaches 3,720 cases Home
Office reveals

The Independent 19/1/2021   MPs try to block Priti Patel's pick to scrutinise
immigration plans, fearing nominee won't stand up to her.

INTERVIEWS

Roy Hackett 6/6/2015 and 17/6/2015

INDEX

vegetarian
perfection

HINKLER
BOOKS

vegetarian
perfection

Food Editor
Jody Vassallo

Creative Director
Sam Grimmer

Project Editor
Lara Morcombe

First published in 2004 by Hinkler Books Pty Ltd
17–23 Redwood Drive
Dingley, VIC 3172 Australia
www.hinklerbooks.com
10 9 8 7 6 5 4 3
10 09 08 07

ISBN: 1865 157 627
EAN: 978 1865 157 627

Printed and bound in China

contents

an introduction to vegetables

Short of curing cancer and promising never-ending longevity, vegetables are accredited with so many health benefits it's a wonder that their daily consumption is not a common obsession. Rich in vitamins, minerals and dietary fibre, vegetables are THE cornerstone of a healthy diet. Once the exclusive domain of vegetarians, vegetable-only meals are being incorporated into a growing number of weekly menu plans. And why not? They're good for your health, they help with weight loss and they're easy on the budget.

With increased demand comes increased availability and today's supermarkets and grocers offer an exciting diversity of vegetables. If you're shopping for lettuce, what type? Good shops will have at least 5 varieties on hand. Check out the cos, iceberg, mignonette, green coral, red coral, butter, endive, rocket and radicchio. And potatoes? Look for the pink eye, desiree, pontiac, king edward , new and sebago. Capsicums are available in a multitude of colours. Asian vegetables such as bok choy, chinese cabbage and ginger are plentiful and fresh.

The recipes in this book showcase the versatility of vegetables. Bolt down a quick snack of tomato and goats cheese bruschetta. Enjoy the lively taste of a red onion and chilli tart. Or savour the flavours of a lemon broccoli risotto. With this book on hand, vegetarian cooking need never be bland again.

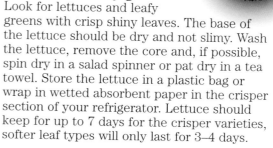

buying and storing

When shopping for vegetables, it's worth remembering that freshness is important. Buy only what you need – shopping for small amounts of vegetables a few times a week is much better than a once weekly shop for everything. Plan meals with vegetables in season. These will be the freshest and most reasonably priced vegetables available. Watch the weather – long periods of rain can reduce the supply and the price will rise. If you establish a good relationship with your fruit and vegetable provider, they will be able to assist you in the best buys from week to week.

Also keep in mind that frozen vegetables can be added to soups and simmering dishes. Despite being frozen, they still contain nutrients and can be extremely handy if you don't have the time to shop every couple of days.

lettuce and leafy greens
Look for lettuces and leafy greens with crisp shiny leaves. The base of the lettuce should be dry and not slimy. Wash the lettuce, remove the core and, if possible, spin dry in a salad spinner or pat dry in a tea towel. Store the lettuce in a plastic bag or wrap in wetted absorbent paper in the crisper section of your refrigerator. Lettuce should keep for up to 7 days for the crisper varieties, softer leaf types will only last for 3–4 days.

Salad leaves deteriorate after a few days, so it's best to only buy what you need; some supermarkets are now selling prepackaged salad mixes that last up to 5 days in the refrigerator.

root vegetables

Avoid root vegetables with blemished skin, green or purple marks, a musty smell or that have started to sprout. Carrots, potatoes, parsnips, pumpkin, sweet potatoes, beetroots, celeriac, swedes, jerusalem artichokes and turnips are all quick to show signs of spoilage. When purchased, carrots should be firm with no sign of wrinkles. Store most root vegetables in the vegetable crisper of your refrigerator for 6–8 days.

There are many different varieties of potatoes available for cooking; the two main groups being floury and waxy. Floury potatoes are suited to baking, mashing and frying while waxy potatoes are good for boiling. Potatoes should be bought with the dirt still on to protect them from bruising and exposure to light. If stored in a cool dark place in a hessian bag, potatoes can last for up to 1 month.

Whole pumpkins will keep for months in a cool dark place. Wedges wrapped in plastic can be refrigerated for up to 3 days. Unless you have a good, sharp and large knife, it is probably best to buy pumpkin by the wedge. Check that the seed area is moist, but not slimy, and that there is no mould.

tomatoes

Store tomatoes at room temperature as refrigerating will soften the flesh. To ripen tomatoes leave them on a window sill in a sunny spot in the kitchen. Unfortunately, the colour of a tomato is no longer indicative of the flavour. Vine ripened tomatoes that have been, as the name implies, left to ripen on the vine usually have a stronger sweeter flavour. Roma or egg tomatoes can also be sweet.

brassicas

Cabbage, broccoli, cauliflower and brussel sprouts are quick to show signs of spoilage. With broccoli and cauliflower, look for tightly packed florets that show no evidence of yellowing or tiny flowers. Cabbages and brussels sprouts should be dense with crisp outer leaves.

onions

Purchase onions with skins intact and no soft spots, green sprouts or any signs of moisture. Spring onions (also known as green onions) should have crisp green stems with moist roots.

peas and beans

The best way to test the freshness of a bean is to bend it – if it snaps it is fresh, if it bends it is on its way out. Try to purchase beans loose as this allows you to pick your own. Store them in a plastic bag in your refrigerator for 2–3 days. Sugar snap and snow peas (also known as mangetout) should be crisp and bright green with no sign of blemishes; they should be eaten on the day of purchase. Buy peas in the pod and shell them just before cooking – 1 kg (2 lb) peas will yield 500 g (1 1b) shelled peas. About the only way to tell the sweetness of a pea is to put it to the taste test.

capsicum

Look for capsicums (also known as peppers) with shiny waxy skins; they should also be heavy for their size with no signs of softening. They can be stored at room temperature for 1–2 days or in the vegetable crisper of the refrigerator for 4–5 days

celery, fennel and asparagus

Stalky vegetables should be crisp with upright stalks. Celery should have bright green leaves. Look for asparagus with firmly closed buds. Store stalky vegetables in the vegetable crisper for 2–3 days.

avocado

To select a ripe avocado, gently press your thumb into the top near the stem and if it gives slightly it's ready to eat. Ripe ones should be eaten within 2–3 days of purchasing. Store unripe avocados at room temperature.

sweet corn

Corn is best purchased in its husk. Peel back the husk and silk and check the kernels for signs of drying. Also, the silk should not be starting to moisten – the whiter the silk the fresher the corn. Corn is best eaten soon after purchase.

mushrooms

Look for clean white mushrooms with a fresh earthy aroma and tight caps. Exotic mushrooms are usually sold in trays covered in plastic so check carefully for any signs of decay. Mushrooms last longer when stored in paper bags in the vegetable crisper in the refrigerator. Do not wash or peel mushrooms; brush clean with a piece of absorbent paper towel.

spring vegetables

artichoke
asian greens
asparagus
avocado
beans
broccoli
cabbage
carrot
choko
cauliflower
cucumber
garlic
ginger
leek
lettuce
mushroom
onion
peas
pumpkin
silverbeet
spinach
sweet corn
watercress
zucchini flower

summer vegetables

asparagus
avocado
beans
capsicum
celery
chilli
choko
cucumber
daikon
eggplant
lettuce
okra
onion
peas
radish
squash
sweet corn
tomato
watercress
zucchini
zucchini flower

autumn vegetables

asian greens
avocado
beans
beetroot
broccoli
brussels sprouts
cabbage
capsicum
carrot
cauliflower
celery
chilli
cucumber
daikon
eggplant
fennel
garlic
ginger
leek
lettuce
mushroom
okra
olive
onion
parsnip
peas
potato
pumpkin
shallot
silverbeet
spinach
squash
swede
sweet potato
tomato
turnip
zucchini

winter vegetables

asian greens
avocado
beetroot
broccoli
brussel sprouts
cabbage
carrot
cauliflower
celeriac
celery
fennel
garlic
ginger
horseradish
jerusalem artichoke
kale
kohlrabi
leek
okra
olive
onion
parsnip
pea
potato
pumpkin
shallot
silverbeet
spinach
swede
sweet potato
turnip
witlof

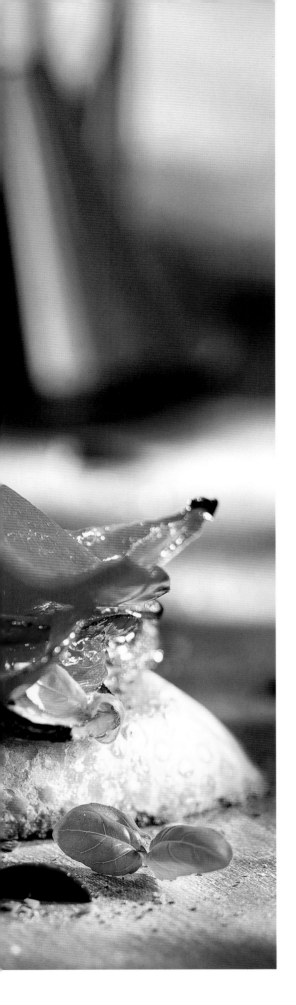

starters

grilled vegetable bruschetta

ingredients

1 red or yellow capsicum (pepper), sliced
1 zucchini (courgette), thinly sliced
1 red onion, thinly sliced
2 large plum tomatoes, thickly sliced
3 tablespoons extra virgin olive oil
2 teaspoons wholegrain mustard
black pepper
1 ciabatta loaf or baguette, cut into 8 slices
1 clove garlic, halved
8 pitted black olives, thinly sliced
fresh basil to garnish

serves 4

i

preparation time
15 minutes

cooking time
20 minutes

nutritional value per serve
fat: 1 g
carbohydrate: 1.8 g
protein: 7 g

1 Preheat grill to high and line with foil. Place capsicum, zucchini, onion and tomatoes in a bowl. In a small bowl whisk together 2 tablespoons of oil, the mustard and black pepper, pour over vegetables and toss gently to coat.

2 Spread vegetables onto grill rack and grill for 3–4 minutes on each side, until lightly browned. Set aside and keep warm.

3 Toast bread on both sides and rub garlic halves over one side. Divide the vegetables between the toast slices, garlic side up. Top with olives and drizzle with remaining oil. Garnish with basil and serve.

roman kebabs

ingredients

1 french bread stick
400 g (13 oz) mozzarella
4 tomatoes
$1/3$ cup (80 ml, $2^3/4$ fl oz) olive oil
1 tablespoon lemon juice
1 teaspoon dried oregano
salt and black pepper
fresh basil to garnish
serves 4

1 Preheat oven to 230°C (450°F, gas mark 8). Soak 4 wooden skewers in water for 10 minutes.

2 Cut bread into thick slices, and cut mozzarella into 12 slices. Slice tomatoes into 3.

3 Combine oil, lemon juice, oregano and seasoning in a shallow dish. Brush both sides of bread with oil, thread bread onto skewers, alternating with mozzarella and tomato and finishing with bread. Pour over any remaining oil.

4 Place kebabs on a baking sheet, cook for 6–8 minutes, turning halfway through, until bread is crisp and cheese has melted. Serve garnished with basil.

i

preparation time
10 minutes, plus 10 minutes soaking

cooking time
15 minutes

nutritional value per serve
fat: 16.8 g
carbohydrate: 7.3 g
protein: 11.8 g

1 Preheat oven to 220°C (425°F, gas mark 7). Cut 4 x 12 cm rounds of pastry. Score a 1 cm border on each – to form a rim. Place the rounds on a greased baking sheet.

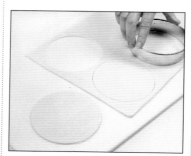

2 Heat oil in a large frying pan. Cook onions on a medium high heat for 10 minutes, until softened, stirring. Add chilli, cook gently for 1 minute, and season.

3 Spread pesto over the pastry rounds, leaving the rim clear. Spoon onion mixture over the pesto and sprinkle with pine nuts. Bake in the oven for 12–15 minutes until golden.

red onion and chilli tarts

ingredients

4 sheets (370 g, 12 oz) ready-rolled puff pastry
1 tablespoon olive oil
200 g (7 oz) red onions, finely sliced lengthways
1 small red chilli, deseeded and sliced
salt and black pepper
2 tablespoons sun-dried tomato pesto
3 tablespoons pine nuts
makes 4

i

preparation time
15 minutes

cooking time
25 minutes

nutritional value per serve
fat: 21.9 g
carbohydrate: 19 g
protein: 4.4 g

bubble and squeak with red onion chutney

3 Place chutney ingredients in a large pan and bring to the boil over a low heat. Simmer, uncovered, for 20 minutes until liquid is almost evaporated.

4 Shape potato into eight flat rounds. Melt butter and oil in a large frying pan, fry cakes on a medium heat for 5 minutes on each side, turning carefully. Cook until golden and heated through. Serve topped with chutney.

i

preparation time
15 minutes

cooking time
20 minutes

nutritional value per serve
fat: 8.1 g
carbohydrate: 12 g
protein: 1.7 g

ingredients

650 g (1 lb 5 oz) potatoes,
  cut into chunks
1 clove garlic, peeled
125 g (4 oz) cabbage, finely shredded
4 spring onions (green onions),
  finely sliced
sea salt and freshly ground black pepper
2 tablespoons butter
1 tablespoon sunflower oil
onion chutney
2 large red onions, finely chopped
4 tablespoons brown sugar
1 tablespoon white-wine vinegar
serves 4

1 Place potatoes and garlic in a large pan of water. Bring to the boil, cover and simmer for 15–20 minutes, until tender. Drain, return to the pan and mash until smooth. Cool and set aside

2 Blanch cabbage in a large pan, drain well. Add cabbage, spring onions and seasoning to the potato and mix well to combine.

artichokes with soured cream sauce

ingredients

4 large globe artichokes
280 ml (9 fl oz) sour cream
5 spring onions (green onions),
  finely chopped
1 tablespoon balsamic vinegar
1 clove garlic, finely chopped
serves 4

i

preparation time
10 minutes

cooking time
50 minutes, plus
30 minutes
standing

**nutritional value
per serve**
fat: 10 g
carbohydrate: 1.6 g
protein: 1.9 g

1 Cut off artichoke stalks, so artichokes stand flat. Place in a large pan of boiling water and simmer, partly covered, for 40 minutes or until tender. To test if artichokes are cooked, pull off an outside leaf – it should come away easily. Remove from pan and set aside for 30 minutes to cool.

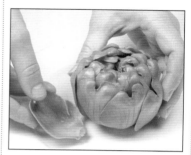

2 In a large bowl combine sour cream, spring onions, vinegar and garlic. Pull central cone of leaves out of each artichoke, leaving leaves around the edge, and discard. Scrape away the inedible core to leave the edible base.

3 Spoon sauce into artichoke centre. Place artichokes on plates and eat by plucking out a leaf and dipping it into the sauce. Use your teeth to pull away the edible fleshy part at the base of the leaf, then discard the rest.

green vegetable terrine with salsa

ingredients

100 g (3¹/₂ oz) peas
100 g (3¹/₂ oz) broad beans
125 g (4 oz) asparagus, cut into
  1 cm pieces
2 cabbage leaves, sliced
sunflower oil for greasing
4 eggs
1 clove garlic, crushed
2 teaspoons ground coriander
360 g (12 oz) ricotta cheese
¹/₂ cup (125 ml, 4 fl oz) coconut milk
3 tablespoons double cream
1 tablespoon chopped fresh coriander
1 tablespoon chopped fresh basil
salt and black pepper
extra basil to garnish

salsa
3 tomatoes
1 avocado, chopped
juice and grated rind (zest) of 1 lime
2 shallots, finely chopped
1 clove garlic, crushed
1 chilli, deseeded and chopped

serves 6

1 Bring a large pan of water to the boil. Cook peas, broad beans, asparagus and cabbage for 3 minutes to soften, refresh under cold water, drain and set aside.

2 Preheat oven to 180°C (350°F, gas mark 4). Grease a 500 g (1 lb) loaf tin with oil, line with baking paper and grease again. Whisk eggs until foamy, stir in garlic, ground coriander, ricotta, coconut milk and cream. Add vegetables, coriander and basil. Mix to combine, season and pour mixture into loaf tin.

3 Place loaf tin in a large baking dish. Pour enough boiling water into the roasting tin to come halfway up the sides of the loaf tin. Cook for

50–55 minutes, until set. Cool for 1¹/₂ hours, cover terrine with foil and refrigerate for 2 hours or overnight.

4 Place tomatoes in a large bowl, cover with boiling water and leave for 30 seconds. Remove, peel, deseed and chop. In a large bowl combine tomatoes, avocado, lime rind and juice, shallots, garlic and chilli, then season. Turn out terrine, garnish with basil and serve topped with salsa.

i

preparation time
20 minutes

cooking time
1 hour 15 minutes,
plus overnight
refrigeration

**nutritional value
per serve**
fat: 4.1 g
carbohydrate: 1.6 g
protein: 2.9 g

watercress roulade with parmesan

ingredients

oil for greasing
2 tablespoons parmesan, grated
90 g (3 oz) watercress, finely chopped
   (thick stems discarded)
4 eggs, beaten
salt and black pepper
filling
210 g (7 oz) cream cheese,
   at room temperature
3 tablespoons milk
90 g (3 oz) watercress, finely chopped
   (thick stems discarded)
5 spring onions (green onions),
   finely chopped
extra watercress sprigs to garnish
serves 4

1 Preheat oven to 200°C (400°F, gas mark 6). Grease a 23 x 30 cm Swiss roll tin, line with baking paper, sprinkle with 1 tablespoon of parmesan.

3 Combine cream cheese, milk, watercress, onions and seasoning. Turn roulade onto a chopping board. Peel baking paper off the base and spread filling over the base. Roll up from the short end, discarding any paper as you go. Refrigerate for 30 minutes, and serve in slices, garnished with watercress.

2 Mix together the watercress and eggs, season and pour into tin. Cook for 7–8 minutes, until the eggs have set. Remove from oven and leave to cool for 5 minutes. Sprinkle with remaining parmesan. Lay a sheet of baking paper over the top and set aside until cool.

i

preparation time
15 minutes

cooking time
1 hour 15 minutes

**nutritional value
per serve**
fat: 13.8 g
carbohydrate: 1.2 g
protein: 8.8 g

ricotta herb dip with garlic toasts

ingredients

6 pitted green olives, finely chopped
1 tablespoon chopped fresh tarragon
1 tablespoon chopped fresh chives
1 tablespoon chopped fresh mint
2 teaspoons finely grated
  lemon rind (zest)
250 g (8 oz) ricotta cheese
black pepper
4 tablespoons sun-dried tomato purée
1 large mixed grain baguette, cut into
  thick slices
1 clove garlic, halved
serves 4

i

preparation time
10 minutes

cooking time
10 minutes

**nutritional value
per serve**
fat: 4.3 g
carbohydrate: 38 g
protein: 8.5 g

1 In a large bowl combine olives, tarragon, chives, mint and lemon rind, and stir in ricotta. Season with pepper, mix well. Add sun-dried tomato purée and stir gently to create a marbled effect. Spoon into a serving dish.

2 Preheat grill to high. Grill baguette slices for 1–2 minutes on each side, until golden. Rub garlic halves over toast slices and serve with ricotta dip.

grilled brie with beetroot salad

ingredients

1 avocado, sliced
250 g (8 oz) cooked beetroot, drained
   and chopped
2 celery sticks, sliced
1 red apple, cored and chopped
1 baguette, sliced into 4
125 g (4 oz) brie, quartered
120 g (4 oz) mixed salad leaves

dressing

3 tablespoons extra virgin olive oil
3 tablespoons apple cider vinegar
1 clove garlic, crushed
1 red onion, finely chopped
1 tablespoon tomato purée
sea salt and freshly ground
   black pepper
3 tablespoons pine nuts

serves 4

1 In a large bowl, place avocado, beetroot, celery and apple. Cover and set aside. Preheat grill to high and lightly toast bread for 2–3 minutes each side. Place a slice of brie on each piece, return to grill. Cook until cheese is melted and slightly golden.

2 Place all dressing ingredients in a small pan, bring to the boil and simmer for 2–3 minutes, until warmed through.

3 Divide salad leaves between four plates, top with beetroot mixture and a cheese toast. Drizzle with warm dressing and serve.

i

preparation time
15 minutes

cooking time
15 minutes

**nutritional value
per serve**
fat: 8.3 g
carbohydrate: 13.1 g
protein: 4.3 g

vine tomatoes and goat's cheese bruschetta

ingredients

450 g (14 oz) small vine-ripened tomatoes (with vine intact)
2 tablespoons extra virgin olive oil
1 clove garlic, crushed
4 sprigs fresh thyme
4 thick slices ciabatta, diagonally cut
4 tablespoons olive tapenade
100 g (3¹/₂ oz) soft goat's cheese, cut into chunks
fresh basil to garnish

serves 4

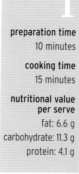

preparation time
10 minutes

cooking time
15 minutes

nutritional value per serve
fat: 6.6 g
carbohydrate: 11.3 g
protein: 4.1 g

1 Preheat oven to 220°C (425°F, gas mark 7). Place tomatoes in a large roasting tin and drizzle with oil. Sprinkle with garlic and thyme sprigs. Roast for 15 minutes, until tender. Divide tomatoes into 4 portions, each with vine intact, and set aside.

2 Preheat grill to high. Toast bread on both sides until golden. Spread each slice with 1 tablespoon of tapenade. Top with goat's cheese and tomatoes. Drizzle with juice from roasting tin and garnish with basil.

mixed mushrooms on herbed muffins

ingredients

500 g (1 lb) mixed mushrooms,
  including wild, oyster and shiitake
2 tablespoons olive oil
salt and black pepper
2 tablespoons butter
1 clove garlic, crushed
3 tablespoons chopped fresh parsley
3 tablespoons finely snipped chives
extra chives for garnish
2 teaspoons balsamic vinegar
4 tablespoons soft cheese
6 white muffins
serves 6

1 Halve any large mushrooms. Heat 2 teaspoons of oil in a large frying pan, add mushrooms, season lightly and cook over a medium-high heat for 5 minutes, until moistened.

2 Remove mushrooms, drain on kitchen towels and set aside. Add remaining oil and half the butter to the pan and heat until butter melts. Add garlic and cook for 1 minute.

3 Return mushrooms to the pan, increase heat to high and fry for 5 minutes, until tender and starting to crisp. Stir in remaining butter and 2 tablespoons each of parsley and chives. Drizzle with vinegar and season.

4 Mix soft cheese with remaining parsley and chives. Split and toast the muffins. Spread cheese mixture over the muffin halves. Top with mushrooms and garnish with chives.

i

preparation time
15 minutes

cooking time
15 minutes

nutritional value per serve
fat: 9.5 g
carbohydrate: 14.1 g
protein: 6.6 g

soups

pea and fresh mint soup

ingredients

4 tablespoons butter
2 rashers bacon, chopped
1 bunch spring onions (green onions), chopped
500 g (1 lb) peas
2 little gem lettuces, shredded
salt and black pepper
2 tablespoons chopped fresh mint
900 ml (1½ pints) water
155 ml (5 fl oz) cream
salt and black pepper
pinch of castor sugar (optional)
lemon juice (optional)
extra cream to serve
fresh chives, snipped to garnish

serves 4

i

preparation time
15 minutes

cooking time
30 minutes

nutritional value per serve
fat: 5.5 g
carbohydrate: 2.5 g
protein: 2.4 g

1 Melt butter in a large pan, add bacon and cook on a medium high heat for 2–3 minutes, add spring onions. Cover, reduce heat and cook gently for 5 minutes, stirring occasionally, until onions have softened.

2 Add peas, lettuce, mint and water. Bring to the boil, reduce heat and simmer for 10 minutes, until vegetables are tender. Cool. In a food processor, combine pea mixture and cream until smooth.

3 Return soup to the pan. Season to taste, add castor sugar and lemon juice, if using. Reheat gently – do not allow soup to boil. Serve in bowls drizzled with cream and garnished with chives.

plum tomato, lentil and basil soup

ingredients

90 g (3 oz) lentils
1 kg (2 lb) plum tomatoes
1 tablespoon olive oil
2 onions, chopped
2 tablespoons sun-dried tomato purée
750 ml (1¼ pints) vegetable stock
1 bay leaf
black pepper
3 tablespoons chopped fresh basil
extra basil leaves to garnish

serves 4

1 Rinse lentils, drain, add to a large pan of boiling water. Reduce heat and simmer, covered, for 25 minutes until tender. Drain, rinse and set aside.

2 Place tomatoes in a large bowl, cover with boiling water, leave for 30 seconds and drain. Remove skins, deseed and chop. Heat oil in a large pan, add onions and cook

on a medium heat for 10 minutes until softened, stirring occasionally. Stir in tomatoes, tomato purée, stock, bay leaf and black pepper. Bring to the boil, reduce heat and simmer, covered, stirring occasionally for 25 minutes until vegetables are cooked.

3 Remove pan from heat and cool for a few minutes. Remove and discard bay leaf. In a food processor, combine soup until smooth. Return to a clean pan, stir in lentils and chopped basil, reheat gently. Serve garnished with fresh basil.

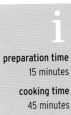

preparation time
15 minutes

cooking time
45 minutes

nutritional value per serve

fat: 1.2 g
carbohydrate: 5.5 g
protein: 2.6 g

mixed bean and vegetable soup

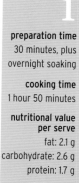

ingredients

110 g (3 ½ oz) dried haricot beans, soaked overnight

110 g (3 ½ oz) dried chickpeas, soaked overnight

3 tablespoons olive oil

1 onion, chopped

1 clove garlic, crushed

1 leek (white part only), diced

1.5 litres (2 ½ pints) vegetable stock

2 sticks celery, sliced

1 carrot, diced

2 sprigs fresh thyme, chopped

1 small fennel bulb, grated

2 zucchini (courgettes), grated

90 g (3 oz) broad beans

3 tomatoes, peeled, deseeded and chopped

salt and freshly ground black pepper

grated parmesan, to serve

serves 4-6

i

preparation time
30 minutes, plus overnight soaking

cooking time
1 hour 50 minutes

nutritional value per serve
fat: 2.1 g
carbohydrate: 2.6 g
protein: 1.7 g

1 Drain the haricot beans and chickpeas. Place in a large pan, cover with water and bring to the boil for 15 minutes. Reduce heat, cover and simmer for a further 30 minutes. Drain well.

2 Heat oil in a large pan, add onion, garlic and leek. Cook on a medium-high heat, stirring, until tender. Add stock, haricot beans and chickpeas. Reduce heat, cover and simmer for 45 minutes until tender. Add remaining ingredients and simmer for a further 15 minutes.

3 Season to taste. Serve with grated parmesan.

spinach and nutmeg soup with cheese toasts

ingredients

2 tablespoons olive oil
2 tablespoons butter
250 g (8 oz) floury potatoes, cut into chunks
250 g (8 oz) spinach leaves
1 teaspoon freshly grated nutmeg
salt and black pepper
1.4 litres (2 1/2 pints) chicken or vegetable stock
4 tablespoons crème fraîche
100 g (3 1/2 oz) gruyère, grated
1 large egg, beaten
day-old narrow french bread stick, cut diagonally into 18 x 1 cm slices

serves 6

i

preparation time
25 minutes

cooking time
35 minutes

nutritional value per serve
fat: 6.4 g
carbohydrate: 11.3 g
protein: 5.6 g

1 Heat oil and half the butter in a large pan. Fry potatoes for 1 minute, add spinach and nutmeg. Cook for 2 minutes, until spinach is wilting.

2 Add stock, season lightly and bring to the boil. Reduce heat, cover and simmer for 10–15 minutes, until potatoes are tender. Leave to cool for 10 minutes.

3 In a food processor, combine until smooth. Stir in half the crème fraîche, season to taste and set aside.

4 Preheat grill. Mix grated cheese, egg and remaining crème fraîche. Lightly toast the bread, spread cheese mixture on one side of each slice. Dot with remaining butter and season with black pepper. Grill for 5 minutes, until bubbling and golden. Return soup to pan and heat gently. Serve topped with cheese toasts.

coconut, sweet potato and spinach soup

ingredients
2 tablespoons butter
500 g (1 lb) sweet potatoes, diced
1 onion, chopped
2 cloves garlic, crushed
1 teaspoon grated ginger
1 tablespoon medium curry paste
600 ml (1 pint) vegetable stock
220 ml (7 1/2 fl oz) coconut milk
juice of 1 lime
1/4 teaspoon dried crushed chillies
185 g (6 oz) spinach, shredded
salt and black pepper
serves 4

1 Melt butter in a large pan, fry potatoes, onion, garlic, ginger and curry paste on a medium-high heat for 5 minutes until lightly golden.

2 Add stock, coconut milk, lime juice and chilli. Bring to the boil, reduce heat, cover and simmer for 15 minutes, until potatoes are tender.

3 Remove from heat and set aside to cool. In a food processor, purée half the soup. Return purée to the pan, stir to combine, add spinach and cook for 1–2 minutes, until spinach has just wilted and soup has heated through. Season to taste.

i

preparation time
20 minutes

cooking time
30 minutes

nutritional value per serve
fat: 5.1 g
carbohydrate: 5.1 g
protein: 1.7 g

chilled yoghurt soup

1 Peel and grate cucumber.

2 Combine cream, yoghurt and vinegars, and whisk lightly until smooth. Stir in cucumber, mint, garlic and seasoning. Cover and chill for 3 hours.

3 Stir and season to taste. Garnish with a slice of cucumber, a sprig of mint and cracked pepper.

ingredients

1 large cucumber
1 cup (250 ml, 8 fl oz) cream
200 g (7 oz) natural yoghurt
2 tablespoons white-wine vinegar
1 tablespoon balsamic vinegar
2 tablespoons chopped fresh mint
1 clove garlic, crushed
salt and freshly ground black pepper
extra mint and slices of cucumber, to garnish.
serves 4-6

i

preparation time
20 minutes

cooking time
3 hours
refrigeration

nutritional value per serve
fat: 26.2 g
carbohydrate: 13.4 g
protein: 5.6 g

carrot and lentil soup

ingredients

2 tablespoons butter
1 tablespoon sunflower oil
500 g (1 lb) carrots, chopped
1 onion, chopped
2 celery sticks, chopped
100 g (3 ½ oz) red split lentils, rinsed
850 ml (1 ½ pints) vegetable stock
sea salt and freshly ground black pepper
natural yoghurt
fresh parsley, chopped to garnish
serves 4

1 Melt butter and oil in a large pan. Fry carrots, onion and celery for 6–8 minutes until lightly golden. Add lentils and 750 ml (1 ¼ pints) of vegetable stock, bring to the boil. Reduce heat, cover and simmer for about 20 minutes, until carrots are tender.

2 Allow soup to cool. In a food processor, combine until smooth. Return to a clean pan with remaining stock, season to taste and reheat gently before serving. Garnish with a swirl of yoghurt and chopped parsley.

i

preparation time
20 minutes

cooking time
40 minutes

nutritional value per serve
fat: 3.4 g
carbohydrate: 5.2 g
protein: 2.4 g

salads

three bean rice salad

ingredients

250 g (8 oz) brown rice
185 g (6 oz) baby broad beans
400 g (13 oz) can black-eye beans, drained and rinsed
200 g (7 oz) can red kidney beans, drained and rinsed
1 red capsicum (pepper), chopped
1 bunch spring onions (green onions), chopped
fresh coriander to garnish

dressing
155 ml (5 fl oz) tomato juice
1 tablespoon olive oil
1 tablespoon white-wine vinegar
2 teaspoons dijon mustard
1 clove garlic, crushed
2 tablespoons chopped fresh coriander
black pepper

serves 4

i

preparation time
20 minutes

cooking time
35 minutes

nutritional value per serve
fat: 1.5 g
carbohydrate: 21.1 g
protein: 5.5 g

1 Bring a large pan of water to the boil. Add rice and cook for 12 minutes, stirring occasionally. Drain. Cook broad beans in a pan of boiling water for 4–5 minutes until tender. Rinse under cold water

and drain, removing skins if desired. Rinse rice under cold water, drain and place in large serving bowl.

2 Place tomato juice, olive oil, vinegar, mustard, garlic, coriander and black pepper in a small bowl and whisk until combined.

3 Pour dressing over the rice and toss to combine. Add broad beans, black-eye beans, kidney beans, capsicum and spring onions and toss well. Cover and refrigerate before serving. Garnish with fresh coriander.

tomato and mozzarella

ingredients

6 plum tomatoes, sliced
250 g (8 oz) mozzarella,
  drained and sliced
2 spring onions (green onions), sliced
90 g (3 oz) black olives
salt and black pepper

dressing

3 tablespoons extra virgin olive oil
1 clove garlic, crushed
2 teaspoons balsamic vinegar
2 tablespoons chopped fresh basil

serves 4

1 Arrange tomatoes, mozzarella, spring onions and olives in layers on serving plates and season.

2 Heat oil and garlic in a small pan over a low heat for 2 minutes until garlic has softened. Remove from heat, add vinegar and basil, whisk to combine and pour over salad.

i

preparation time
10 minutes

cooking time
15 minutes

**nutritional value
per serve**
fat: 13.6 g
carbohydrate: 3.5 g
protein: 8.5 g

1 Preheat grill to high. Place walnuts on a baking sheet and grill for 2–3 minutes, until golden, turning often. Place herbs, walnut oil, olive oil, garlic, vinegar and honey in a food processor and process until smooth. Season to taste and set aside.

2 Arrange salad leaves, beetroot and pear slices on serving plates. Sprinkle with walnuts. Top with shavings of parmesan. Spoon dressing over salad and garnish with whole chives.

beetroot, pear and bitter leaf salad

ingredients

5 tablespoons walnut pieces
200 g (7 oz) mixed salad leaves
250 g (8 oz) cooked beetroot, sliced
2 pears, unpeeled and sliced
2 tablespoons parmesan
fresh chives to garnish
dressing
2 tablespoons chopped fresh herbs
   (basil, parsley, chives and mint)
4 tablespoons walnut oil
2 tablespoons extra virgin olive oil
1 clove garlic, crushed
2 teaspoons red-wine vinegar
1 teaspoon clear honey
salt and black pepper
serves 4

i

preparation time
15 minutes

cooking time
15 minutes

**nutritional value
per serve**
fat: 10.6 g
carbohydrate: 9 g
protein: 1.7 g

roasted vegetable salad

ingredients

preparation time
20 minutes

cooking time
35 minutes

nutritional value per serve
fat: 4.7 g
carbohydrate: 7.4 g
protein: 1.3 g

3 red onions, quartered
3 potatoes, cut into wedges
2 zucchini (courgettes), thickly sliced
2 yellow capsicums (peppers) ,
   thickly sliced
4 tomatoes, halved
2 tablespoons olive oil
sea salt and freshly ground black pepper
parmesan shavings (optional)
dressing
3 tablespoons extra virgin olive oil
2 tablespoons clear honey
1 tablespoon balsamic vinegar
juice and finely grated rind (zest)
   of ¹/₂ lemon
serves 2–4

1 Preheat oven to 200°C (400°F, gas mark 6). Place all vegetables in a shallow roasting tin, drizzle with oil and season. Shake tray gently to coat vegetables. Bake for 35 minutes, until vegetables are tender and lightly browned.

2 In a small bowl combine all dressing ingredients. Pour over roasted vegetables, tossing gently to coat. Serve topped with parmesan shavings.

zucchini and hazelnut salad

ingredients

650 g (1 lb 5 oz) small zucchini
  (courgettes)
2 tablespoons sunflower oil
extra sunflower oil for frying
$^1/_2$ cup (125 ml, 4 fl oz) walnut oil
1 tablespoon white-wine vinegar
salt and black pepper
100 g (3$^1/_2$ oz) whole blanched
  hazelnuts
170 g (5$^1/_2$ oz) watercress (thick stalks
  removed)
90 g (3 oz) feta, crumbled
serves 6

i

preparation time
25 minutes

cooking time
25 minutes

nutritional value
per serve
fat: 19.0 g
carbohydrate: 1.4 g
protein: 3.6 g

1 Pare zucchini into
lengthways slivers, using a
vegetable peeler. In a bowl,
combine sunflower oil, walnut
oil and vinegar, and season.
Add half the zucchini slivers to
the mixture, toss lightly
and set aside.

2 Brush a large frying pan
with a little sunflower oil
and heat. Lay the remaining
slivers in the pan and cook for
2 minutes on each side, until
lightly charred. Remove,
season and set aside. Wipe
the pan clean.

3 Roughly crush hazelnuts,
using a pestle and mortar.
Place in the frying pan and cook
for 1–2 minutes, until golden.

4 Divide the watercress
between serving plates.
Spoon some of the marinated
zucchini into the centre,
reserving some of the
marinade. Scatter over half the
toasted hazelnuts and the feta.
Arrange the charred zucchini
on top, sprinkle over the rest
of the hazelnuts and the
reserved marinade.

baby spinach, feta and artichoke salad

ingredients

1 red capsicum (pepper), quartered
olive oil
100 g (3 ½ oz) walnuts
200 g (7 oz) baby spinach, washed
200 g (7 oz) feta, cubed
300 g (10 oz) artichoke hearts, quartered
70 g (2 ¼ oz) pitted black olives
pita bread, to serve

dressing

½ cup (125 ml, 4 fl oz) extra virgin olive oil
4 tablespoons lemon juice
2 teaspoons honey
2 teaspoons chopped oregano
freshly ground black pepper

serves 4–6

i

preparation time
20 minutes

cooking time
20 minutes

**nutritional value
per serve**
fat: 19.7 g
carbohydrate: 3.6 g
protein: 5.3 g

1 Preheat grill. Grill capsicum skin side up for 10–15 minutes, until skin blisters and blackens. Transfer to a plastic bag, seal and leave to cool. Remove skins, deseed, cut into strips and set aside.

2 In a small jar combine all dressing ingredients. Shake well and set aside.

3 In a frying pan, heat one tablespoon olive oil, add walnuts, and cook on a medium-high heat for 1–2 minutes, until lightly browned. In a large serving bowl combine all salad ingredients, drizzle with dressing, and serve with pita bread.

warm bulgur salad with walnuts

ingredients

250 g (8 oz) bulgur wheat
2 yellow capsicums (peppers), quartered
250 g (8 oz) green beans, halved
2 tomatoes
4 spring onions (green onions), sliced
90 g (3 oz) brazil nuts, roughly chopped
4 tablespoons chopped fresh parsley
sea salt and freshly ground black pepper
dressing
4 tablespoons extra virgin olive oil
1 tablespoon wholegrain mustard
1 clove garlic, crushed
1 teaspoon balsamic vinegar
1 teaspoon white-wine vinegar
serves 4

i

preparation time
20 minutes

cooking time
25 minutes, plus
20 minutes
soaking

**nutritional value
per serve**
fat: 11 .3g
carbohydrate: 7.9 g
protein: 3.2 g

1 Place bulgur wheat in a large bowl and cover with 2 cm boiling water above bulgur wheat. Soak for 20 minutes. Preheat grill to high. Grill capsicum skin-side up for 10–15 minutes, until skin blisters and blackens. Transfer to a plastic bag, seal and leave to cool. Remove skins, deseed and roughly chop flesh.

2 Blanch the green beans in boiling water for 3–4 minutes. Drain, refresh under cold running water and set aside. Place tomatoes into a large bowl, cover with boiling water and leave for 30 seconds. Peel, deseed and roughly chop flesh. Set aside.

3 In a large bowl, combine dressing ingredients and mix well. Drain bulgur wheat and transfer to a large serving bowl. Pour over dressing and toss well. Add reserved beans, capsicums, tomatoes, spring onions, brazil nuts, parsley and seasoning, toss gently to combine. Season to taste.

mains

mixed mushrooms risotto

ingredients

2 tablespoons butter
500 g (1 lb) mixed mushrooms (oyster, shiitake, flat, enoki, swiss), sliced
2 tablespoons olive oil
2 cloves garlic, crushed
1 leek, finely sliced
1 litre (1²⁄₃ pints) chicken stock
440 g (14 oz) arborio rice
½ cup (125 ml, 4 fl oz) white wine
grated rind (zest) of 1 lemon
60 g (2 oz) pecorino cheese, grated
60 g (2 oz) parmesan, grated
2 tablespoons chopped parsley
serves 4-8

i

preparation time
25 minutes

cooking time
45-50 minutes

nutritional value per serve
fat: 4.6 g
carbohydrate: 15.3 g
protein: 4.2 g

1 Heat butter in a large pan, add mushrooms and cook on a medium-high heat for 2 minutes. Remove from heat and set aside.

2 Heat oil in a large pan, add garlic and leek. Cook on a medium heat for 5–6 minutes, until cooked. Heat stock in a large pan, cover and keep at a low simmer.

3 Add rice to garlic and leek, stir until rice is coated. Add ½ cup of stock and stir constantly over a medium heat until all liquid is absorbed. Add white wine, stir until absorbed. Continue adding stock ½ cup at a time until all liquid is absorbed and rice is tender and creamy. This will take around 25–30 minutes.

4 Stir in mushrooms, lemon rind, cheese and parsley. Serve.

tomato, mustard and brie tart

ingredients

185 g (6 oz) plain white flour
pinch of sea salt
90 g (3 oz) butter, diced
½ cup (125 ml, 4 fl oz) milk
2 egg yolks
1 clove garlic, crushed
1 tablespoon wholegrain mustard
60 g (2 oz) mature cheddar, grated
4 tomatoes, sliced
125 g (4 oz) brie, thinly sliced
sea salt and freshly ground black pepper
herb oil
1 tablespoon finely chopped fresh basil
1 tablespoon finely chopped fresh parsley
1 tablespoon finely chopped
  fresh coriander
2 tablespoons extra virgin olive oil
serves 4

1 Preheat oven to 190°C (375°F, gas mark 5). Sift flour and a pinch of sea salt into a large bowl. Using your fingertips, rub butter into flour until it resembles fine breadcrumbs. Add 2 tablespoons of cold water and mix to dough. Cover and refrigerate for 20 minutes. Roll pastry to line a deep 20 cm metal flan tin. Chill for a further 10 minutes.

2 Line pastry with baking paper and baking beans, bake blind for 10–12 minutes. Carefully remove paper and beans. Bake pastry for a further 5 minutes and set aside. Reduce oven temperature to 180°C (350°F, gas mark 4).

3 In a jug, place milk, egg yolks, garlic and seasoning. Whisk to combine. Spread mustard over pastry base and sprinkle with cheddar. Arrange tomatoes and brie on top, pour over egg mixture. Cook for 30–35 minutes, until just set and golden. In a small bowl, combine remaining ingredients and drizzle over tart. Serve warm.

i

preparation time
25 minutes

cooking time
1 hour 30 minutes

**nutritional value
per serve**
fat: 13.8 g
carbohydrate: 11.4 g
protein: 5.7 g

tortellini with tomato and cream sauce

ingredients

4 tablespoons butter
1 small onion, finely chopped
1 stick celery, finely chopped
400 g (13 oz) tomato paste
1/2 teaspoon castor sugar
155 ml (5 fl oz) crème fraîche
600 g (1 1/4 lb) fresh spinach and
  ricotta tortellini
salt and black pepper
parmesan, grated to serve
serves 4

i

preparation time
15 minutes

cooking time
45 minutes

nutritional value
per serve
fat: 8 g
carbohydrate: 4 g
protein: 1.3 g

1 Melt butter in a large pan. Add onion, celery, tomato paste and sugar, and bring to the boil. Reduce heat and simmer, uncovered, for 30 minutes or until sauce has thickened.

2 Spoon in crème fraîche, season and bring back to the boil, stirring. Simmer for 1 minute and season to taste.

3 Cook pasta in a large pan of boiling water until al dente. Drain well, transfer to a serving bowl and pour over sauce. Garnish with parmesan.

harvest vegetable bake

ingredients

1 onion, sliced
2 leeks, sliced
2 sticks celery, chopped
2 carrots, thinly sliced
1 red capsicum (pepper), sliced
500 g (1 lb) mixed root vegetables
   (sweet potato, parsnip, turnip etc), cubed
185 g (6 oz) mushrooms, sliced
400 g (13 oz) can tomatoes, chopped
1/2 cup (125 ml, 4 fl oz) dry cider
1 teaspoon dried thyme
1 teaspoon dried oregano
black pepper
fresh herbs of choice to garnish
serves 4

1 Preheat oven to 180°C (350°F, gas mark 4). Place the onion, leeks, celery, carrots, capsicum, root vegetables and mushrooms in a large ovenproof casserole dish and mix well. Stir in the tomatoes, cider, thyme, oregano and black pepper.

2 Cover and bake in centre of oven for 1–1½ hours until the vegetables are cooked through and tender, stirring once or twice. Garnish with fresh herbs.

i

preparation time
30 minutes

cooking time
1½ hours

nutritional value per serve
fat: 0 .5 g
carbohydrate: 5.4 g
protein: 1.5 g

mixed vegetable cheese bake

ingredients

1 large butternut pumpkin,
  cut into chunks
salt and black pepper
3 tablespoons olive oil
1 large (about 800 g, 1 lb 10 oz)
  cauliflower, cut into florets
360 g (12 oz) mushrooms, sliced
2 tablespoons fresh white breadcrumbs
2 tablespoons grated parmesan

sauce

2 tablespoons butter
30 g (1 oz) plain flour
pinch of cayenne pepper
300 ml (10 fl oz) milk
1 teaspoon english mustard
100 g (3 1/2 oz) cheddar, grated
extra butter for greasing
black pepper

serves 4

i

preparation time
30 minutes

cooking time
1 hour 15 minutes

**nutritional value
per serve**
fat: 5.1 g
carbohydrate: 4.3 g
protein: 3.2 g

1 Preheat oven to 200°C (400°F, gas mark 6). Place pumpkin into an ovenproof dish, season, drizzle with half the oil. Roast for 25 minutes, stirring once, until tender.

Cook cauliflower in a large pan of boiling water for 5 minutes, until just tender. Drain, reserving 220 ml (7 1/2 fl oz) of the cooking water, refresh in cold water and set aside. Heat remaining oil in a large frying pan. Cook mushrooms on a medium-high heat until just tender, tossing gently.

2 Melt butter in a large pan, stir in flour and cayenne pepper. Cook on a medium low heat for 2 minutes, gradually stir in reserved cooking liquid. Cook for 2–3 minutes, until thick, gradually stir in the milk. Simmer, stirring, for 10 minutes. Remove from heat, stir in mustard and cheese, until melted. Season to taste.

3 Reduce oven temperature to 180°C (350°F, gas mark 4). Add cauliflower to pumpkin, toss gently to combine. Divide between four individual ovenproof dishes, top with mushrooms and pour over sauce. Combine breadcrumbs and parmesan, and sprinkle over each dish. Bake for 30–35 minutes.

noodles with broccoli and carrots

ingredients

250 g (8 oz) dried stir-fry noodles
3 tablespoons vegetable oil
1 tablespoon finely chopped ginger
2 red chillies, deseeded and finely chopped
4 cloves garlic, crushed
2 onions, thinly sliced
2 tablespoons honey
300 ml (10 fl oz) vegetable
 or chicken stock
3 tablespoons white wine vinegar
650 g (1 lb 5 oz) broccoli, cut into florets
300 g (10 oz) carrots, cut into ribbons
fresh chives, snipped to garnish
serves 6

i

preparation time
25 minutes

cooking time
1 hour

nutritional value
per serve
fat: 3.9 g
carbohydrate: 7.3 g
protein: 2.5 g

1 Cook noodles in a large pan of boiling water until al dente, and drain. Heat oil in a large wok or frying pan, add ginger and chillies and stir-fry on a medium-high heat for 1–2 minutes to soften.

2 Add garlic and onions. Cook on a medium high heat for a further 5–6 minutes until onions have browned. Reduce heat and stir in honey and cook for 6–8 minutes until the honey starts to caramelise.

3 Add stock and vinegar. Bring to the boil, reduce heat and simmer, uncovered, for 8 minutes until the liquid has slightly reduced. Stir in broccoli and carrots, cover, and simmer for 5 minutes, until vegetables are just cooked.

4 Stir in the noodles and mix well. Cook, stirring, for 1–2 minutes until noodles are heated through. Sprinkle with chives.

pasta with double tomato sauce

ingredients

1 tablespoon extra virgin olive oil
1 red onion, finely chopped
2 celery sticks, finely chopped
400 g (13 oz) can tomatoes, chopped
1 tablespoon tomato purée
280 ml (9 fl oz) vegetable stock
250 g (8 oz) cherry tomatoes, halved
1 teaspoon brown sugar
340 g (11¼ oz) dried gemelli or penne
2 tablespoons crème fraîche
sea salt and freshly ground
   black pepper

serves 4

i

preparation time
20 minutes

cooking time
35 minutes

**nutritional value
per serve**
fat: 2 g
carbohydrate: 2.4 g
protein: 0.8 g

1 Heat oil in a large pan, add red onion and celery. Cook, uncovered, for 5 minutes on a medium heat, until vegetables are tender. Add chopped tomatoes, tomato purée and stock. Bring to the boil and simmer, uncovered, for 15 minutes, stirring occasionally until reduced and thickened.

2 Add cherry tomatoes, sugar and season to taste. Stir gently for about 3 minutes until heated through.
Cook pasta in a large pan of boiling water until al dente, and drain. Pour the sauce over the pasta, toss gently to combine and serve topped with crème fraîche.

bean, lentil and eggplant moussaka

ingredients

90 g (3 oz) lentils, rinsed and drained
1 eggplant (aubergine), thinly sliced
2 tablespoons olive oil
2 leeks, sliced
2 sticks celery, chopped
2 cloves garlic, crushed
1 yellow capsicum (pepper), diced
400 g (13 oz) can tomatoes, chopped
½ cup (125 ml, 4 fl oz) dry white wine
2 tablespoons tomato purée
400 g (13 oz) can black-eye beans,
  drained and rinsed
2 teaspoons dried mixed herbs
black pepper
300 g (10 oz) low-fat natural yoghurt
2 eggs
4 tablespoons grated parmesan
fresh herbs to garnish

serves 4

i

preparation time
30 minutes

cooking time
1 hour 30 minutes

**nutritional value
per serve**
fat: .3.1 g
carbohydrate: 6.6 g
protein: 4.5 g

1 Add lentils to a large pan of boiling water, cover, reduce heat and simmer for 30 minutes, until tender. Drain, rinse, drain again and set aside.

2 Preheat oven to 180°C (350°F, gas mark 4). Cook eggplant slices in a pan of boiling water for 2 minutes. Drain, pat dry and set aside.

3 Heat oil in a large frying pan, add leeks, celery, garlic and capsicum and cook on a medium-high heat for 5 minutes, until softened. Add cooked lentils, tomatoes, wine, tomato purée, beans, mixed herbs and black pepper. Stir to combine, cover and bring to the boil. Reduce heat and simmer for 10 minutes, until vegetables have softened.

4 Spoon half the bean and lentil mixture into a shallow ovenproof dish and layer top with half the eggplant. Repeat. Combine yoghurt and eggs, and pour over the top. Sprinkle with parmesan. Cook for 40 minutes, until golden and bubbling. Garnish with fresh herbs.

lemon and broccoli risotto

ingredients

1 tablespoon olive oil
1 onion, chopped
1 clove garlic, crushed
330 g (11 oz) arborio rice
1 cup (250 ml, 8 fl oz) dry white wine
1 litre (1 ²/₃ pints) hot chicken stock
125 g (4 oz) broccoli florets
2 tablespoons chopped fresh parsley
finely grated rind (zest) and juice
   of 1 lemon
crushed black peppercorns
walnut pesto (optional)
3 tablespoons walnut pieces, roasted
1 tablespoon chopped green olives
2 teaspoons grated parmesan
2 teaspoons olive oil
2 teaspoons balsamic vinegar
serves 4-6

1 Place walnuts, olives, parmesan, oil and vinegar in a food processor. Process to make a coarse paste. Set aside.

2 Heat oil in a large pan over a medium heat. Add onion and garlic. Cook, stirring, for 1–2 minutes, until onion is translucent.

3 Stir in rice. Cook for 1–2 minutes, stirring to coat rice.

Add wine. Cook, stirring, until liquid is absorbed. Add 1 cup chicken stock and cook, stirring occasionally, until liquid is absorbed. Repeat this adding ¹/₂ cup of stock at a time and cook until all stock is used and rice is tender and creamy. Add broccoli with last addition of stock, stirring occasionally. This will take around 25–30 minutes.

4 Stir in parsley, lemon rind, juice and black pepper to taste. Remove pan from heat. Cover. Stand for 3 minutes. Serve with pesto.

i

preparation time
20 minutes

cooking time
40-45 minutes

**nutritional value
per serve**
fat: 1.2 g
carbohydrate: 14.6 g
protein: 2.1 g

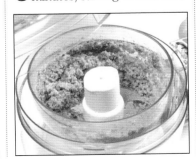

chilli mushroom stir-fry with noodles

ingredients

15 g (½ oz) dried porcini mushrooms
200 g (7 oz) fresh chinese noodles
2 tablespoons sunflower oil
4 cloves garlic, crushed
1 red chilli, deseeded and chopped
2 teaspoons grated ginger
450 g (14 oz) mixed fresh mushrooms, sliced
4 spring onions (green onions), sliced
4 tablespoons sake or dry sherry
4 tablespoons dark soy sauce
2 tablespoons lemon juice
1 tablespoon sugar
2 tablespoons chopped fresh coriander

serves 4

i

preparation time
25 minutes

cooking time
30 minutes

nutritional value per serve
fat: 6.7 g
carbohydrate: 13.9 g
protein: 3.8 g

1 Cover dried porcini mushrooms with 90 ml (3 fl oz) of boiling water and soak for 15 minutes, until softened. Strain and reserve liquid, slice mushrooms. Cook noodles in a large pan of boiling water. Drain well and set aside.

2 Heat oil in a wok or large frying pan, add garlic, chilli and ginger and stir-fry for 15 seconds, until fragrant. Add porcini and mixed mushrooms and stir-fry for 2 minutes, until softened.

3 Add spring onions, sake or sherry, soy sauce, lemon juice, sugar, coriander, reserved liquid from mushrooms and noodles, and heat for 1–2 minutes, tossing gently to combine.

linguine with leeks and mushrooms

ingredients

500 g (1 lb) leeks, sliced
290 g (10 oz) button mushrooms, sliced
1 bay leaf
3 tablespoons butter
45 g (1½ oz) plain flour
2 cups (500 ml, 16 fl oz) low-fat milk
2 tablespoons snipped fresh chives
extra chives to garnish
black pepper
500 g (1 lb) fresh linguine or tagliatelle
serves 4

1 Steam leeks, mushrooms and bay leaf over a large pan of boiling water for 10–15 minutes until tender. Discard bay leaf and keep vegetables warm.

2 Melt butter in a large pan, add flour and cook gently for 1 minute, stirring. Remove from heat and gradually add milk. Return to heat and bring to the boil, stirring, until thickened. Reduce heat and simmer for 2 minutes, stirring. Add leek and mushrooms, chives and black pepper, heat through.

3 Cook pasta in a large pan of boiling water until al dente. Drain well, return to pan, add leek and mushroom sauce and toss lightly to combine. Garnish with fresh chives.

i

preparation time
20 minutes

cooking time
30 minutes

nutritional value per serve
fat: 3 g
carbohydrate: 23 g
protein: 5.9 g

classic herb omelette

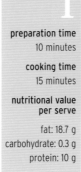

ingredients

2 eggs
salt and black pepper
1 tablespoon butter
2 tablespoons chopped fresh mixed herbs
  (parsley, chives etc)
serves 1

i

preparation time
10 minutes

cooking time
15 minutes

**nutritional value
per serve**

fat: 18.7 g
carbohydrate: 0.3 g
protein: 10 g

1 Whisk eggs in a small bowl until combined.

2 Heat butter in a small non-stick frying pan, covering the base of the pan with butter as it melts.

3 Pour eggs into the pan, tilt pan so that eggs cover the base. After about 10 seconds, use a wooden spatula to pull the cooked egg gently from the edge of the pan towards the centre, allowing any uncooked egg to run underneath and set. Continue pulling the edges until all the egg has set; this will take 2–3 minutes.

4 Sprinkle herbs evenly over omelette. Using a spatula, gently fold omelette in half and slide onto a plate.

rich bean and vegetable stew

ingredients

125 g (4 oz) dried porcini mushrooms
3 tablespoons olive oil
250 g (8 oz) large mushrooms, chopped
2 carrots, finely diced
1 large potato, diced
250 g (8 oz) baby beans, chopped
$^1/_2$ tablespoon dried thyme
$^1/_2$ tablespoon dried sage
2 cloves garlic, crushed
300 ml (10 fl oz) red wine
2$^1/_2$ cups, (600 ml, 1 pint) vegetable stock
250 g (8 oz) broad beans
300 g (10 oz) can cannellini beans
225 g (7$^1/_2$ oz) can flageolet beans
salt and black pepper
serves 4

1 Cover porcini mushrooms with 2$^1/_2$ cups (600 ml, 1 pint) of boiling water, soak for 20 minutes. Heat oil in a large pan, add fresh mushrooms, carrots, potato and green beans. Fry gently for 3–4 minutes, until slightly softened.

2 Add thyme, sage and garlic, the porcini mushrooms and liquid, the red wine, stock and seasoning. Bring to the boil, reduce heat and simmer, uncovered, for 20 minutes, until vegetables are tender.

3 Add broad beans, simmer for a further 10 minutes until tender. Drain and rinse the cannellini and flageolet beans, add to mixture, stir to combine. Simmer for 2–3 minutes, until heated through.

i

preparation time
30 minutes

cooking time
1 hour

nutritional value per serve
fat: 2.3 g
carbohydrate: 5.1 g
protein: 3.5 g

asparagus, ricotta and herb frittata

ingredients

500 g (1 lb) fresh asparagus
12 eggs
2 cloves garlic, crushed
4 tablespoons chopped fresh mixed
 herbs (basil, chives, parsley etc)
salt and black pepper
4 tablespoons butter
100 g (3½ oz) ricotta
squeeze of lemon juice
olive or truffle oil to drizzle
parmesan to serve
extra whole chives to garnish
serves 4

i

preparation time
20 minutes

cooking time
30-35 minutes

nutritional value
per serve
fat: 10 g
carbohydrate: 0.8 g
protein: 8 g

1 Preheat grill to high. Char grill asparagus on a griddle pan, until browned. Set aside and keep warm.

2 In a large bowl, whisk together eggs, garlic, herbs and seasoning. Melt half of the butter in an ovenproof frying pan, immediately pour in a quarter of the egg mixture and cook for 1–2 minutes, until almost set.

3 Place under preheated grill for 3–4 minutes, until egg is cooked through and top of frittata is set, transfer to a plate. Keep warm whilst making remaining frittatas, adding more butter when necessary.

4 Place frittatas on 4 serving plates and arrange a quarter of asparagus and a quarter of ricotta over each frittata. Squeeze over lemon juice, season and drizzle with oil. Top with shavings of parmesan and garnish with fresh chives.

sides

sweet potato puree

ingredients

750 g (1 1/2 lb) sweet potatoes, cut into large chunks
3 tablespoons milk
1 clove garlic, crushed
45 g (1 1/2 oz) mature cheddar, finely grated
1 tablespoon chopped fresh parsley
1 tablespoon snipped fresh chives
black pepper
extra chives to garnish
serves 4

i

preparation time
10 minutes

cooking time
20 minutes

**nutritional value
per serve**
fat: 2 g
carbohydrate: 11.7 g
protein: 3.5 g

1 Cook sweet potatoes in a large pan of boiling water for 10–15 minutes, until tender. Drain thoroughly, mash until smooth.

2 Heat milk in a small pan, add to potato along with garlic, cheddar, parsley, chives and black pepper. Beat until smooth and well combined. Serve garnished with fresh chives.

sweet and sour red cabbage

1 Preheat oven to 160°C (315°F, gas mark 3). Place oil, vinegar, chilli, orange rind and juice, orange-flower water and sugar into a small pan, bring to the boil, reduce heat and simmer for 5 minutes.

2 Place cabbage in an ovenproof casserole dish, pour over oil and vinegar mixture, reserving about 2 tablespoons. Cover and bake for 3 hours, until cooked through. Toss with reserved oil and vinegar mixture.

ingredients

3 tablespoons olive oil
2 tablespoons red-wine vinegar
1 red or green chilli, sliced, seeds and pith included
grated rind (zest) and juice of 1 orange
1 tablespoon orange-flower water
3 tablespoons light muscovado sugar
1 red cabbage, thinly sliced

serves 4

i

preparation time
20 minutes

cooking time
3 hours

nutritional value
fat: 6.2 g
carbohydrate: 8.6 g
protein: 1.4 g

green beans with walnut dressing

ingredients

450 g (14 oz) green beans
2 tablespoons walnut oil
1 tablespoon olive oil
1 tablespoon white-wine vinegar
1 teaspoon dijon mustard
black pepper
serves 4

i

preparation time
10 minutes

cooking time
15 minutes

**nutritional value
per serve**
fat: 7.2 g
carbohydrate: 1.9 g
protein: 1.9 g

1 Cook beans in a large pan of boiling water for 5–6 minutes until tender.

2 Place walnut oil, olive oil, vinegar, mustard and black pepper in a small bowl, whisk to combine. Drain the beans and serve hot or cold drizzled with dressing.

snowpeas and carrots with sesame seeds

ingredients

½ cucumber
2 tablespoons sesame seeds
1 tablespoon sunflower oil
4 carrots, julienned
250 g (8 oz) snow peas (mangetout)
6 spring onions (green onions), chopped
1 tablespoon lemon juice
black pepper
serves 4

i

preparation time
20 minutes

cooking time
20 minutes

nutritional value
per serve
fat: 3.5 g
carbohydrate: 4.5 g
protein: 1.8 g

1 Peel cucumber, cut in half lengthways and scoop out seeds. Slice into half moons.

2 Heat a non-stick wok or large frying pan. Add sesame seeds and dry-fry on a medium heat for 1 minute until toasted,

tossing constantly. Remove and set aside. Add oil and heat. Add cucumber and carrots, and stir-fry over a high heat for 2 minutes. Add snowpeas and spring onions and stir-fry for a further 2–3 minutes, until vegetables are tender but crunchy.

3 Add lemon juice and sesame seeds, toss gently to combine. Season with pepper and serve.

spinach with sesame seeds

ingredients

500 g (1 lb) fresh spinach,
  stalks removed
1 tablespoon peanut oil
1 teaspoon sesame oil
3 cloves garlic, crushed
2 tablespoons sesame seeds
juice and rind (zest) of ½ lemon
salt and black pepper

serves 6

1 Place spinach in a large bowl, cover with boiling water and stand for 2–3 minutes. Drain and refresh under cold running water. Squeeze out any excess water, and coarsely chop.

2 Heat peanut and sesame oil in a wok or large frying pan. Add garlic and sesame seeds and on a medium heat fry for 1–2 minutes, until garlic is lightly brown and seeds have started to pop.

3 Stir in spinach and cook for 1–2 minutes, until heated through. Add lemon juice and rind, season to taste and mix well.

preparation time
15 minutes

cooking time
15 minutes

nutritional value per serve
fat: 8.5 g
carbohydrate: 0.8 g
protein: 3 g

1 Place eggs in a small pan of cold water, bring to the boil and cook for 10 minutes. Run under cold water, peel, halve and remove yolks, discarding the whites.

2 In a food processor combine yolks, pickled cucumber, capers, mustard and gradually add oil until well combined. Add lemon rind, juice and sugar, if using. Process until combined. Stir in parsley and crème fraîche, and set aside.

3 Cut ends off asparagus, peel the lower half using a vegetable peeler to expose flesh. Fill a large pan with about 4 cm water, bring to the boil. Stand asparagus spears in the pan, keeping tips out of the water. Reduce heat and simmer for 5–6 minutes, until just tender, drain. Serve asparagus topped with sauce and season with black pepper.

asparagus with lemon sauce

ingredients

2 bunches (about 500 g, 1 lb) asparagus
salt and black pepper
sauce
2 eggs
2 tablespoons chopped pickled cucumber
1 teaspoon chopped capers
1 teaspoon dijon mustard
1/2 cup (125 ml, 4 fl oz) olive oil
finely grated rind (zest) and juice
   of 1/2 lemon
pinch of castor sugar (optional)
2 tablespoons chopped fresh parsley
2 tablespoons crème fraîche
serves 4

i

preparation time
20 minutes

cooking time
20 minutes

**nutritional value
per serve**
fat: 16.5 g
carbohydrate: 1.9 g
protein: 3.2 g

potato and onion dauphinoise

i

preparation time
20 minutes

cooking time
1 hour 10 minutes

nutritional value per serve
fat: 14.1 g
carbohydrate: 8.5 g
protein: 2 g

ingredients

1 tablespoon butter
extra butter for greasing
750 g (1½ lb) baking potatoes, thinly sliced
3 onions, thinly sliced
1 teaspoon freshly grated nutmeg
450 ml (14 fl oz) cream
salt and black pepper
serves 2–4

1 Preheat oven to 180°C (350°F, gas mark 4). Grease a shallow ovenproof dish with butter.

2 Arrange potatoes and onions in alternate layers in baking dish. Lightly season each layer with salt, pepper and nutmeg. Finish with a potato layer, pour over cream and dot with butter. Place on lower shelf of oven and cook for 1 hour until golden.

zucchini polenta slices

ingredients

1 tablespoon butter
extra butter for greasing
3 tablespoons olive oil
250 g (8 oz) zucchini (courgettes), grated
3 cups, 750 ml (1¼ pints) chicken or vegetable stock
185 g (6 oz) instant polenta
salt and black pepper
2 tablespoons grated parmesan

serves 4

i

preparation time
15 minutes

cooking time
20 minutes

nutritional value per serve
fat: 6.3 g
carbohydrate: 10.5 g
protein: 2.4 g

1 Grease a shallow 22 cm square roasting tin. Heat the butter and 1 tablespoon of oil in a large frying pan. Fry zucchini on a medium heat for 3–4 minutes, until softened but not browned, stirring frequently. Remove from heat and set aside.

2 Bring stock to the boil in a large pan. Sprinkle in polenta, stirring with a wooden spoon, and continue to stir for 5 minutes, until polenta

thickens and begins to come away from the sides of the pan. Remove from the heat and stir in zucchini. Season to taste.

3 Turn polenta mix into the roasting tin, spreading evenly, sprinkle with parmesan and leave for 1 hour to cool and set.

4 Heat a ridged cast-iron grill pan over a high heat. Cut polenta into slices, brush with remaining oil and cook for 2–4 minutes on each side, until golden.

glossary

al dente: Italian term to describe pasta and rice that are cooked until tender but still firm to the bite.

bake blind: to bake pastry cases without their fillings. Line the raw pastry case with greaseproof paper and fill with raw rice or dried beans to prevent collapsed sides and puffed base. Remove paper and fill 5 minutes before completion of cooking time.

baste: to spoon hot cooking liquid over food at intervals during cooking to moisten and flavour it.

beat: to make a mixture smooth with rapid and regular motions using a spatula, wire whisk or electric mixer; to make a mixture light and smooth by enclosing air.

beurre manié: equal quantities of butter and flour mixed together to a smooth paste and stirred bit by bit into a soup, stew or sauce while on the heat to thicken. Stop adding when desired thickness results.

bind: to add egg or a thick sauce to hold ingredients together when cooked.

blanch: to plunge some foods into boiling water for less than a minute and immediately plunge into iced water. This is to brighten the colour of some vegetables; to remove skin from tomatoes and nuts.

blend: to mix 2 or more ingredients thoroughly together; do not confuse with blending in an electric blender.

boil: to cook in a liquid brought to boiling point and kept there.

boiling point: when bubbles rise continually and break over the entire surface of the liquid, reaching a temperature of 100°C (212°F). In some cases food is held at this high temperature for a few seconds then heat is turned to low for slower cooking. See simmer.

bouquet garni: a bundle of several herbs tied together with string for easy removal, placed into pots of stock, soups and stews for flavour. A few sprigs of fresh thyme, parsley and bay leaf are used. Can be purchased in sachet form for convenience.

caramelise: to heat sugar in a heavy-based pan until it liquefies and develops a caramel colour. Vegetables such as blanched carrots and sautéed onions may be sprinkled with sugar and caramelised.

chill: to place in the refrigerator or stir over ice until cold.

clarify: to make a liquid clear by removing sediments and impurities. To melt fat and remove any sediment.

coat: to dust or roll food items in flour to cover the surface before the food is cooked. Also, to coat in flour, egg and breadcrumbs.

cool: to stand at room temperature until some or all heat is removed, eg, cool a little, cool completely.

cream: to make creamy and fluffy by working the mixture with the back of a wooden spoon, usually refers to creaming butter and sugar or margarine. May also be creamed with an electric mixer.

croutons: small cubes of bread, toasted or fried, used as an addition to salads or as a garnish to soups and stews.

crudite: raw vegetable sticks served with a dipping sauce.

crumb: to coat foods in flour, egg and breadcrumbs to form a protective coating for foods which are fried. Also adds flavour, texture and enhances appearance.

cube: to cut into small pieces with six even sides, eg, cubes of meat.

cut in: to combine fat and flour using 2 knives scissor fashion or with a pastry blender, to make pastry.

deglaze: to dissolve dried out cooking juices left on the base and sides of a roasting dish or frying pan. Add a little water, wine or stock, scrape and stir over heat until dissolved. Resulting liquid is used to make a flavoursome gravy or added to a sauce or casserole.

degrease: to skim fat from the surface of cooking liquids, eg, stocks, soups, casseroles.

dice: to cut into small cubes.

dredge: to heavily coat with icing sugar, sugar, flour or cornflour.

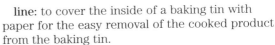

dressing: a mixture added to completed dishes to add moisture and flavour, eg, salads, cooked vegetables.

drizzle: to pour in a fine thread-like stream moving over a surface.

egg wash: beaten egg with milk or water used to brush over pastry, bread dough or biscuits to give a sheen and golden brown colour.

essence: a strong flavouring liquid, usually made by distillation. Only a few drops are needed to flavour.

fillet: a piece of prime meat, fish or poultry which is boneless or has all bones removed.

flake: to separate cooked fish into flakes, removing any bones and skin, using 2 forks.

flame: to ignite warmed alcohol over food or to pour into a pan with food, ignite then serve.

flute: to make decorative indentations around the pastry rim before baking.

fold in: combining of a light, whisked or creamed mixture with other ingredients. Add a portion of the other ingredients at a time and mix using a gentle circular motion, over and under the mixture so that air will not be lost. Use a silver spoon or spatula.

glaze: to brush or coat food with a liquid that will give the finished product a glossy appearance, and on baked products, a golden brown colour.

grease: to rub the surface of a metal or heatproof dish with oil or fat, to prevent the food from sticking.

herbed butter: softened butter mixed with finely chopped fresh herbs and re-chilled. Used to serve on grilled meats and fish.

hors d'ouvre: small savoury foods served as an appetiser, popularly known today as 'finger food'.

infuse: to steep foods in a liquid until the liquid absorbs their flavour.

joint: to cut poultry and game into serving pieces by dividing at the joint.

julienne: to cut some food, eg, vegetables and processed meats into fine strips the length of matchsticks. Used for inclusion in salads or as a garnish to cooked dishes.

knead: to work a yeast dough in a pressing, stretching and folding motion with the heel of the hand until smooth and elastic to develop the gluten strands. Non-yeast doughs should be lightly and quickly handled as gluten development is not desired.

line: to cover the inside of a baking tin with paper for the easy removal of the cooked product from the baking tin.

macerate: to stand fruit in a syrup, liqueur or spirit to give added flavour.

marinade: a flavoured liquid, into which food is placed for some time to give it flavour and to tenderise. Marinades include an acid ingredient such as vinegar or wine, oil and seasonings.

mask: to evenly cover cooked food portions with a sauce, mayonnaise or savoury jelly.

pan-fry: to fry foods in a small amount of fat or oil, sufficient to coat the base of the pan.

parboil: to boil until partially cooked. The food is then finished by some other method.

pare: to peel the skin from vegetables and fruit. Peel is the popular term but pare is the name given to the knife used; paring knife.

pith: the white lining between the rind and flesh of oranges, grapefruit and lemons.

pit: to remove stones or seeds from olives, cherries, dates.

pitted: the olives, cherries, dates etc, with the stone removed, eg, purchase pitted dates.

poach: to simmer gently in enough hot liquid to almost cover the food so shape will be retained.

pound: to flatten meats with a meat mallet; to reduce to a paste or small particles with a mortar and pestle.

simmer: to cook in liquid just below boiling point at about 96°C (205°F) with small bubbles rising gently to the surface.

skim: to remove fat or froth from the surface of simmering food.

stock: the liquid produced when meat, poultry, fish or vegetables have been simmered in water to extract the flavour. Used as a base for soups, sauces, casseroles etc. Convenience stock products are available.

sweat: to cook sliced onions or vegetables, in a small amount of butter in a covered pan over low heat, to soften them and release flavour without colouring.

conversions

measurements differ from country to country, so it's important to understand what the differences are. This Measurements Guide gives you simple 'at-a-glance' information for using the recipes in this book, wherever you may be.

Cooking is not an exact science – minor variations in measurements won't make a difference to your cooking.

equipment

There is a difference in the size of measuring cups used internationally, but the difference is minimal (only 2–3 teaspoons). We use the Australian standard metric measurements in our recipes:

1 teaspoon ....5 ml	1 tablespoon....20 ml
½ cup......125 ml	1 cup.....250 ml
4 cups...1 litre	

Measuring cups come in sets of one cup (250 ml), ½ cup (125 ml), ⅓ cup (80 ml) and ¼ cup (60 ml). Use these for measuring liquids and certain dry ingredients.
Measuring spoons come in a set of four and should be used for measuring dry and liquid ingredients.
When using cup or spoon measures always make them level (unless the recipe indicates otherwise).

dry versus wet ingredients

While this system of measures is consistent for liquids, it's more difficult to quantify dry ingredients. For instance, one level cup equals: 200 g of brown sugar; 210 g of castor sugar; and 110 g of icing sugar.

When measuring dry ingredients such as flour, don't push the flour down or shake it into the cup. It is best just to spoon the flour in until it reaches the desired amount. When measuring liquids use a clear vessel indicating metric levels.

Always use medium eggs (55–60 g) when eggs are required in a recipe.

dry

metric (grams)	imperial (ounces)
30 g	1 oz
60 g	2 oz
90 g	3 oz
100 g	3½ oz
125 g	4 oz
150 g	5 oz
185 g	6 oz
200 g	7 oz
250 g	8 oz
280 g	9 oz
315 g	10 oz
330 g	11 oz
370 g	12 oz
400 g	13 oz
440 g	14 oz
470 g	15 oz
500 g	16 oz (1 lb)
750 g	24 oz (1½ lb)
1000 g (1 kg)	32 oz (2 lb)

liquids

metric (millilitres)	imperial (fluid ounces)
30 ml	1 fl oz
60 ml	2 fl oz
90 ml	3 fl oz
100 ml	3½ fl oz
125 ml	4 fl oz
150 ml	5 fl oz
190 ml	6 fl oz
250 ml	8 fl oz
300 ml	10 fl oz
500 ml	16 fl oz
600 ml	20 fl oz (1 pint)*
1000 ml (1 litre)	32 fl oz

*Note: an American pint is 16 fl oz.

oven
Your oven should always be at the right temperature before placing the food in it to be cooked. Note that if your oven doesn't have a fan you may need to cook food for a little longer.

microwave
It is difficult to give an exact cooking time for microwave cooking. It is best to watch what you are cooking closely to monitor its progress.

standing time
Many foods continue to cook when you take them out of the oven or microwave. If a recipe states that the food needs to 'stand' after cooking, be sure not to overcook the dish.

can sizes
The can sizes available in your supermarket or grocery store may not be the same as specified in the recipe. Don't worry if there is a small variation in size—it's unlikely to make a difference to the end result.

cooking temperatures	°C (celsius)	°F (fahrenheit)	gas mark
very slow	120	250	1/2
slow	150	300	2
moderately slow	160	315	2-3
moderate	180	350	4
moderate hot	190	375	5
	200	400	6
hot	220	425	7
very hot	230	450	8
	240	475	9
	250	500	10

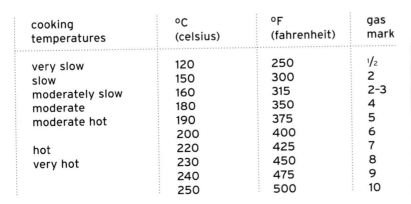

index